METAPHYSICAL PATTERNS IN PLATONISM

Ancient, Medieval, Renaissance and Modern Times

Edited by John F Finamore & Robert M Berchman

The Prometheus Trust

In association with the

International Society for Neoplatonic Studies

The Prometheus Trust
28 Petticoat Lane
Dilton Marsh, Westbury
Wiltshire, BA13 4DG, UK

A registered charity, number 299648

Metaphysical Patterns in Platonism
Ancient, Medieval, Renaissance and Modern Times

Prometheus Trust edition: 2014

Originally published in 2007 by University Press of the South: the Prometheus Trust gratefully acknowledges their permission to reprint this work.

ISBN 978 1 898910 831

Cover: The Sun and its atmosphere, with acknowledgements to NASA

British Library Cataloguing-in-Publication Data.
A catalogue record for this book is
available from the British Library.

Printed in the UK by Berforts Information Press, King's Lynn

TABLE OF CONTENTS

PREFACE

On 22-26 June 2005, the third annual conference of the International Society for Neoplatonic Studies convened in New Orleans. The papers in this volume trace the history of Platonism from the Middle Platonist Galen (c.129-c.216 C.E.) to the philosophy's lasting effects in the present. The authors explore the writings of Galen, Plotinus, Iamblichus, Julian, Augustine, Eriugena, Ficino, Copernicus, Emerson, Hegel, Adorno, and Lutoslawski. The vast scope of time and the intricate ways in which philosophers make use of Platonism bring further evidence that the Platonic tradition is alive and flourishing. The articles in this collection are designed to be readable in sequence, but each chapter is self-contained and makes no presuppositions about the order in which it should be read. Nothing can substitute an unmediated encounter with the primary texts discussed, but we shall be pleased if our readers find many of the ideas presented here challenging. We shall be disappointed if our articles are found difficult or if the encounter with the philosophical traditions discussed in this book does not trigger the *theoria* which Aristotle claimed was the *aitia* of philosophy.

The contributors to this book were given a free hand within the limits of space to present their topic as they saw fit. The authors revised their papers for publication, and the editors sent the revised versions out anonymously for peer review. The editors thank those peer reviewers, all of whom selflessly gave of their time. We also wish to commend the editors and staff at the University Press of the South, especially its hard-working director Dr. Alain Saint Saëns.

This conference occurred approximately two months before Hurricane Katrina made landfall in New Orleans on 29 August. Katrina was the third largest hurricane ever to come ashore in the continental United States, and its devastation was staggering in the beautiful city of New Orleans. As New Orleans continues to bear the scars of Katrina and slowly emerges again from its wake, we dedicate this volume to the city and its people. May the city be reborn like the souls Plato describes in his Myth of Er.

John F. Finamore
Robert M. Berchman

THE PLATONIC TRIPARTITE SOUL AND THE PLATONISM OF GALEN'S *ON THE DOCTRINES OF HIPPOCRATES AND PLATO*

John F. Finamore

Galen of Pergamum (129-c.210 CE) was the physician of the Emperor Marcus Aurelius. During his first stay in Rome (162-166 CE), he came to fame by conducting public dissections of animals before learned audiences of physicians and philosophers, in which he sought to display his expertise especially concerning the system of nerves in the body. During this stay he also began writing his *De Placitis Hippocratis et Platonis* (*On the Doctrines of Hippocrates and Plato*), in which he intended to demonstrate that these two writers were in agreement concerning the nature of the tripartite soul. He wrote the first six books at that time, and completed the final three books during his second Roman sojourn in 169-176 CE.[1] In this paper I wish to consider Galen's arguments for the tripartite soul. I will argue that Galen's interpretation of Plato's *Timaeus* while not always accurate is nonetheless a kind of interpretation generally found in the later-Platonic period, and I will defend him against some recent scholars who have seen him as unphilosophical.

A. Galen on the three parts of the soul

The beginning of *PHP* has been lost, and so we do not have Galen's statement of purpose. De Lacy in his edition and translation of the *PHP* has collected passages from elsewhere in the *PHP*, which show that Galen's intention was to demonstrate that Hippocrates and Plato were in agreement, among other matters, on the question of the tripartition of the soul into the rational, spirited, and desiderative.[2] As is well known, Plato makes his case for these three aspects of soul in book 4 of the *Republic*. The concept is

[1] For Galen's biography, see Tieleman (1996) xiii-xiv, Tracy (1976), 48-50; Harkins and Riese (1963), 1-3. On the dates of the composition of *PHP* as well as some possible internal conflicting evidence, see De Lacy (1978) Vol. 1, 46-48.

[2] *PHP* 64.6-14; 68.20-25.

repeated in the *Phaedrus* myth, where the soul is compared to a charioteer (rational aspect) controlling two horses (spirited and desiderative aspects). In the *Timaeus*, Plato apportions each of these elements to three separate parts of the body: the rational to the head (*Tim.* 44d3-6), the spirited to the chest (69d6-70a2), and the desiderative to the area between the midriff and navel (70d7-71a3).

As a doctor, Galen constructs his arguments in physical terms, writing in favor of what he sees as the Hippocratic/Platonic conception of the tripartite soul. He seeks to prove the tripartite nature of the soul via dissections of animal bodies. Against the views of Chrysippus and Aristotle, he sets out to show that the view that the heart is the seat of the controlling power of the soul is wrong and that the Platonic tripartite structure is correct.

Galen explains his position in *PHP* 2, 110.1-14. Arguing against the Stoic view that the heart is the seat of the soul's controlling power, he states that "as even they [i.e., Stoics] agree, the governing part is the source of perception and drive" (ἔστι δὲ τὸ ἡγεμονικόν, ὡς καὶ αὐτοὶ βούλονται, τὸ κατάρχον αἰσθήσεως τε καὶ ὁρμῆς, 110.1-2). Thus, the proof about the governing part, that motions start there and perceptions are carried back to it, requires the proof of dissection (110.2-6).

> For if this [faculty] transmits the power of perception and motion to every individual part [of the body], then it is altogether necessary that some vessel issues from it for the purpose of serving them (εἰ γὰρ αὕτη τοῖς κατὰ μέρος ἅπασιν ἐπιπέμπει δύναμιν αἰσθήσεώς τε ἅμα καὶ κινήσεως, ἀποπεφυκέναι τι πάντως ἀπ᾽ αὐτῆς ἀγγεῖον ἀναγκαῖόν ἐστι εἰς τὴν αὐτῶν ὑπηρεσίαν, 110.6-8).

Thus, dissection and dissection alone will answer the philosophical and medical questions involved.

Earlier in book I, at 78.26-80.15, Galen argues that when pressure is applied to the left ventricle of the brain of an animal, "the animal will immediately be without motion, perception, breath, and voice" (ἀκίνητόν τε καὶ ἀναίσθητον, ἄπνουν τε καὶ ἄφωνον εὐθὺς ἔσται τὸ ζῷον, 78.32-33). He adds that the same results are obtained in human beings when they undergo trepanning (33-34). When such pressure is applied to the heart, however, there is no such impairment. He cites an instance in which an assistant held the animal's heart in tongs and the animal "cried out loudly, breathed without difficulty, and excessively moved all its limbs" (ἐκεκράγει τε μεγάλα καὶ ἀκωλύτως ἀνέπνει καὶ πάντα ἐκίνει σφοδρῶς τὰ κῶλα, 80.7-8). When pressure is applied to the heart, the arteries alone are affected; when to the brain, the arteries function. Thus, Galen concludes, the heart does not need the brain for the exercise of its arterial motions, and the brain does not need the heart for its motions. The two are separate, and the brain controls the motions that Galen claims are associated with reason.[3]

Further, he criticizes Aristotle and the physician Praxagoras for mistakenly arguing that the source of nerves is in the heart (80.24-82.10). Praxagoras had argued that the arteries issuing from the heart eventually thinned and became nerves;[4] Galen refutes him at length (82.11-90.25), using his expertise in dissection and observation. After arguing against Aristotle's statement (*De Partibus Animalium* 3.4) that the heart has many nerves (νεύρων πλῆθος) and motions begin from the heart (90.26-98.35), Galen concludes that the brain, not the heart, is the source of the nerves (ἀρχὴν τῶν νεύρων ἐγκέφαλον, 100.2-3); the heart is the source of the arteries. Thus, by the end of the first book, Galen can claim to have shown that the seats of two of the powers of the soul, the rational and the spirited, are in the brain and heart respectively.

In book 3, Galen presents further evidence for the heart being the seat of the spirited part of the soul, arguing from the effect of anger and fear on it. He berates Chrysippus, who used quotations from the poets to show that the heart was the seat of affections, for selecting poetic passages that did not show that the heart was the seat of reason but rather that of anger. Since Plato agreed that this was the case, Chrysippus' arguments were misdirected. Galen complains that Chrysippus is illicitly assuming that "wherever the affective aspect of the soul is, there too is the rational" (ὡς ἔνθ ἂν ῃ τὸ παθητικὸν

[3] See also 120.29-128.8, where Galen argues that speech is not caused by pneuma from the heart. Again using evidence from his dissections, he argues that the respiration and voice are caused by muscles that are in turn connected to nerves from the brain. At 124.13-32, he directs the reader to other of his works for exact information about which muscles and nerves perform which precise tasks. At 124.33-126.17, he argues that manipulating the heart of a live animal does not stop its breathing or speech, but manipulating the brain does. In particular, he describes what happens in animal sacrifices, where (he assures us) the heart is separated and lying on the altar yet the animal is still breathing and lowing and even running; but when the animal is cut where the spinal cord comes from the brain, the animal loses breath, voice, and motion (126.18-128.2). Galen concludes (128.2-8) that the brain and heart control different functions and represent different psychic powers. Cf. 2.148.26-152.8; 3.210.10-212.4.

[4] For Praxagoras of Cos, see Tieleman (1996), 83-84 and 189; De Lacy (1984), vol. 3, 619-620.

τῆς ψυχῆς, ἐνταῦθα καὶ τὸ λογιστικὸν ὑπάρχειν, 176.24-25).[5] In reality, Chrysippus is agreeing with Plato's assertions in the *Timaeus* 70a7-c5 that the heart makes use of the boiling blood near it when it is angry at some injustice and that the lungs cool the heart agitated by fear (174.10-24).[6]

Galen takes up the third part of the soul in book 6. He argues that the liver, which he believes to be the source of the veins in the body, is where the desiderative soul resides. He admits, however, that he can provide neither as clear evidence (οὐκ ἐξ ὁμοίως ἐναργῶν, 372.20) as for the other two parts nor a demonstration from the very nature of the part itself (οὐδ ἐξ αὐτῆς . . . τῆς φύσεως ἡ ἀπόδειξις, 372.20-21) but rather from accidents pertaining to the part's own individual nature (ἀλλ ἐκ τῶν τούτῳ συμβεβηκοτων ἰδίᾳ, 372.21-22). Galen explains his meaning by pointing out that whereas in the case of the nerves coming from the brain and the arteries coming from the heart, ligatures and incisions had an immediate effect on the animal's motions and voice (in the former case) and on the pulsations (in the latter),[7] pressing on the liver or cutting the veins produces no such immediate visible results. Time, he explains, is needed to bring any changes to light. (372.32-374.8).

Within these boundaries, Galen gives several arguments that the liver is the source of veins and therefore the seat of the desiderative soul. He begins, however, with a matter of terminology (374.14-19). Aristotle used three terms of the desiderative power: nutritive, vegetative, reproductive (θρεπτικὴν ἢ φυτικὴν ἢ γεννητικὴν, 374.15). These terms designate the three activities of this part of the soul: growing (φύειν), nourishing (τρέφειν) and generating (γεννᾶν). Plato, however, considering only the sheer numbers of the part's desires, called it "desiderative" (ὁ Πλάτων δ ἀπὸ τοῦ πλῆθους τῶν ἐπιθυμίων ἐπιθυμητικήν, 374.17). In this way, Galen identifies Aristotle's lower psychic powers with Plato's third psychic

[5] At 176.13-18, Galen quotes Chrysippus as saying that since anger arises in the breast, so too do the other affections and "ratiocinations" (dialogismouv", 176.15). Galen accuses Chrysippus of assuming what he must prove. At 182.27-184.10, Galen notoriously ridicules Chrysippus for not at least choosing passages where a poet writes lines in conformity with Chrysippus' thesis; Galen kindly offers one from Hesiod and three from Homer.

[6] Cornford (1937), 283-284 sees the influence of the Hippocratean "On the Heart" in the passage from Plato. Note that whereas Plato believes (and Galen concurs) that the lungs cool the heating around the heart (*Tim.* 70cd), Aristotle thinks that the brain serves this purpose for the heart via the blood (*De Partibus Animalium* II.7).

[7] Galen adds an important feature of the spirited faculty: anger (θυμός) and fear cause the heart to fluctuate, that is to say, beat faster (372.27-29).

part. We should not differ over terms, Galen says, but debate over the realities behind them.[8]

In his proofs concerning the desiderative part, Galen draws an analogy between the part of plants from which the roots and the stalk grows. Larger parts are the sources of the smaller. As in a tree, the trunk is the largest part growing out of that spot and as in the heart its largest artery is like the trunk of a tree (branching out to the head and spine), so too the largest growths from the liver are the veins that go from the liver to the stomach and to the whole body (376.24-382.32). Galen goes on to argue that since the veins come out of the liver and do not go to the heart, the heart cannot be the source of the veins (386.10-392.5). Further, Galen adds that a certain unnamed man would not accept Galen's conclusion without visual proof. Through dissection, Galen showed him that the veins started from the liver and went all over the body and that none could be seen starting from the heart. They could not find a single vein whose source was not the liver (390.32-392.1). Thus, Galen can conclude that the liver is the source of the veins and, as such, it is the seat of the desiderative part of the soul.

In book 8, Galen summarizes what he has shown in the earlier books. On the higher two parts of the soul, he breaks his arguments down into two simple syllogisms:

(1) Where the beginning of the nerves is, there is the governing part. The beginning of the nerves is in the brain. Therefore, the governing part is there. (484.35-486.2)

(2) Where the affections of the soul move the parts of the body more obviously, there is the affective part of the soul. But in the case of anger and fear the heart clearly possesses a great change of motion. Therefore the affective part of the soul is in this [i.e., in the heart]. (486.4-7)

About the third part of the soul, Galen writes that he showed the following:[9]

[8] 374.20-21: ονομαζέτω μὲν ουν ἕκαστος ὡς ἂν ἐθέλῃ, περὶ δὲ τῶν ἐν αὐτοῖς τοῖς πράγμασι διαφορῶν ἀποδείξει πιστούσθω. Of the adjectives θρεπτικός, φυτικός, and γεννητικός, only θρεπτικός and γεννητικός appear in Aristotle's *De Anima*. See 416a19, where the two capacities are called "the same," and 432b10-11, where they are said to be found in all animals. The term φυτικός is used by Aristotle in the *Nicomachean Ethics* (I.13.17) and in the *Eudemian Ethics* (II.1.17). The three terms as used by Galen most likely grouped together in later interpretations of Aristotle. Galen has chosen to equate them with Plato's third part of the soul. We may doubt that Aristotle's and Plato's categories fit as closely as he suggests.

[9] Galen gives three additional arguments for the liver being the source of veins at 486.30-488.33.

(3) In plants as in the nerves and arteries, the thickest part grows out of its source and branches off later. The veins that go down to the stomach originate in the liver; the vena cava originates from the liver and goes to all parts of the body. Thus the liver is the source of veins and the source of the nutritive power, which Plato called "desiderative." (486.17-29)

B. Galen the Middle-Platonist

Galen has boldly used medical evidence to bolster Plato's arguments for the tripartite nature of the soul, but how well has he succeeded? Scholars are not in general supportive. Tieleman in the introduction to his important work *Galen and Chrysippus on the Soul* states that Galen's use of specific organs as the three seats of the psychic parts distorts Plato's looser placement.[10] Carlos Steel in a recent article in *Phronesis* claims that Galen—and indeed anyone looking for a medical text in the *Timaeus*—is mistaken.[11] But their arguments seem wrongheaded to me. Of course Galen is stretching the evidence when he argues that (a) Plato and Hippocrates are in agreement on the tripartite nature of the soul and that (b) Galen's dissections will prove conclusively where Plato intended the three seats of the psychic parts to be. Stretching the evidence is exactly what Middle Platonic and Neoplatonic authors did. To them it was not falsification or a clever way of re-writing the facts. Rather it was a way of doing philosophy. The goal was not to show your originality and innovation but to argue instead that your ideas were in keeping with the masters of the past, especially Plato. But Galen goes one step beyond this later-Platonic credo as well. At 198.23-33, while attacking Chrysippus for his use of poets in his arguments, Galen expresses his belief that not only are the poets not sufficient evidence in place of a demonstration of the facts but neither are Hippocrates himself, by common consent the best of all physicians, nor Plato, the first of all philosophers (ἀλλ̣ οὐδ̣ αὐτὸς ὁ πάντων ἰατρῶν ὁμολογουμένως ἄριστος Ἱπποκράτης, ὥσπερ οὐδὲ ὁ πρῶτος ἁπάντων φιλοσόφων Πλάτων, 198.25-27). One should instead wait for the demonstration (ἀναμένει τὴν ἀποδείξιν, 198.33). Thus, authorities are fine, but even their doctrines require testing and proof. As we shall see, Galen lives up to this precept.

A better place to begin to assess what Galen has accomplished was expressed by Theodore Tracy in his 1976 article in the *Illinois Classical Studies*. Tracy asked why Galen would plump for Plato and found an answer

[10] Tieleman (1996) xxix-xxxi.

[11] Steel (2001), 120-123.

precisely in "Galen's investigations in neuroanatomy and their applications to the center of consciousness."[12] In other words, Galen's medical investigations led him to believe that the brain was the seat of the soul, and the only philosopher of any importance who supported this position was Plato.[13] We know that Galen studied with teachers from all the major philosophical schools, including Platonists: a student of Gaius taught him when he was young as did Albinus later at Smyrna.[14]

When we turn to Galen's assignment of the seats to the psychic parts, we find that Plato made the identification easy. Neither Tieleman (xxix) nor Steel (121) finds fault with Galen's claim that Plato designated the brain as the seat of the rational soul. Plato, however, does not mention the brain at all at *Tim* 44d3-6 or 69c5-6, where he discusses the placement of the rational soul in the head, but rather at 73c6-d1 in the discussion of the marrow, where Plato says that the rational soul is set in the marrow that became the brain. Thus, it was an easy task for Galen to identify the brain with its nerves as the seat of the rational soul.

It was still an anachronistic claim, however, since the nerves were not discovered until the 3rd Century BCE by Herophilus and Erasistratus. Alcinous in his *Handbook of Platonism* 17.173.8-9 clearly adapts *Tim.* 73c6-d1 to this updated knowledge when he says that the head is the origin of the marrow and nerves. Galen, however, is more circumspect, admitting that Plato is ignorant of the nerves as he is of other medical data.[15] Thus, Galen is willing to admit that Plato is correct even when Plato does not have all the evidence to hand. Galen, then, is not merely relying on Plato's vagary. He is also claiming the philosopher's expertise *in matters of philosophy*, to which he can then add other evidence of his own, such as that from dissection. Galen is a more perspicacious reader of Plato than has been thought, certainly willing to give credit to Plato but also willing to acknowledge the philosopher's lack

[12] Tracy (1976), 45; cf. 49-50. This one doctrine, of course, is not and cannot be the whole reason for Galen's acceptance of Plato, as Tracy also sees. The *PHP* makes clear that Galen agreed with Plato on many points, including the providential role of the Demiurge among others. Medically, however, the doctrine of the brain must have been the most compelling.

[13] For earlier philosophers who opted for the brain as the seat of the soul, see Tracy (1976), 46.

[14] De Lacy (1972) 28.

[15] See Tieleman (1996), xxix and notes 68 and 69; Dillon (1977), 289 and (1993), 140. Galen believed that Plato had limited knowledge of medical information; see De Lacy (1992), 33-35.

of expertise. We find Galen claiming that Plato was correct (the rational soul is indeed seated in the brain) and offering further evidence of his own that this is the case.

Let us turn to the heart as the seat of the spirited faculty. Tieleman and Steel point out that Plato is vague, placing the spirited soul "between the midriff and neck" (*Tim.* 70a4).[16] Plato continues, saying:

> the heart, the bundle of veins (ἅμμα τῶν φλεβῶν) and the source of blood traveling vigorously through all the limbs, they [i.e., the younger gods] placed in the guardhouse in order that, when the anger of the spirit boils (because reason announces that some unjust action is occurring around these [limbs], whether externally or from the desires internally), quickly through all the narrow channels every such perceptive element in the body perceiving the exhortations and threats will pay attention and obey completely, and in this way allow the best element among all to rule (τὴν δὲ δὴ καρδίαν ἅμμα τῶν φλεβῶν καὶ πηγὴν τοῦ περιφερομένου κατὰ πάντα τὰ μέλη σφοδρῶς αἵματος εἰς τὴν δορυφορικὴν οἴκησιν κατέστησαν, ἵνα, ὅτε ζέσειεν τὸ τοῦ θυμοῦ μένος, τοῦ λόγου παραγγείλαντος ὥς τις ἄδικος περὶ αὐτὰ γίγνεται πρᾶξις ἔξωθεν ἢ καί τις ἀπὸ τῶν ἔνδοθεν ἐπιθυμιῶν, ὀξέως διὰ πάντων τῶν στενωπῶν πᾶν ὅσον αἰσθητικὸν ἐν τῷ σώματι, τῶν τε παρακελεύσεων καὶ ἀπειλῶν αἰσθανόμενον, γίγνοιτο ἐπήκοον καὶ ἕποιτο πάντῃ, καὶ τὸ βέλτιστον οὕτως ἐν αὐτοῖς πᾶσιν ἡγεμονεῖν ἐῷ, 70a7-c1).

There are two problems facing Galen here. First, Plato clearly connects the heart to the veins and not to the arteries. Galen, however, explains (*PHP* 418.1-8) that Plato and earlier medical writers called the arteries "veins," but that Plato makes his meaning clear here when he says that it is the source of blood that *travels vigorously* through all the limbs.[17] Indeed, a little earlier (416.16-36), Galen explained that Hippocrates called arteries "veins" as well, showing there that the learned physician also placed the seat of the spirit in the heart.[18] The second obstacle Galen faces is that Plato's own words may make it seem that the heart is separate from the spirit, since the heart is positioned to pass on the spirit's agitated state. Nevertheless, Plato's words may be taken as Galen suggests: the spirit is in the heart, so placed as to move the heart easily. There is evidence that this is indeed the way the

[16] Tieleman (1996) xxix-xxx; Steel (2001), 121.

[17] See also 416.6-15.

[18] See Tieleman (1996) xxx note 73 and xxxii-xxxiii note 85.

Middle –Platonic philosophers took Plato's words. Alcinous (176.19) and Apuleius (*De Platone* 207) both place the spirited faculty in the heart.[19]

Galen comes in for the harshest criticism for his placing the desiderative faculty in the liver. Plato (*Tim.* 70d7-71a3) confined the desiderative element to the area between the midriff and navel. Tieleman and Steel think that Galen is taking advantage of Plato's vagueness to situate the seat of appetite in the liver and also is creating wholesale the notion of the liver's role in digestion.[20] Again, Galen's case is more subtle.

Let's begin with the role of the liver in digestion. It is, of course, perfectly true that in Plato's discussion of digestion (*Tim.* 80d1-81e5), the liver is not mentioned. Later Platonists, however, would never let such a minor obstacle stand in the way. What is required is a passage in which the Plato connects the liver with digestion, and Galen finds one at *Tim.* 70d7-e3:

> The part of the soul desirous of food and drink and of as many things of which it has a need because of the nature of the body, this they housed between the midriff and the boundary by the navel, having constructed as it were a manger in all this place for the nourishment of the body. (τὸ δὲ δὴ σίτων τε καὶ ποτῶν ἐπιθυμητικὸν τῆς ψυχῆς καὶ ὅσων ἔνδειαν διὰ τὴν τοῦ σώματος ἴσχει φύσιν, τοῦτο εἰς τὸ μεταξὺ τῶν τε φρενῶν καὶ τοῦ πρὸς τὸν ὀμφαλὸν ὅρου κατῴκισαν, οἷον φάτνην ἐν ἅπαντι τούτῳ τῷ τόπῳ τῇ τοῦ σώματος τροφῇ τεκτηνάμενοι.)

Galen cites this passage at 418.9-16, and uses it to show that the blood from the liver is used to nourish the whole body and quotes especially the words "desirous of food and drink" to demonstrate that Plato intended the nutriment to travel from the stomach through the liver and then to the heart.[21] Thus. the desiderative element can be said to be involved with digestion because one of its desires is for nourishment, which it attains through the blood in the veins.

[19] Galen does, however, run afoul of Plato when he asserts that the brain/rational soul is the seat of perceptions. See Tieleman (1996) xxx and note 75. Even here, however, one should note that Galen could have read the passage as saying only each of the limbs is, qua *αἰσθητικόν,* perceptive of the spirit, not of actual sensations. Galen ignores *Tim.* 69d4-6, where sensations are clearly aligned with the lower two parts, as Tieleman says.

[20] Tieleman (1996) xxx-xxxi; Steel 121. Cornford (1937), 288 note 1 points to *Tim.* 71d2 as evidence that Galen is correct is assigning the seat of the appetitive part of the soul to the liver. The phrase that Plato employs, however, shows rather that the seat is *near* the liver (τὴν περὶ τὸ ἧπαρ ψυχῆς μοῖραν κατῳκισμένην) not the liver itself. Cf. 71a7-b1, where the god (not the Demiurge, but the lower gods) placed the liver in the area of the appetitive soul. Indeed, the soul must be apart from the liver in order to be "perceive" the images on the liver.

[21] Cf. 420.32-422-19.

Galen has a retort for those who say that he is taking advantage of Plato's looseness of expression to establish the desiderative part in the liver. He proceeds by comparing Hippocrates and Plato, and arguing that they are saying the same things about the liver but the former qua physician and the latter qua philosopher (418.17-422.19). In speaking of the liver, it is as if Hippocrates and Plato:

> apportioned out the arguments, the one speaking of the organs and the other of the faculty controlling them (νειμάμενοι τοὺς λόγους ὁ μὲν ὑπὲρ τῶν ὀργάνων, ὁ δὲ ὑπὲρ τῆς διοικούσης αὐτὰ δυνάμεως διελέχθη, 422.10-11).[22]

Thus Hippocrates can be used to further explain Plato. This again, as we saw in the case of the rational part, shows us that Galen's method is not uncritical. He sees failings in Plato's method (in this case, he is not medical enough) but he also finds a means of giving Plato credit. This may not inspire conviction in the modern reader,[23] but it is again in keeping with the Middle-Platonic method.

I have thus far been arguing that Galen is firmly in the Platonic tradition as he makes his case that Hippocrates and Plato agree that there is a tripartite soul and further that they are right to do so. Galen uses the classic middle-Platonic and Neoplatonic device of showing that Plato (and indeed Hippocrates) supports the author's view by arguing that Plato must be read with care. Seen in this way, Galen is as cunning a philosopher as he is a doctor.

But he is a doctor and this fact colors the kind of interpretation of tripartism that Galen makes, and this in turn places him outside the mainstream of Platonic interpretation. Notoriously, Galen remains obstinately agnostic about matters that cannot be proved through clear evidence. Thus, he refuses to state whether the soul is immortal or not and what its substance may be.[24] But the soul, whether corporeal or incorporeal and whether mortal or

[22] With regard to the heart as the seat of spirit, they both use both kinds of arguments (422.11-12).

[23] But see Hankinson's arguments in Galen's favor (1991), 229-231.

[24] The topic recurs in the *PHP*: 442.36-444.11, where Galen says that the pneuma in the brain is either the incorporeal soul's οἰκητήριον or is the soul itself if the soul is corporeal; 474.22-29, where the soul is either an ethereal body or an incorporeal substance and the pneuma is its first vehicle; 599.19-25, where Galen cites *Tim.* 72d4-8 to show that Timaeus in the *Timaeus* accounts the soul's immortality merely a likely story; 598.26-600.30, where Galen distinguishes what he has proven (that the soul has three parts, etc.) from what is not provable (the soul's substance, whether it or any of its parts is immortal, and whether Plato speaks literally about the mortality of the two lower parts). Cf. Tieleman (1996), xviii; DeLacy (1992), 35-36; Hankinson (1991), 201-204.

immortal, does reside in the body and does have three different seats with three different functions. The corporeality of his medical arguments requires that the soul has a physical structure to work through. The nerves, originating from the brain and going to all parts of the body, provide the corporeal conduit for the rational psychic activity, the arteries for the spirited activity, and the veins for the desiderative activity (in its wide sense which includes nutrition and growth). Galen's interpretation of Plato's tripartism, is physical therefore, and concentrates on the *Timaeus* and its placement of the parts of the soul in different parts of the body. Galen does admire the arguments in book 4 of the *Republic*. He says that they produce knowledge that soul has three *powers* (ἐπιστημονικαί, *PHP* 600.23) and summarizes Plato's argument at length (336.16-358.22). But his interest is medical and corporeal, and as such it had limited appeal to later Platonists, such as Porphyry and Iamblichus, who were concerned not with the soul's physical seats in the body but with the soul's unity in its tripartition.

But this is not to say that Galen denied unity to the tripartite soul, as Steel wrongly concluded (212):

> Further, in Galen's view the three commanding souls (διοικούσαι) function quasi-independently, the one from the other, as is demonstrated by some medical experiments. Plato, on the contrary, wants to keep the commandment of the whole psychic life under the rational soul.

This is surely a misreading of Galen's thesis. In *PHP* 5.294.26-304.32, Galen takes Chrysippus to task for not recognizing that parts are necessary for a soul to be at odds with itself: a rational soul qua rational cannot come into conflict with itself. In an extended comparison of vice with disease of the body, Galen points out that Plato follows this path and that disease of the soul involves both conflict among the three parts and health proportion:

> For when the three parts are in harmony with one another and differ not at all, it brings about the health of the soul, but when they are in disharmony and conflict, disease. (συμφωνοῦντα μὲν γὰρ ἀλλήλοις τὰ τρία καὶ κατὰ μηδὲν στασιάζοντα τὴν ὑγίειαν τῆς ψυχῆς ἀπεργάζεται, διαφωνήσαντα δὲ καὶ στασιάσαντα τὴν νόσον, 302.14-16).

At 302.18-19, Galen quotes Plato's *Sophist* 228a7-8 as a definition of disease ("the destruction of what is naturally akin because of some conflict," ἡ τοῦ φύσει συγγενοῦς ἔκ τινος <διαφορᾶς> διαφ<θ>ορά), and then argues that rebellion against reason is disease of the soul (302.29-30, ἡ τοῦ λογιστικοῦ στάσις οὐδενὸς τῶν ἄλλων ἐστι πλὴν ψυχῆς νόσος). A few pages later (312.11-12), he quotes Plato's *Sophist* again: "One must posit that the unintelligent soul is shameful and without measure" (ψυχὴν ἄρ ἀνόητον αἰσχρὰν καὶ ἄμετρον θετέον). This is ample evidence that Galen holds to the Platonic view that vice is disorder among the three parts and virtue is order under the hegemony of reason. Thus, he holds, as one would expect, Plato's view that the soul's unity is in direct proportion to its rationality. Indeed the idea of unity arising from the harmony of the three parts is apparent in Galen's discussion of the arguments of book 4 of the *Republic* (5.336.16-358.22).[25] If Galen presents the three parts as exerting separate desires, he found this in Plato as well. The problem of unity versus division is in both Plato and Galen, as indeed it is in the later Platonists generally.

C. Conclusion

Galen's position on the tripartite soul is both recognizably Platonic and yet idiosyncratic. Later generations of Platonists were much less concerned with the body and its corporeal vessels. To them the problem will become how what is divided into parts can be a unity. Galen, however, had already answered that question satisfactorily for himself. The soul has three separate faculties located in three separate parts of the body. It is a functioning moral unity only when the commands of reason, coursing through the whole body via the nerves, are heeded and obeyed by the spirited faculty in the heart and the desiderative faculty in the liver. The heart echoes reason's message and transmits it through the blood in the arteries. The liver, having calmed its raging desires and (following the instructions of the other two parts) having sent correct messages through the blood in its veins, thereby satisfies the needs of the body in an appropriate manner. Thus, Galen is indeed a Platonist. He follows Plato's teachings, though not unthinkingly. He is a Platonist of his time, reinterpreting Plato in accordance with his own doctrines.[26]

[25] See, e.g., Galen's argument that if there were not the rational and irrational parts of the soul, the virtue of *sophrosyne* would not exist (342.13-16).

[26] I wish to thank Svetla Slaveva-Griffin for her helpful suggestions. Any remaining errors are my own responsibility.

WHO THOUGHT THE STARS ARE CAUSES? THE ASTROLOGICAL DOCTRINE CRITICIZED BY PLOTINUS

Marilynn Lawrence

I. Introduction

In the Hellenistic and Late Antique eras, astrology was a widespread phenomenon of great cultural, political, religious, and philosophical significance. Its political and cultural significance,[1] and its role in the development of Greek astronomy and mathematics,[2] have been discussed by a number of scholars, though with a few rare exceptions such as David Amand's *Fatalisme et Liberté*,[3] discussion of the philosophical import of Hellenistic astrology has been lacking, even though philosophers from Carneades to Thrasyllus to Iamblichus have had some position on astrology. Plotinus is

[1] For astrology's political significance, see Frederick H. Cramer (1959) and Tamsyn Barton (1994b). The role of astrology, or astral symbolism, has also invigorated the field of Mithraic studies in works such as Roger Beck's "Interpreting the Ponza Zodiac" (1976).

[2] These studies were primarily initiated by Otto Neugebauer, who created the history of mathematics department at Brown University. See, for instance, Otto Neugebauer and H.B. van Hoesen (1959). David Pingree made several groundbreaking contributions to the field, such as his commentary and translation of *Yavanajataka of Sphujidhavaja*, 2 Vols. (1978), and *From Astral Omens to Astrology from Babylon to Bikaner* (1997). Alexander Jones has produced many publications analyzing Babylonian and Greek astronomical methods used in astrological practice, including the three-part *Studies in the Astronomy of the Roman Period*, in *Centaurus* 39 (1997).

[3] *Fatalisme et Liberté dans L'Antiquité Grecqué* (1945). Tamsyn Barton also provides some excellent preliminary research on some philosophical foundations of astrology in *Ancient Astrology* (1994a). The present author has also made an attempt to fill in this gap in "Hellenistic Astrology" (2005). A. Bouché-Leclercq (1899) argues for philosophical precedence for Greek astrology in pre-Socratic cosmologies. However, at the expense of more detailed information on ancient astrology, the work is bloated with hostile commentary on every ancient philosophy, particularly Platonism, which he believed did not result in rapid 'progress' of the natural sciences.

certainly not alone in confronting astrology as a philosophical theory,[4] though his discussion of it in *Enneads* 2 and 3 provides a cogent example of the problems astrology and astral fatalism presented for philosophy in general, and Neoplatonism in particular.

Hellenistic astrologers, in developing methods of categorizing planets and signs, and the predictions that can be made from them, or *apotelesmatika*,[5] did not exclusively follow one theoretical school. Making predictions on the basis of astral phenomena was primarily a late Babylonian import.[6] However, against the backdrop of the scientific developments and philosophical theories of Middle Platonists, Neopythagoreans and Stoics, astrologers wove an elaborate tapestry of methods and meanings assigned to various configurations and calculations.[7]

Astrology's relationship to schools of philosophy was complicated by a number of factors. For instance, the *practice* of astrology preceded and sometimes developed simultaneously with *theories* of astral causality and fatalism. Astrology also developed and spread during a period in which certain inherent connections between cosmology, fatalism, epistemology, and divination were established. These connections colored the lens by which it was scrutinized by philosophers. Writers of astrological manuals rarely discussed their theoretical leanings (though these can sometimes be teased out), making it difficult to determine which onto-cosmological theories were held by practicing astrologers. Furthermore, astrological predictions and

[4] Other philosophers who have offered lengthy discussion of astrology include, but are not limited, to Sextus Empiricus (*Pros Astrologous*, in *Adversus mathematicos* vol. IV), Cicero (*De divinatione*, 41), Augustine (*De civitate dei*, 5.1-7), and Origen (*Philocalia*, 41).

[5] *Apotelesmatika* was a common word for astrological texts, used by Ptolemy (mid-2nd C.E.), Antiochus of Athens (late-2nd C.E.), Pseudo-Manetho (3rd? C.E.) and Hephaistion of Thebes (4th C.E.). While the placement of planets relative to the horizon and the fixed stars was the primary material for astrologers, these positions resulted in additional entities, such as *kleroi*, which are discovered through various mathematical calculations.

[6] The earliest surviving Babylonian horoscopes date to the early fifth century B.C.E. See F. Rochberg (1998) for translation and commentary on these cuneiform tablets.

[7] These developments are discussed in M. Lawrence (2005).

astral causality are to be distinguished from astral piety.[8] One need not be an astrologer to think of the planets and stars as divine beings, preservers of number, time, and the orderly cosmos. A particular problem for the relationship between Neoplatonism and astrology is the prominence of the planets and stars in Plato's *Timaeus* (38c ff), *Republic* (10.616c-617d), and *Laws* (7.817ff; 10.886 ff), and the mysterious role of these young gods (*Tim.* 40b ff) in the descent of the souls. It is not the intention of this paper to explore these issues here, but to note that the practice of astrology was a sounding board for philosophical issues, particularly centered on causality and fatalism.

By outlining Plotinus' arguments against astrological theory and practice (while noting his acceptance of astral divination), the intention of this paper is to address the question whether or not astrologers really thought that the stars *cause* temperament, appearance, and character, and to illustrate some of the theoretical background that prompted the attention given by Plotinus to this issue. The author also intends to demonstrate the complexity of the issue of astrology's place in Neoplatonism, so that meaningful questions can arise for further discussion. This field of questioning can only emerge when we dismiss an earlier false dichotomy between 'rational' and 'irrational' in Greek thinking – a dichotomy that superficially places divination, magic, and astrology on the side of the irrational.[9]

II. Plotinus' Arguments in *Ennead* 3.1.

Plotinus' discussion of astral causality and astrology can primarily be found in two places: in his early treatise "On Fate,"[10] (*Ennead* 3.1; chronologically the 3rd), and in the late *Ennead* 2.3, "On Whether the Stars

[8] Plato's position on the study of astronomy as preparation for philosophy may have led to the prominence of astral piety in his Academy, as evident in the *Epinomis* dialogue. Cf. Alan Scott (1991), pp. 20-23.

[9] E.R. Dodds (1951) shares in the responsibility for this dichotomy as does Bouché-Leclercq mentioned above. The present author rather sees the treatment of astrology, magic, and divination as an outgrowth of rationality. The systematization of astrology is a perfect example of a concern for rationality, for it was an expression of an orderly and predictable cosmos.

[10] *Peri Heimarmenês*. *Ennead III*, tr. A.H. Armstrong (1967, reprint with corrections, 1993), pp. 1-35. This edition, and others of this series, will be referenced throughout.

Are Causes,"[11] (chronologically the 52nd). In "On Fate," Plotinus dismisses the Epicurean atomic notion of causality that does not explain individual fate, particularly, concerning one's occupation, temperament, and all differences in human affairs. In sections 4 and 7, he also points out a definition of fate that treats the cosmic soul as a single cause, but considers fate to be the direction of this principle to all activities including our own.[12] He argues that such a definition of fate not only contradicts the notion of interwoven causes, but attributes good and evil actions to the cosmic All. This view, that all matters are directed by the universal Soul, ignores the freedom of the individual soul, which has the ability to gain control of impulses and to be the internal source of its thoughts and actions.

Plotinus spends more time on a third theory by 'others' who think that:

> ...each and every thing comes to be from the universal circuit (*pantos phoran*), that encompasses and causes everything by its movement and by the positions and configurations of the planets and fixed stars toward one another (*schêmatismois pros allêla*)..."[13]

These others trust that "everything thereafter would occur as expected from these predictions (*prorrêseôs*)."[14] According to this view, divination from the activities of the universal circuit can lead one to knowledge of the fortune, thoughts, desires, impulses, and character of an individual.

At this point in the treatise, we have the introduction of a theory with two parts: 1) all things are caused by the universal motion of the heavens; and

[11] *Peri tou ei poiei ta astra. Ennead II*, tr. A.H. Armstrong (1966), pp. 56-101.

[12] In *Ennead.III*, pp. 18-19, n. 1, Armstrong points out the similarities of this notion of fate and that found in the commentary by Calcidius on the *Timaeus* and in Pseudo-Plutarch's *De fato*. He then argues that because Plotinus differentiates theories of fate that is caused by a world-soul from the causal chain of determinism, the world-soul fate must be one espoused by earlier Stoic-influenced Platonists. However, Susanne Bobzien (1998) argues that the late Stoic fatalism took a different form than the early Stoa, and holds to a particular compatibility between that which depends on us and causal determinism (pp. 358-412). She argues that this view may have arisen out of Peripatetic and Middle Platonic criticisms of early Stoic fatalism (p. 359). While the target of Plotinus' criticisms in this section, in fact, may be a Platonic theory of fate, it may not be entirely distinct from a certain late Stoic compatibilist version.

[13] *Ennead* 3.1.2.26-8. Author's translation unless noted otherwise.

[14] *Ennead* 3.1.2.6-30.

2) predictions from the study of configurations of planets and stars to one another are possible. The first part precedes the development of Hellenistic astrology by at least two centuries. In *On Generation and Corruption* (336a33 ff), Aristotle places the real cause of generation and corruption in the zodiacal ecliptic - the path of the Sun. This notion that the circular motions of the heavens cause perpetual growth and decay provided one among several entrance points for the successful importation of astrology in Greco-Roman thinking. More specifically, however, the relationship between astral causality and astrology may have been established in the context of the Neopythagorean works such as *On the Nature of the Universe* by Ocellus Lucanus.[15] In this work, Ocellus draws the supralunar/sublunar division of worlds, with the harmonious and regular movements of the heavenly bodies signifying the unchanging and incorruptible supralunar realm. Included in his list of indicators of the self-subsistence of the cosmos are the "order, symmetry, configurations (*skhêmatismoi*), positions (*theseis*), intervals (*diastaseis*), powers (*dunameis*), swiftness and slowness with respect to one another, their numbers, and temporal periods."[16]

Plotinus mentions these positions and configurations of the planets[17] in *Ennead* 3.1.5.1-4. He also alludes to 'powers' when admitting that planets do contribute something to bodily temperaments (*kraseis*),[18] while not determining the character and thoughts (*êthesi*, *dianoiais*) of an individual.[19] These powers, being at the heart of the theory that stars are causes, particularly of temperament in living beings, are further described by Ocellus as pairs of contrary qualities, namely, hot, cold, wet, and dry. The powers being incorporeal, ungenerated and incorruptible are aided by contraries, which ensure the immutability of the powers. Through the yearly solar revolution along the ecliptic, the active nature of hot and cold and the passive

[15] *Peri tês tou pantos phuseôs* (1926). Translated by K.S. Guthrie (1987) as "On the Nature of the Universe," pp. 203-211. This spurious work of Aristotelian influence dates to around the mid-second century B.C.E.

[16] Ocellus Lucanus. *De universi natura*, 1.6.1-3 (Harder).

[17] The Greek word that is often translated as star, *astêr*, included and often primarily meant planet which was differentiated from what we today call a star by the designation of fixed or stationary (*aplanos*).

[18] This word for 'temperature' as a mixture of qualities means temperament, as well (e.g., Galen's *Peri Kraseôn*, '*On Temperaments*').

[19] *Ennead* 3.1.6.4-7.

nature of moist and dry produce changes in the four elements or substances,[20] which are of a lower ontological status than the powers, due to their position in the generated realm of strife and nature. This realm of generated beings is demarcated by the Fates from the ungenerated realm of divinities at the path of the Moon.[21] In keeping with Aristotle, the sun's seasonal path through the zodiacal signs is the more proximate cause, by causing changes in the atmosphere.

By admitting that temperament is caused by the stars, Plotinus accepts this naturalistic cosmology; however, he also considers temperament to be a result of material influence on the lower part of the soul, a part that may be mastered by the higher, the soul in communion with *Nous*.[22]

With one prominent exception, Claudius Ptolemy, there is little in the surviving astrological texts to indicate that this particular notion of astral causality was the dominant one during and after the period in which astrology became systematized in the second century B.C.E.[23] The assignment of planets to pairs of qualities, such as Saturn being cold and dry, Jupiter being warm and moist, is not directly present in surviving astrological works prior to and independent of Ptolemy.[24] In some cases, however, certain natural

20 The elements are called *ousiai* by Ocellus. *De universi natura*, ed. R. Harder (Berlin: Weidmann, 1926), 2.5. It is a Peripatetic notion that even fire suffers action and is itself moved (*On Generation and Corruption*, 336a8).

21 Ocellus Lucanus. *De universi natura*, 2.2 (Harder).

22 Cf. *Enneads* 2.2.3 and 2.4.3.4-6.

23 Other cosmological theories, such as Stoic determinism and universal sympathy of Greek medicine, also had a great impact on Hellenistic astrological doctrine. These theories are discussed in M. Lawrence, "Hellenistic Astrology." The relationship between astrology and Stoicism is complicated. Many Stoics did accept a type of astral causality, and most accepted divination as an indicator of a chain of fated causes, but the relationship between individual Stoics and astrology is on a case-by-case basis. Numenius, (Frag. 17, Guthrie, 1917), indicates that the Stoics believed that everything arises from the motions of the stars, but this does not necessarily lead to predictive astrology. Middle Platonic theories that one finds in pseudo-Plutarch (*Peri Heimarmenês*) and Hermetic literature (e.g., *Stobaei Hermetica*, Excerpts VII, XXIII, and XXIX) demonstrate other ways, those in line with interpretations of the *Timaeus*, in which planets and stars contribute to fate and to temperament.

24 These authors include the fragments and works of Nechepso and Petosiris (2nd B.C.E.), Teukros of Babylon (1st? B.C.E.), Dorotheus of Sidon (1st B.C.E.–1st C.E.), Marcus Manilius (1st C.E.), Vettius Valens (2nd B.C.E.), and in the skeptic Sextus Empiricus' account of astrological doctrine. For more on astrological techniques independent of Ptolemy, see Manilius, *Astronomica* (1977). Also see T.S. Barton (1994a) for basic information on Hellenistic astrologers and their techniques.

affinities of planets and qualities are expressed in writers such as Vettius Valens, who noted that Saturn is responsible for ailments related to an imbalance of cold,[25] and Dorotheus of Sidon, who considered the pairing of Mars with the Moon as productive of warmth,[26] likely due to the caustic nature of Mars. These and other astrologers do not, however, systematically pair the five planets with the four qualities, as does Ptolemy. He describes the nature of each of the fixed stars and planets as a combination of these powers, hot, cold, moist, and dry; the powers of the planets are modified in a variety of ways through their positions.[27] These produce physical effects on individuals and nations as filtered through the course of the Sun, and the physical body remains in sympathy with the quality of the moment in which an individual is born. Given Ptolemy's extensive account of the powers of planets and fixed stars,[28] his *Apotelesmatika* was likely the immediate source for Plotinus' second century association of astrological practice with the causal theory of powers affecting the elements and the realm of generation.

Additional arguments that Plotinus uses in *Ennead* 3.1 - those not necessarily related to his own philosophy of freedom of the individual soul over its lower nature - are classic New Academy arguments that likely originated with Carneades.[29] Plotinus mentions three of these traditional arguments. The first is the expectation that other people born at the same time and under the same configurations should have the same fate (but in fact do not). The second argument is that animals born at the same time as humans should likewise share the same destiny (but obviously do not). The third is against astro-geography or astro-chorography. This is the notion that zodiac signs or planets have dominion over certain geographical zones, and affect the people of these zones. Plotinus notes that even if these regions affect appearance in general of those born in them, it does not account for the variety of character within each group.

[25] Vettii Valentis, *Anthologiarum libri ix*, ed. Kroll (1908, rpt 1973), 2.16-19.

[26] Dorotheus, *Fragmenta Graeca* (1976), 356.12-13.

[27] Claudius Ptolemy. *Tetrabiblos*, tr. F. E. Robbins (1956), 1.4-8, pp. 35-45.

[28] Ptolemy also had considerable familiarity with Aristotle's works, as is evident in his philosophical preface to *Syntaxis mathematica* (*Almagest*). He breaks from Aristotle by demonstrating empirical skepticism of the theoretical sciences of theology and physics; he embraces mathematics as the only true science – again, revealing possible Neopythagorean influence. See G.J. Toomer (1998), pp. 35-37.

[29] See F.H. Cramer (1959), pp. 52-56.

There is little to indicate that Plotinus had more than a surface knowledge of astrology at the time of the earlier work, "On Fate." He does show awareness of the use of 'derived' charts - that is - reading the fate of another person from one's own chart. Such a technique can be found in Book 3 of Ptolemy's *Apotelesmatika*.[30] He also states that it should not be said that the planets become or do good or bad from the way they *look* at one another and are positioned relative to one another.[31] He returns to this in more detail in *Ennead* 2.3. We might ask why Plotinus returned to the issue of astrology towards the end of his career. Perhaps he had been worrying about the enthusiasm that some of his students, such as Porphyry,[32] had for astrology. By the time of his late criticisms, which are particularly centered on the ontological status of the planets, Plotinus demonstrated a better acquaintance with astrological jargon.[33] Turning now to this late treatise on "Whether the Stars are Causes," we'll find that the arguments are directed specifically against astrologers, and not simply against those who might suppose a fatalistic astral causality.

III. Plotinus' Criticism of Astrology in *Ennead* 2.3.

In his later treatise, *Ennead* 2.3, Plotinus is not speaking of general effects that one might find in Aristotle or the Neopythagoreans, but of a language of causality found in astrological manuals such as the *Anthology* of Vettius Valens or the *Apotelesmatika* of Ptolemy. One of the primary doctrines of Hellenistic astrology is that planets, when placed in certain zodiac

[30] Claudius Ptolemy. *Tetrabiblos*, tr. F.E. Robbins (1956), 3.4-5, pp. 241 ff.

[31] *Ennead* 3.1.6.16-18.

[32] See *Introductio in Tetrabiblum Ptolemaei*, eds. Aemilia Boer and Stephen Weinstock, *CCAG* 5.4 186-228, in D. Olivieri, et al. (1898-1953). A large portion of this work is actually a copy or paraphrase of the *Thesaurus* by late second century astrologer Antiochus of Athens. See D. Pingree (1977). pp. 203-223.

[33] The earlier treatise indicates some exposure to the language of technical astrology, but this does not mean that he directly read astrological manuals. As stated above, most of the arguments in "On Fate" are concerning a general theory of causal effects from the stars. Many of his arguments identified as against predictive astrology are standard skeptical New Academy observations. He does not appear in this treatise to use the technical vocabulary found in astrological texts. Plotinus uses forms of *horaô* (2.3.4.1; 3.1.6.16), while the more common words used by astrologers are *epimartureô* and *theôreô* (see below).

signs, are thought to relate to one another in ways that modify their significations. The technical words used to describe planets interacting with one another are often words of seeing, such as *theôreô*, *epimarturô*, and *katopteuô*. These modifications of the planets, either in activity or emotional state, would then correspond to an individual whose moment of birth or place in time synchronizes with the conditions of planets and signs.

In the Platonic tradition, the power of sight is productive through the act of contemplation. The agent of this activity may be the Soul (e.g. *Ennead* 2.9.2) or the creator god (e.g. Numenius Fr. 12.17-22, des Places). Such doctrines arose from interpretations of Plato's *Timaeus*, particularly of the creative/contemplative/copying activity of the demiurge (28a-b, 29a-b), as well as of our own sight of the heavens, which produce concepts of time and number, while leading to wonder and eventually to philosophy (47a-b). It is quite possible that the astrologers had a Platonic optical theory in mind when they developed their technical vocabulary. However, for the astrologers, it appears that the direction of the seeing, upward or downward, is irrelevant to the planets when they look upon each other.

For Plotinus, the absurdity of the planets' contemplation of one another is not in the improper application of optical theory, Platonic or otherwise. It is rather a joint matter of astrophysics and the preservation of the divine nature of these celestial residents. Plotinus first cleverly argues that the notion that planets are 'in' zodiac signs is meaningless, for they are not 'in' the signs but below them in their own circuits. Furthermore, it should not be possible for planets to change their emotional state based on their rising and setting relative to the *kentra* - the four turning positions of the eastern and western horizons, the midheaven, and the anti-midheaven. Each planet will be declining or rising relative to another of the four points, resulting in conflicting emotional states such as glad and sad at the same time.[34] Plotinus is speaking from the perspective of the planets in their course, while astrologers are speaking from our perception of them on earth and from our measurements of the sky relative to our position on earth. Another example, in which Plotinus speaks from the perspective of the planets rather than us, is his criticism of the astrological doctrine of *hairesis*. In astrological language, each planet has chosen its diurnal or nocturnal preference, so that Saturn delights in the day when it is warmed, and Mars delights at night when its

[34] In this criticism, Plotinus seems to be confusing the function of the four angles, that of increasing or decreasing the capability of the planets, with the doctrine that planets in particular places (*topoi*) and signs 'rejoice' or are 'depressed'.

burning nature is cooled.[35] Plotinus responds that it is always day for the planets (although the astrologers think that the *hairesis* of a planet is again relative to our horizon).[36] Likewise, Plotinus points out that the Moon cares not whether she is waxing or waning, for the half of her facing the Sun will always be lit.[37]

Plotinus then asks whether the stars are with or without souls. Supposing that the planets are without souls, they only contribute degrees of heat (and not cold). This causal contribution will only affect one's body. Plotinus modifies his earlier admission (in *Ennead* 3.1) that the planets do have an effect on temperament (although the genetic contribution from the parents would be greater),[38] with the addition that even if the planets do have influences on the body, these physical effects are far too mixed when they reach the lower realm for any claims to identify them though knowledge of the configurations of the planets.[39] Nor would it be possible to determine from this mixture anything concerning one's praxis, wealth, etc. Nevertheless, he maintains that the motions of the heavens conform to the *logos* of the whole and do have some productive capacity, not for bringing about complete changes but for inessential changes. He counters the claim that the beings in the heavens make or cause everything below, with an appeal to the Forms that are beyond the heavens. It is the form of Horse that makes a horse, though effects caused from without, such as a bodily illness or even a 'cold' of the soul, make an ill-tuned lyre.[40]

If, though, the planets *are* ensouled, they are capable of making deliberate choices. However, their choices have nothing to do with decisions to act for good or evil that we might face, for planets do not have the will to deliberately harm us. As Plotinus says, "they are always serene and rejoice in the goods they have and in what they see."[41] Furthermore, any virtuous character trait that is sent down from above would become vice below. For example, a "kindly disposition" becomes a less refined sort of love; courage

[35] Cf. Vettius Valens, *Anthologiarum libri ix*, 2.22, 3.14-15; Claudius Ptolemy, *Tetrabiblos*, 1.7.

[36] *Ennead* 2.3.5.7-9.

[37] *Ennead* 2.3.5.11-17.

[38] *Ennead* 3.1.5.24-29.

[39] *Ennead* 2.3.12.1-3.

[40] *Ennead* 2.3.13.11-17.

[41] *Ennead* 2.3.3.22-24. Armstrong translation (1966), p. 63.

becomes unbridled passion; and intelligence becomes trickery.[42] Plotinus also makes the point that we can do nothing to affect the planets, for their effluences (*aporroiai*)[43] flow in only one direction - from the supralunar to the sublunar. This position is also explained in his "On the Heavens."[44]

Regardless of whether the planets are ensouled and have deliberate choice, the technical vocabulary of astrology leads Plotinus to believe that the theoretical position of astrologers is that planets are compelled by their places and figures. The astrological causality that he attacks in this work is one that places the planets themselves at the mercy of a system that compelled them to be affected and to do good or bad things. Plotinus interprets this system as a chain of causality rather than as a method of interpretation, for he analyzes the language of astrology quite literally.

Unfortunately it is difficult to say on the basis of surviving texts whether or not the astrologers themselves really thought that Venus in trigonal aspect to Saturn actually *produces* those who are austere and lacking a sense of humor (*agelastous*).[45] In fact, it seems that astrologers often used linguistic shortcuts. Vettius Valens would at one time refer to the star of Hermes or Ares in the genitive,[46] though in the course of giving examples, the planets are simply identified with their godly names. Words such as 'cause' (*aitia*) (e.g., 40.31, 41.12) and 'make' (*poiei*) (e.g., 3.7, 3.17) are used by Valens, interchangeably with signifying words such as *sêmainei* (e.g., 1.5, 2.24, 2.35).

[42] *Ennead* 2.3.11. Incidentally, these examples correspond to the astrological characteristics of Venus, Mars, and Mercury (cf. Vettius Valens, *Anthologiarum libri ix*, 3.16-24; 2.35-3.10; and 4.9-11).

[43] *Aporroia* is also a technical word in astrology for the effluence from the Moon, which occurs when it has recently made an aspectual configuration with a planet and is within a certain range from it. It is paired with *sunaphê*, the approaching contact with a planet, which does not have the implication of any effluence upward from the atmosphere to the stars (cf. Ptolemy, *Apotelesmatika*, 1.24; Dorotheus, *Fragmenta Graeca*, 387.16-17). However, Plotinus' criticism may indicate that there was such a word in astrology that, when taken literally, translates into such a concept.

[44] *Ennead* 2.1.6.55-57. Plotinus asks whether anything flows away from heavenly bodies so that they need nourishment from below. His answer is that because the stars do not have an elemental mixture, they do not in fact need nourishment. This does not mean that they could not possess the quality of heat – but the fire in question is of a different order.

[45] Vettius Valens, *Anthologiarum libri ix*, 75.11-13. Even Ptolemy, who comes closest to expressing a theory of astral causality, uses other manners of correspondence, such as sympathy and familiarity (cf. *Tetrabiblos*, 1.2.3; 1.11.31) that cannot be pinned down as efficient or physical causality.

[46] Cf. *Anthologiarum libri ix*, 2.35; 4.4.

We must not forget that after all of his attacks on astral causality and technical astrology, Plotinus not only accepts astral divination, but also thinks that the stars are best and brightest of all for giving signs of the future to those who can read such celestial writing.[47] Acceptance of divination may seem to be an odd position for someone who attempts to avoid fatalism and to preserve freedom of the soul. This is particularly so given the close ties between divination and fatalism in Stoicism, particularly that of Chryssipus.[48] By knocking down both material astral causality and astrology (as based on astral causality), Plotinus draws a distinction between astrology and divination. His astral divination, then, could have nothing to do with the multitude of complex signifiers in astrology. Although he says stars or planets give signs of the future (*ta mellonta*), the future indicated by this analogical writing in the sky appears to be less deterministic than that of astrologers. Even if astrologers treated their language as a tool of divinatory interpretation, the systematization of astrology in the Hellenistic era was an attempt to capture the signifiers; to hold them down in *time* and place, while expecting them to be repeatable and knowable. Astrologers had numerous methods for predicting events within *any* period in life, as well as several methods for calculating one's day of death. No matter what language astrologers employed, this would be reason enough for Plotinus to exclude their doctrine from his notion of astral divination.[49]

IV. Porphyry's Response

In Porphyry's preface to *Introduction to Ptolemy's Apotelesmatika*,[50] the author addresses the necessity for this compilation, namely, that Ptolemy fails to give adequate definitions for the obscure astrological vocabulary. This

[47] *Enneads* 2.3.7.1-14; 3.1.6.20-25.

[48] For a detailed reconstruction of Chryssipus' arguments on divination, see, S. Bobzien (1998), pp. 87-96; 144-179.

[49] Toward the end of *Ennead* 2.3, Plotinus turns to Plato's Spindle of Fate myth in the *Republic* for guidance on astral causality. It is not apparent that Plotinus successfully squares his criticisms with Plato's notions that descending souls are linked to the stars and necessity, receiving from the stars character (*êthê*), characteristic actions (*êthê praxeis*) and emotions (*pathê*). Plotinus accepts from his master some astral fatalism that applies to all but the individual souls who free themselves and fly away toward the Good. The idea that the planets contribute something to descending souls is one which would play a greater part in the astrological theories of other Neoplatonists, as well as in Hermetic philosophy.

[50] Porphyry. *Introductio in Tetrabiblum Ptolemaei*, eds. Aemilia Boer and Stephan Weinstock, *CCAG* 5.4, in Olivieri, et. al (1898-1953), pp. 186-228.

work contains short chapters defining the astrological terms, including those left out by Ptolemy.[51] In the preface, he says that Ptolemy would have done better to separate out and define each of the obscure terms from the ancients. Of the terms that Ptolemy fails to explain, Porphyry says, one is "reminded of the witnessing [planets] (*marturias*), the [planetary] guards, (*doruphopias*), the prevailing ones (*kaphuperterêseôs*), and the predominant ones (*epikratêseôs*)."[52] Porphyry writes, "[We] set forth this timely introduction to be a fulfillment of a debt, and by these words to make it easy for the uninitiated to take it in at a glance."[53]

This author can only speculate at this point and suggest that the debt Porphyry attempted to fulfill is to be found in his response to Plotinus' inadequately informed critique of astrological language. Plotinus, who was not initiated into the practice of astrology, had perhaps glanced at Ptolemy, and there found in the mixture of causal language and obscure words of seeing and rejoicing, an easy target for his piercing logic.

[51] Notable is a longer section on a method for calculating the *oikodespotês*, the planetary ruler of the chart, which is discussed in Porphyry's *Letter to Anebo*.

[52] *Introductio in Tetrabiblum Ptolemaei*, p. 190.

[53] Ibid.

THE TRANSCENDENCE OF SOPHIA IN PLOTINUS' TREATISE ON INTELLIGIBLE BEAUTY, V.8 (31)

Daniele Bertini

I will consider an argument by Plotinus to show how the notion of transcendence is used in explaining the nature of knowledge. The argument is set forth in the section 4-6 of the treatise V.8 (31).[1] In my opinion this argument provides a good example of the philosophical frame of Platonism. I sum up this frame in the following theses: a) for a thing being is being real and true; so that for a thing being real and being true is equivalent; but b) for a thing being real and true means being intelligible; that is to say: a thing could be understood because that thing is a being; thus c) for a thing being is the identity of its ontological and epistemological nature.[2]

I.

Plato's texts provide many passages to prove this conceptual notion of Platonism. I will briefly consider the best known, *Republic* 508d and following. Socrates invites his interlocutor to call the idea of Good (τὴν τοῦ ἀγαθοῦ ἰδέαν) that being (τοῦτο) giving: a) to things knowable their truth (τὴν ἀλήθειαν παρέχον τοῖς γιγνωσκομένοις); and b) to the knowing subject the possibility to know (τῷ γιγνώσκοντι τὴν δύναμιν). The assumption of the argument is plainly that the sourceal being accounts simultaneously for objective truth and subjective cognition. Indeed this source is said to be the causal reason (αἰτίαν οὖσαν) both of knowledge and truth (ἐπιστήμης καὶ ἀληθίας).

Anyway, at this stage, it is not very clear what Plato really means; since he simply asserts a kind of transcendental condition of *epistéme* and *aletheia*,

[1] Porphyry entitled the treatise ΠΕΡΙ ΤΟΥ ΝΟΗΤΟΥ ΚΑΛΛΟΣ. The actual body of the text was part of a major work against gnosticism divided by Porphyry into four treatise. The sequence would have been the following: III.8; V.8; V.5; II.9. See Harder (1936); Cilento (1971).

[2] On the double features of a thing in Plotinus, see Emilsson (1996).

without arguing in relation to the ontological status of this condition. Moreover, what does he think when he says knowledge? And truth? Are we sure truth is objective and knowledge subjective? Can truth be understood as a logical concept? Or does it have an ontological value too? It seems clear that the notion of truth assumed in the text is the main philosophical problem of the argument.[3]

[3] Notoriously an influential reading of the myth of cave by M.Heidegger attributes to Plato a germinal theory of truth as representation (See Heidegger [1976]). Now, although we have good reasons to refute the Heideggerian interpretation from a purely exegetical standpoint (See, J.Barnes [1990]), I think that a philosophical consideration of the text shows undoubtedly how Heidegger could not achieve the inner essence of Plato's thought. Heidegger's thread is grounded in the distinction between the condition of man. in and out of the cave. In the cave the being of man is determined by falsity; while out of the cave by truth (See M.Heidegger [1976], p. 214). But, for Heidegger, this assertion is just a superficial comprehension of the myth. (See M.Heidegger [1976], p. 215). The crucial point of the reading is the observation that in the Greek text preceding Plato's philosophizing this truth is not understood as a quality of the epistemological process of the human acquisition of knowledge, but as the evidence of every particular being, of ta onta. (See M.Heidegger [1976], p. 223). Heidegger translates aletheia with the German neologism Un-Verborgenheit; truth is everything that is not-hidden, because truth is everything positively appearing in the horizon of being. (See M.Heidegger [1976], p. 238). Now, the man delivering himself from the chains imprisoning human kind in the cave attains a right view of truth out of the cave, since he moves from the ontological space of falsity to that of truth. In this way he draws out things from their Verborgenheit, hiddeness, making them public for his comrades. Heidegger thinks then that for Plato the truth acquires an instrumental value for the laying of life: in the cave, where we spend most of our human condition, we need to regard the true beings subsisting outside of the cave; since these are the epistemological criteria to judge correctly of the nature of things. Things in the cave represent in fact the ideas out of the cave, and truth consists in the right understanding of our conceptions as images of certain true archetypal causes. Thus Heidegger reduces the journey of man through the degrees of reality, described by Plato, to an epistemological process. But this is the real source of his unsatisfying comprehension of Platonism. Had he read the passage in the Republic immediately preceding the myth of cave, with the same accuracy he dedicates to that containing the myth, he could have maybe seen how the idea of Good has for Plato simultaneously an epistemological and an ontological causal activity; so that it would be deceiving to distinguish, with a modern attitude, between epistemology and ontology, subjectivity and objectivity, in Plato's philosophy. (On the philosophical understanding of the relation between Plato and Heidegger see H.G.Gadamer [1976]).

Now, the subsequent passage of the text, treating the causal action of the first principle, the idea of Good, gives to the reader some helpful suggestions for understanding the presumed nature of aletheia.

Plato explains the epistemological and ontological role peculiar to the source by comparing how the principle acts with the activity of the epistemological and ontological principle of the visible world (see *Respublica*, 509b). This second principle is the sun. The sun gives to the visible things the possibility to be viewed (τοῦ ὁρᾶσθαι δύναμηιν), but it is also the cause of their actual being: of their birth, growth, and nourishment (τὴν γένεσιν καὶ αὔξην καὶ τροφήν). The sun plays in this way a twofold function: while enlightening the sensible world, it makes the object able to be seen; but in this enlightment the sun provides the ontological condition for the existence of things too. In a similar way the idea of Good, a kind of sun of the intelligible world, gives to the knowable things not only the possibility of being known, but also their existence (τὸ εἶναί) and essence (τὴν οὐσίαν).

If we collect all these assertions, it will appear evident how, for Plato, things are true in the same sense in which they simply subsist. Being is being real and being true; since reality and truth are caused with the same act by a single principle, the idea of Good. In their ontological subsistance, depending on their actual relation to the source, true things are possible objects of knowledge because of their being, enlightened by the intelligible sun. Consequently the same conditions of the existence of a thing accounts for our knowledge of it too: in being real things are true.

Naturally Plato just asserts all these theses, without giving a philosophical justification of the reasons why the principle should and could act in this way. Indeed, he paradoxically says that the principle gives existence and essence to things, being itself beyond being (οὐκ οὐσίας ὄντος τοῦ ἀγαθτοῦ, ἀλλ'ἔτι ἐπέκεινα τῆς οὐ σίας). How is it possible? How can a principle act without having a kind of subsistence? And what does it mean, that the principle is beyond being? What is it then? Or where is it? Now, since Plato's argument is the place where the notion of transcendence appears in the horizon of western philosophy, in my opinion, it would be difficult to overestimate its importance. The history of Platonism find here its spring: Plato's assumption of a principle transcending the wholeness of beings grounded, constitutes the permanent *leit-motiv* of every neoPlatonic philosophy.

Consequentely Plotinus too finds in this passage of the Republic a source for his understanding of the relation among hypostasis. In his book on the Plotinian doctrine of *Nous*, T.Szlezák has proved the sourceal importance of the textual source offered by Plato's argument.[4] The notion of transcendence seems in this way the centre around which gravitates the Platonic conflagration of reality, truth and being.

II.

Many Plotinian treatises concern transcendence among the hypostasis.[5] But, instead of taking a general survey of these, I prefer analyse the use of the notion in an argument where Plotinus does not focus it: so that the notion implicitly assumed could be particularly clear from its use.

I begin then the consideration of Plotinus' text. The first passage (V.8.4, lines 1-7) treats the ontological determinations of the *Nous*. Plotinus speaks in this place a mythical language. While elsewhere he defines rationally the structure of the Intellect, here he prefers adopting an allusive proceeding concerning the kind of life peculiar to the superior gods.[6] In conformity with the Homeric verse, these gods *live at ease* in the Intellect (καὶ γὰρ τὸ ρεῖα ζώειν ἐκεῖ), since the truth is the cause of their birth, provides to them nourishment, and constitutes their substantiality (ἀλήθεια αὐτοῖς καὶ γενέτειρα καὶ τροφὸς καὶ οὐσία καὶ τροφή). They stay there contemplating all things (ὁρῶσι τὰ πάντα) in clearness; because in the Intellect every being is shining (διαφανῆ). An intelligible light is the efficient cause of this clearness: every being shows itself in its depth core completely (ἀλλὰ πᾶς παντὶ φανερὸς εὶς τὸ εἴσω καὶ πάντα· φῶς γὰρ φωτὶ).

Evidently in this passage Plotinus refers to Plato's argument concerning the idea of Good.[7] Some elements prove this impression: the role of light is a direct quotation of the epistemological activity of the sun; the Platonic pattern

[4] See T.A.Szlezák (1979), passim.

[5] See V.4 (7); V.1 (10); V.2 (11); V.6 (24); V.5 (32); VI.7 (38): VI. (39); V.3 (49).

[6] In V.8.3, lines 27 and following, Plotinus distinguishes among two kinds of gods. Those of them "ἐν οὐρανῷ ὄντες...θεῶνται ἀείε οἷον δέ πόρρωθεν, τὰ ἐν ἐκείνῳ", that is to say the objects in the Intellect. In some sense they are spatially under the intellect, so that their nature could be determined as inferior, because of the distance qualifying their imperfect contemplation. Others gods, "οἱ... ἐν ἐκείνῳ ὄντες" ,stay in the Intellect, "ἐπ' αὐτῶν ἐν αὐτῷ, ἐν παντὶ οἰκοῦντες τῷ ἐκεῖ οὐρανῷ". These could be said superior, since they live the same life of the Intellect, directly touching it.

[7] I. Crystal states persuasively that Plotinus used the light analogy since influenced by *Respublica* passage quoted above. See Crystal (1998).

of thought asserting a twofold causation, both epistemological and ontological, is applied to the explanation of the life of the gods; the relationship between knowledge and vision is explicitly set forth with a metaphorical language, the language of myth, stated by the quotation by Homer. Plotinus, in this way, introduces the reader into a Platonic world, inhabited by intelligible beings, whose subsistence is to be self evident to some superior understandings, those of the gods. Obviously, the reader could ask: why does Plotinus speak mythically? Has he rethorical reasons as in other treatises? Or do philosophical motives incline him to this choice? In my opinion the reference to the mythical horizon has a rigorous epistemological source (V.8.3, lines 11 and following): to inquire the nature of the *Nous* (τίνα εἰκόνα τις αὐτοῦ) a philosopher needs to apprehend his object directly from the inside. If he looks for an image of that, he could find just something inferior, derivative. Indeed, he really attains the Intellect, only purifying the *nous* in him. Just because we are in the *Nous*, we can understand the *Nous*.[8] But this purified understanding is similar to the life of gods: so Plotinus wants the reader to have a comprehension of the Intellect by a kind of phenomenology of the understanding peculiar to the divine part of our soul; that is to say that part of our soul similar to soul of the gods.[9] The use of myth in this passage is therefore justified by the necessity to involve the reader in the search, referring to a world familiar to him, the commonly granted context of the Greco-Roman religious culture.

Because of this proceeding Plotinus describes the *Nous* as it appears to the gods (V.8.4, lines 7-9). There every thing is everything else, and the gods see every thing in every otherness (ἔκει πᾶς πάντα ἐν αὐτῷ, καὶ αὖ ὁρᾷ ἐν ἄλλῳ πάντα). There are no determinations in the extension, since all things are everywhere. Every being is in relationship with all the others, and the evidence of the every being is infinite (ἄπειρος). The structure of the Intellect is then a whole wherein all beings subsist; and such subsistence consists in being a part referred to the whole: a part who mirrors in itself every otherness (... ἐν ἑκάστῳ ἄλλο, ἐμφαίν, ... πάντα). Now, the same gods are to be understood, not as subject of the process of intellection, but as part of this intelligible world. Their mythical connotation is gradually lost, while their true nature becomes clear: they are simply a kind of beings subsisting in the Intellect; and when they contemplate the *Nous* they just contemplate everything in themselves; since they actually contemplate themselves, the otherness and the relationships between themselves, the otherness, and among

[8] Plotinus states clearly this epistemological principle in III.7.7, lines 1-9.5.

[9] V.8.3, lines 17-18.

other othernesses. Plotinus states in this way the general ontology of the second hypostasis. Every being in the Intellect is intelligible because its being is to be an understanding, and the Intellect is its substance (τὸ ὑποκείμενον νοῦς καὶ αὐτὸς νοῦς). In the activity of the *Nous* subject and object are then the same, since what thinks is thought too; and every part is sustained by its relationship to the wholeness.

After having laid down this ontological structure, Plotinus goes on comparing this whole with the sensible order appearing to us (V.8.4, lines 22 and following). While in the sensible world everything springs from other (ἄλλο ἄλλου), and to be a singular thing means to be a part (μόνον ἕκαστον μέρος), in the intelligible world every part has in itself all other beings (φαντάζεται μὲν γὰρ μέρος, ἐνορᾶται δὲ τῷ ὀξεῖ τὴν ὄψιν ὅλον). The text assumes then a difference in predicating the term part (μέρος) of an object of the *Nous* and of a sensible object. The second is an actual part, because sensible beings are composition of many different elements. The first is a part just because it inheres in a substance; but this substance, the Intellect, is not a composition of its object: every object is every other object too.

The third step of the argument is the most controversial, and the most important (V.8.4, lines 35 and following). Here Plotinus characterizes the ontological structure of the *Nous* by the comprehension of the kind of life proper to this hypostasis. In this way he stops enumerating the intelligible objects and their relationships and begins considering the dynamical subsistence of the whole of those objects. This subsistence is that life whose living is a particular kind of knowledge (῾Η δὲ ζωὴ σοφία): the first knowledge, the absolute knowledge, the knowledge in itself (ἀλλ'ἔστιν ἡ πρότη καὶ οὐκ ἀπ'ἄλλης). The very being of this knowledge is to be nothing else than knowledge: differently from any human science, inferred by reasonings and occasioned by a lack, the life of *Nous* is always complete and never faulty (... ἀεὶ ἦν πᾶσα καὶ ἐλλείπουσα οὐδενί), a kind of absolute contemplation of objects, self-evident in their appearance (Πάντα γὰρ τὰ τοιαῦτα ἐκεῖ οἷον ἀγάλματα παρ'αὐτῶν ἐνορώμενα). Now, this knowledge is the very source of every thing (πεποίηκε τὰ ὄντα), since it is itself every thing (ἔστιν αὐτὴ τὰ ὄντα); so that the *prote sophia* and being in general are the same (ἡ οὐσία ἡ ἐκεῖ σοφία).

It seems then to me clear enough how Plotinus is here plainly stating the Platonic identity between being, reality and truth. The life of the *Nous*, the first knowledge, is the very spring of the real things: the whole of these inheres indeed in it. But this inherence can not be understood simply by the relationship between a part and the whole: every thing in the Intellect is every other thing, since the whole appears in every part. In this sense the *Nous* is the same with its parts; every part is a part related to the whole, because this relationship is a sort of mirroring, wherein the otherness appears completely.

But if every part shows itself inhering in the whole and subsisting as an expression of the whole, since the life of the whole, the *Nous*, is a kind of knowledge, the first and absolute knowledge, whose being is to be knowledge, so that the all is truth, then in being real every part shows its truth, appearing as the same truth.

III.

The main problem of this passage, about which controversies arose, concerns the issue of non- discursive thought. Recent scholarship has paid particular attention to Plotinus' theory that the knowledge peculiar to the upper *Nous* would be non-propositional.[10] In the argument on which I'm commenting there are some ideas referring to the theory: a) the first knowledge is not acquired by reasoning (σοφία δὲ οὐ πορισθεῖσα λογισμοῖς); b) at the last lines of V.8.4 Plotinus says that we cannot understand the nature of the *prote sophia* because we are used to think sciences composed by theorems (θεωρήματα), while the first knowledge has not this kind of composition; c) at line 20 of the subsequent section (V.8.5, 20 and following), the text states that gods and people contemplating the truth do not know axioms (Οὐ τοίνυν δεῖ νομίζειν ἐκεῖ ἀξιώματα ὁρᾶν τοὺς θεοὺς οὐδὲ τοὺς ἐκεῖ ὑπερευδαίμονας), but the real appearance of the things (... ἀγάλματα δὲ οὐ γεγραμμένα, ἀλλὰ ὄντα); d) at the beginning of section six (V.8.6, lines 1 and following), Plotinus says that the old Egyptian system of notation, the hierographical scripture, was grounded on the understanding of the non-propositional nature of knowledge (... οἱ Αἰγυπτίων σοφοί, ... ἐβούλοντο διὰ σοφίας δεικνύναι, μὴ τύποις γραμμάτον διεξοδεύουσι λόγους καὶ προτάσεις, ... ἀγάλματα δὲ γράψαντες).

In my opinion all these elements should incline the reader to think that Plotinus does maintain a non-propositional theory of absolute knowledge. Not only he is arguing about the possibility of knowing something without using a written or a spoken discourse: he is really thinking about a kind of knowledge other than a propositional one.[11] Naturally that knowledge could be, in some intelligible sense, non-propositional is really puzzling. In our philosophical culture we are used to believe a sourceal dogma: every knowledge has a propositional nature; that is to say, only those theses which could be set forth by a language could be thought. Anyway, differently from the contemporary linguistic pattern, Plotinus adopts a visual approach to knowledge: while our ordinary knowing experience is of a propositional kind, the knowledge

[10] See A.C.Lloyd (1970); R.Sorabji (1982); A.C.Lloyd (1986); M.Alfino (1989).

[11] Plotinus treats the argument many other times. See in particular V.5.

peculiar to the *Nous* is something like a vision. Indeed the *prote sophia* is an apprehension of self evident objects. The semantic context of the argument is constituted by terms related to the phenomenon of vision. Things are shining in clearness (διαφανῆ). The light is mentioned at V.8.4, line 7. In a quotation of the myth of Lynceus (V.8.4, lines 25 and following) Plotinus makes the reader think the right understanding is a kind of deep view. And the key-word of the passage is the term *agalma*, recurring twice as a predication of the intelligible objects at V.8.4, line 43 and V.8.5, lines 22-24, and once in the sense of the identity of sign and meaning proper to the elements of the absolute scripture used by the old Egyptian wise men, at V.8.6, line 6. Now, *agalma* means *statue, ornament, image*.[12] Plotinus says then that absolute knowledge is a kind of vision of images, both real and true; vision wherein the viewer and the viewed are not ontologically separated.

If this is the case, we will not really understand Plotinus' doctrine if we do not take off our glasses: our prejudices about the linguistic nature of knowledge. Before asking about the possible consistency of a so unusual system, we should then try to apprehend its visual pattern. Actually, this is the first reason of unsatisfaction with the recent scholarly literature about the theory. For example: Lloyd, Sorabji, and Alfino all inquire into Plotinus' doctrine of the absolute knowledge from the standpoint of the linguistic conception. While Sorabji seems troubled to save Plotinus from the presumed absurdities of a non-propositional theory of knowledge, Lloyd and Alfino provide textual evidence that he did hold the theory; but all the three commentators read the text assuming that knowledge has something to do with language: that the issue of the non-discursive thought of the *Nous* should be approach by the relationship between knowledge, language, intellection or meaning.[13]

Obviously we should ask the reason why Plotinus states that the *first knowledge* is a kind of vision. Some difficulties indeed seem arise from Plotinus' statement. E. K. Emilsson speaks, for example, of a basic problem: every vision presumes a distinction between subject and object--exactly what

[12] Faggin (1992) translates the three occurences of the term with statue, immagini, and figure; S.McKenna (1991) translates with visible images, noble image, and pictures.

[13] Lloyd defines the Plotinian issue of non-discursiveness an *enigma*; wherein Plotinus could be read as asserting a doctrine regressive comparing with Aristotle and the middle platonists (Lloyd, 1970). The author focuses his reading around the notion of intellection; aiming at showing how Plotinus tries to escape from the fallibilism proper to the aristotelic concept of first mover. Alfino reads Plotinus theory directed by a model of consciousness escluding discursiveness, in relation to the issue of meaning (see Alfino, 1989).

Plotinus intends to deny for *Nous'* knowledge--so that the *light analogy* would be unable to prove the consistency of a visual epistemology.[14] Anyway, I think that here Emilsson is completely missing the point. Firstly, Plotinus cannot understand subject-object opposition in knowledge as we are used to do, that is as a skeptical topic; since the epistemological problems of Platonism are not dealing with this kind of opposition. Moreover, vision is the very *paradeigma* of this attitude, since it is understood as a kind of immediate assimilation between the soul and the object in a *medium*; so that vision, for Plotinus, proves the identity of subject and object. Secondly, Plotinus does not introduce a visual pattern to refute epistemological dualism, but simply because it is an example of a non-propositional way to know; a way in which the simple being of a thing, its being viewed, is the source of its being real and truth. In my opinion all this is proved by his use of the doctrine set forth in the Platonic similitude of the sun. Plotinus' topic is here to assert the identity of epistemology and ontology, and not that of explain how the soul knows an object. Thus, it would be wrong to treat Plotinus' visual knowledge as a kind of theory of perception: it is an ontological model of the second hypostasis. To understand this model we should then change our epistemological approach.

Now, we could go along a different path. In asserting the Platonic identity between being, reality and truth, Plotinus refers also to the other notion peculiar to Platonism: transcendence. In my opinion, we could achieve better results examining the text from the point of view of the role transcendence plays in the explanation of the nature of the *prote sophia*.

IV.

At the beginning of section five (V.8.5, lines 1 and following) Plotinus asserts that all sensible beings (Πάντα τὰ γινόμενα, εἴτε τεχνητὰ εἴτε φυσικὰ εἴν) are occasioned by a certain knowledge (σοφία τις ποιεῖ). This knowledge is in conformity to the kind of beings occasioned, since it accomplishes the process of producing. The artisans, in framing the objects of their arts, refer to the knowledge of nature: this is in fact the cause of the same arts (καθ'ἕν γεγένηται). Nature too, in framing sensible beings, acts by some rational principles, proceeded from other, from the *Nous*. This last knowledge, being not derived by other, can be said first.

The argument assumes therefore that every determined knowledge cannot be founded in itself, since it needs to refer to something other. This reference is made necessary because no knowledge has in itself the principles of its truth, except the first knowledge, whose being is to be truth. Plotinus then

[14] See Emilsson (1996).

defines a scale of knowledge where the upper degree accounts for the inferior, because the true principles of the inferior are ontologically subsisting in the superior: the human knowledge is so grounded in the upper level, the natural knowledge; the natural knowledge is grounded in the first knowledge; and, lastly, the first knowledge is self-grounded. The transcendence is the relative ontological situation of a degree in respect to the others, so that the first knowledge is that knowledge that is not transcended by other knowledge: this knowledge in fact does not refer to anything other than itself.

Now, the argument seems however problematic. Why does every knowledge refer to something other? And why must this reference be thought as an ascensional dialectics of trascendent degree? And why is the first knowledge self-grounded when the *Nous* proceeds from the One?

The answer to these questions involves in some sense a sympathetic reading of Plotinus' visual model of knowledge. The first knowledge transcends all the other because is the source of the Platonic identity between being, reality and truth. This knowledge is a self-intellection of the *Nous*.[15] The One is beyond being: it is not ontologically real, neither true, nor knowable. Obviously this does not mean that the One has a privative nature; but that its transcendence is more sourceal than that degree wherein reality, truth, and the absolute knowledge acquire an ontological subsistence; since the One is the source, while being is the substantiality of the true reality. The first knowledge is this very ontological determination of the power of the One to give being in reality and in truth. The first knowledge is the same wholeness of being (H... ἀληθινὴ σοφία οὐσία, καὶ ἡ ἀληθινὴ οὐσία σοφία). Now, this knowledge could not be discursive, since it is not propositional; indeed it is not rational.[16] In being real and true all objects just show their self evidence to the *Nous*, contemplating them; that is to say, touching intellectually with a clear vision in the identity in which things come into being as real and true. In being known, indeed, things come into being as something that is viewed: without distinction with the viewer, and without mediation; simply as beings. This identity between *Nous* and the being real and true of the objects is the absolute appearance of the ontological degree in the procession from the One: and for this reason it transcends all the derivative lower degrees, being in this way the source of their necessity to refer to it. In some sense every object has an ontological meaning, preceding the linguistic one: because the truth and reality proper to every sensible is not self evident in the sensible order, but in the intelligible order where the object really and truly appears.

15 See Crystal (1998).

16 See C.Guidelli, (1991).

THE GOOD'S BEAUTY IS ABOVE BEAUTY. PLOTINUS' ARGUMENT IN *ENNEAD* VI.7[38].32-33.

Martin Achard

Plotinus' remarks about the relationship between the Good or the One and beauty or the beautiful can appear quite puzzling. Already in *Ennead* I.6 [1], *On Beauty*, we find three sets of conflicting statements on this relationship. First, near the end of Chapter 6, Plotinus would seem, as Davide Susanetti puts it:

> to mark out the structure of transcendent reality, by proposing a terminological distinction.[1]

Indeed, in lines 25-27, Plotinus says:

> And first we must posit beauty (*tên kallonên*) which is also the Good (*tagathon*); from this immediately comes Intellect (*nous*), which is the beautiful (*to kalon*); and Soul is given beauty by Intellect.

In other words, the One or the Good should be called *kallonê*, "beauty," while the Intellect, the place of Forms and true being, should be called *to kalon*, "the beautiful." This neat and clear-cut distinction, however, is disregarded just a few lines later, in Chapter 7, where Plotinus describes the rising of the Soul toward the Good by drawing heavily on the conclusion of Diotima's speech in Plato's *Symposium*.[2] In that chapter, Plotinus uses without reservation the adjective *kalos* to describe the Good, saying, in lines 2-3, that:

> Anyone who has seen [the Good] knows what I mean when I say that it is beautiful (*kalon*).

And then, in lines 15-16, that:

[1] Susanetti (1995) 135. This is my translation of Susanetti: all translations of secondary literature in this paper are mine. Translations of Plotinus are taken from Armstrong (1966-88), which I sometimes slightly modify. I quote the lines of Plotinus' text, however, according to Henry and Schwyzer (1964-82), and not according to the Greek text given in Armstrong's translation. I would like to thank Robert M. Berchman, Catherine Collobert, Gerard Naddaf, Jean-Marc Narbonne, Frederic M. Schroeder, and especially Gregory MacIsaac, who commented on a first draft of this paper, and whose insights have been very helpful.

[2] 211c-212a. See especially 211d-e, where Plato uses twice the expression *auto to kalon*.

> The man ... who has seen [the Good] glories in its beauty (*epi kalôi*).

And then, more strikingly, in lines 21-22, that the Good is "the beautiful in itself" (*auto to kalon*); and accordingly, in line 29, that the Good

> is beauty most of all, and primary beauty (*malista kallos on auto kai to prôton*).

Finally, in Chapter 9, at the very end of the treatise, Plotinus seems content to propose two tentative solutions. He writes:

> You must become first all godlike and all beautiful if you intend to see God and beauty. First the soul will come in its ascent to Intellect and there will know the Forms, all beautiful, and will affirm that these, the Ideas, are beauty (*to kallos*); for all things are beautiful by these, by the products and essence of Intellect. That which is beyond this (*epekeina toutou*) we call the nature of the Good, which holds the beautiful (*to kalon*) as a screen before it. So in a loose and general way of speaking the Good is the primary beautiful (*to prôton kalon*); but if one distinguishes the intelligibles [from the Good] one will say that the place of the Forms is the intelligible beauty (*to...noêton kalon*), but the Good is That which is beyond (*to epekeina*), the "spring and origin" of the beautiful (*pêgên kai archên tou kalou*); or one will place the Good and the primary beautiful (*kalon prôton*) on the same level: in any case, however, the beautiful (*kalon*) is in the intelligible world (32-43).

In his book *The Philosophy of Plotinus*, W.R. Inge put forward the idea that the first of these passages, which seems to place *hê kallonê* and *to kalon* on different levels, gave the true and definitive view of Plotinus.[3] The same interpretation was adopted and defended by J.M. Rist in his *Plotinus: The Road to Reality*. To explain why Plotinus sometimes applies, as in Chapter 7 of *Ennead* I.6 [1], the word *kalon* to the Good, Rist offers a simple explanation: in those passages, Plotinus was "tremendously indebted to the terminology of Plato's *Symposium*," where of course "the Beautiful is the aim of the philosopher's quest."[4] The problem of the relationship between the Good, beauty and the beautiful, was examined anew in 1981 by Massimo Massagli, in a paper that is seldom quoted, but that still offers in some ways the most substantial treatment of the matter: "L'Uno al di sopra del bello e della bellezza nelle *Enneadi* di Plotino." Massagli showed convincingly that we should not lend importance — as Inge and Rist do — to the distinction

[3] See especially Inge (1968[3]) 124. The first edition of Inge's book was published in 1918.

[4] Rist (1967) 56.

seemingly put forward in Chapter 6 of *Ennead* I.6 [1]. In reality, the word *kallonê*, which appears three times in Chapter 6, reappears only twice in the rest of the *Enneads*; and the distinction between *hê kallonê* and *to kalon* is nowhere to be found outside of I.6 [1].[5] Hence, the word *kallonê* is used in an "unforeseen and sporadic"[6] way by Plotinus; and it most certainly never becomes his habit to use it to refer to the One. It is therefore better to ask ourselves, as Massagli does, why Plotinus sometimes says that the One is *kalon* or *to kallos*, while he sometimes says that it is "beyond beauty or the beautiful."

In *Ennead* V.5 [32].12, Plotinus explains that the desire (*ephesis*) for the Good is "more ancient" (*archaiotera*) than the desire for the beautiful, and that the Good itself is thereby "more ancient (*archaioteron*) and prior (*proteron*) to the beautiful" (17-19). A proof of this, according to him, is the fact that people "do not want to have the Good in seeming only," while "it is enough for them to seem to be beautiful, even if they are not really (23-24)." It could of course be tempting, when we read such strong statements, to downplay the meaning and importance of those passages where Plotinus applies the words "beauty" or "beautiful" to the One. This is what Massagli wanted to do.[7] He tried to show that:

[5] See Massagli (1981) 122. It should also be pointed out that the immediate context of I.6[1].6.25-27 does not necessarily suggest that, in these lines, Plotinus is speaking *ex professo*, for in the immediately preceding lines, he has also equated, seemingly at random, "beings" (*ta onta*) with "beauty" (*hê kallonê*) (line 21), "good" (*agathon*) with "beautiful" (*kalon*) (line 23 and lines 24-25), and "the Good" (*tagathon*) with "beauty" (*kallonê*) (lines 23-24). This could certainly lead one to suppose that, in the whole passage which runs from lines 21 to 27, Plotinus is only juggling with ideas. Gerson's claim that in "I.6.6.18-24 … the identification of beauty and good is strongly made" (1994) 290 is an oversimplification.

[6] Massagli (1981) 122.

[7] As he writes: "V.5[32].12 is the chapter where Plotinus proposes the most complete analysis of the relationship between *to agathon* and *to kalon*" (1981) 125. The notion that V.5[32].12 must be given priority over other passages that concern the relationship between the Good and beauty seems to have been held already by Marsilio Ficino. In his commentary on I.6[1], for instance, he writes, in a passage that he presents as a summary of Plotinus' position (but which really is a defense of the view that "Beauty is Intellect"): "Tu ergo memento … omnia quidem appetere bonum: non omnia pulchrum, sed eos duntaxat, qui judicium quoddam pulchritudinis habent: atque hos quidem semper appetere bonum, non tamen semper pulchritudinem affectare" (This quotation is from the edition of the *Commentary* published by Creuzer and Moser [1835] 92a). This argument clearly echoes V.5[32].12.7-14.

> at first, because of the subjects dealt with in the first treatises and due to the influence of Plato, Plotinus was willing to call his Absolute [i.e. the One] *kallonê* or *kalon*.[8]

And that:

> [after] developing ... his own metaphysical conceptions, Plotinus saw the Absolute [the One] as Cause of beauty, and did not see it anymore as *hê kallonê* or *to kalon*.[9]

In other words:

> the attributions of the words *kallonê* and *kalon* ... to the Absolute are only stages (*episodi*) of the influence of Plato on the thought and language of the "first Plotinus."[10]

And they would be "stages" where, furthermore, Plotinus would not even try to describe what Massagli calls "the structure of the Absolute itself" (*la struttura dell'Assoluto stesso*).[11] Put in a different way: in Plotinus' eyes, those passages wouldn't even have counted as parts of a true "metaphysics of the One."[12]

We can easily dismiss Massagli's idea of a chronological evolution on the part of Plotinus. It will be sufficient to quote just one of his arguments. According to him, the expression *prôton kallos*, which is used by Plotinus in I.6 [1].7 to refer to the Good:

> after being used with the same meaning two more times in I.6 [1].9 (with the adjective *kalon* instead of the substantive *kallos*), doesn't reappear anywhere in the *Enneads*.[13]

This would be a proof that Plotinus stopped seeing the Good as a form of beauty or as the first beauty. But in *Ennead* VI.2, the 43rd treatise in chronological order, we read the following passage:

> As for the beautiful (*peri...tou kalou*), if the primary beauty (*hê prôtê kallonê*) is that [transcendent First], what could be said about it would be the same and similar to what was said about the Good (*epi tou agathou*) (18.1-3).

[8] Massagli (1981) 124.

[9] Massagli (1981) 124 (see also 121).

[10] Massagli (1981) 124.

[11] Massagli (1981) 120.

[12] The same idea is defended by Chrétien (1989) 313-314.

[13] Massagli (1981) 119.

Massagli doesn't take into account these lines, where the expression *prôtê kallonê*, which is of course a substitute for *prôton kallos* or *prôton kalon*, is clearly applied to the One. This counter example is sufficient to show that Plotinus did not make a point of never calling the One "beauty" or "the beautiful."

Hence, we are left with the assumption that in those places where Plotinus does apply the words *kallonê*, *kallos* or *kalon* to the Good, he would not really try to describe the nature of the Good, that is, he would not try to formally set up a "metaphysics of the One."

In spite of passages like V.5[32].12, which seem to bring out a sharp difference between the Good and the beautiful, I don't think that we can easily dismiss the passages where Plotinus equates the two. This is especially true of Chapters 32 and 33 of *Ennead* VI.7[38], which, if we take a close look, turn out to be a formal demonstration of the assertion that *tagathon* is (*to*) *kalon*.[14] The fact that, in these chapters, Plotinus is treating expressions like "beauty," "the really beautiful," "the super-beautiful," "the primary beautiful" or " the first beauty," as labels that are no less unsuitable to the First Principle of all than "the Good" or the "the One,"[15] has been fully recognized in a number of recent publications.[16] I would simply like to add to this recognition by displaying the exact form of the argument developed in these chapters. It would seem that, owing to the intricacy of Plotinus' writing, the precise nature of that argument has sometimes been misunderstood.[17] We shall nevertheless see that the structure of Plotinus' reasoning is simple, and should have amounted for him to a cogent proof.

First of all, of course, it will be useful to recall in outline the context in which the argument is made. In Chapter 31, Plotinus has established that the soul loves the Good, and that it is:

[14] Or, as Plotinus himself puts it, following in his own peculiar way the *Philebus* 64e (where Plato writes: "the power of the good has taken refuge in the nature of the beautiful"): "Beauty is … the nature of the Good" (VI.7[38].33.22). We should also note, as a possible source of Plotinus, *Republic* 509 a, where "the nature of the Good" is referred to as an "extraordinary beauty" (*amêchanon kallos*).

[15] We shall of course always remember that, properly speaking, the First is for Plotinus ineffable (see, among others, VI.9[9].4-5).

[16] See especially Hadot (1988) 24, 49, 320, 324, and the remarkable papers by Stern-Gillet (2000) 38, 46, 49-60, and Hubler (2002) 194, 204. See also Hendrix (2004) 39.

[17] A case in point is the account given in O'Meara's otherwise valuable introductory book (1993) 98.

> moved by it [i.e. by the Good] to love from the beginning (*ex archês*) (17-18).

He has also described in some detail the first two stages of the ascent of the soul toward the Good. First, the soul has gone beyond the beauty of the sensible world, without even waiting, says Plotinus in a most striking formula, that would seem to contradict Plato, "for a reminder from the beauties here" (19-20).[18] Indeed, the innate love for the Good that is in the soul is so strong that it renders such a reminder unnecessary.[19] Then, the soul has reached the Intelligible World, and it has seen that all things there are "beautiful (*kala*) and true" (31-32). This vision, however, did not put an end to its quest. Rather, at that stage, the soul feels like it is "close" (34) to what it has been seeking for so long. Then, at the start of Chapter 32, Plotinus writes:

> Where then is he who made the beauty which is so great and the life which is so great, he who is the generator of substance? You see the beauty which rests upon the very Forms, all of them richly varied. It is beautiful to abide here; but when one is in beauty one must look to see whence these Forms come and whence they derive their beauty (1-5).

The development that follows this exhortation, and which is of interest to us, falls into four parts. In the first (32.5-24), Plotinus shows that the Principle of Forms has to be formless (*aneideon*), otherwise it would be one of the Forms, it would only be a "part" (*meros*) of them. It follows from this, as we would expect, that the First Principle is "unbounded" or "infinite" (*apeiros*). These points are nothing but constant and well-known plotinian metaphysical tenets.[20]

The second part of the argument (32.24-28), however, brings something new. In it, Plotinus shows that what is formless and infinite shall arouse a love that is itself infinite. In other words, he makes a point of tying

[18] In the *Symposium*, as is well-known, the "beautiful things here" constitute a necessary step in the upward path of the soul (211c-d).

[19] In actual fact, Plotinus seems to be talking here of only one specific kind of soul: that of the philosopher (see I.3[20].1-3, where the souls of the philosopher, the lover and the musician, are distinguished and described). This implicit detail, however, has no bearing on the argument.

[20] On the fact that the First is *aneideon*, see V.5[32].6.4-5, VI.7[38].28.28 and VI.9[9].3.43-44 (see also VI.7[38].17. 18, 40 and VI.9[9].3.36-39, where *amorphon* is used instead of *aneideon*). On the fact that it is *apeiros*, see V.5[32].10.19-21, 11.1, and VI.9[9].6.10.

the nature of the love prompted by an object with the nature of that object itself.[21] It is worth quoting in full, here, lines 24 to 28:

> Truly, when you cannot grasp the form or shape of what is longed for, it would be most longed for and most lovable, and love (*ho erôs*) for it would be immeasurable (*ametros*). For love is not limited here, because neither is the beloved, but the love of this would be unbounded (*apeiros*).[22]

In short, these first two parts of the argument expound two principles or premises which were undoubtedly held by Plotinus:
(1) The First Principle, the Good, is formless and infinite.
(2) An infinite object of love will arouse an infinite love.

From these two principles, Plotinus infers, in the third (32.28-34) and fourth (32.34-33.22) parts, two overlapping conclusions, basing himself tacitly on another principle that was for him, as well as for all the Greeks, a self-evident truth: that which is worthy of love is beautiful, and conversely.[23] Right after the lines just quoted, which make explicit the second principle, he goes on to write:

> So his beauty [i.e. the First Principle's beauty] is of another kind and beauty above beauty (*ôste kai to kallos autou allon tropon kai kallos huper kallos*) (32.28-29).

This sentence is often quoted out of context to support the view that, according to Plotinus, when we apply the words "beauty" or "beautiful" to the Good, we are not talking about a genuine beauty, but about some sort of "beauty above beauty."[24] But the conjunction that is used at the beginning of the sentence, *ôste* ("so," "in such a way that"), makes it clear that the sentence

[21] This point was seen by Hadot (1988) 331. For a thorough discussion of some of the philosophical aspects of this idea, see Theiler (1972) and Sweeney (1992).

[22] Hadot is right to note that "Plotinus cannot be using here the word 'unbounded' in a negative sense, for he wants to show the infinity of the love brought about by the infinite Good" (1988) 49. Also, as Bussanich has independently observed: "the lack of limitation both in this love and its object suggests that we are dealing here with the reality of the One itself" (1988) 187.

[23] The role played in the argument by this implicit premise has been seen by Stern-Gillet (2000) 55, 58. The necessary link between "love" and "beauty" is brought out in *Ennead* III.5[50].1.

[24] The best example might be given by Trouillard (1955) 161-162, but see also Kremer (1966) 169-170, Beierwaltes (1980) 300 and O'Meara (1993) 99. The phrase *kallos huper kallos* is a *hapax legomenon* in Plotinus.

is the logical consequence of what was said earlier in the text, where we find absolutely nothing that could support the idea that the Good is not really beautiful, or is not beauty in a proper sense of the word. Quite the contrary, the preceding remarks would concur to show that it is legitimate to call the Good "Beauty," or to say that it is beautiful. Indeed, as we have seen, The Good is infinite, and, by that very fact, it can be the object of an infinite love. But what is loveable must also be beautiful. Therefore, the Good must be beautiful.[25]

If we pay attention to the whole context, it becomes possible to get a better handle on what Plotinus means when he says that the First Principle's beauty "is of another kind," and that the Good is "beauty above beauty." In that third part of the argument, he is trying to specify the relationship between the beauty of the Good and the beauty of the Intelligible Universe. This is shown by the remarks that immediately follow the assertion that the Good is "beauty above beauty." Plotinus writes:

> If the Good is lovable (*erasmion*), it would be the generator (*to gennôn*) of beauty. Therefore the productive power of all is the flower of beauty (*kalou anthos*), a beauty which makes beauty (*kallos kallopoion*). For it generates beauty and makes it more beautiful by the excess of beauty which comes from it, so that it is the principle of beauty and the term of beauty (32.30-34).

Put differently, the Good is indeed *kallos*, "beauty," in the sense that it is the "height" or "flower" of beauty; but since it must be *epekeina nou kai ousias* in order to be the generator of Intellect and Being,[26] his beauty will be "of another kind" than the beauty of *nous*: it will be beauty "above" (*huper*) the beauty of the Intellect.

The fourth part of the argument brings a clear confirmation of that reading. In this part, Plotinus first explains that the beauty of *nous*, which is produced by the Good, must itself be, in a way, "formless" or "shapeless"[27]

[25]. It may be mentioned in passing that this conclusion certainly fits with other principles endorsed by Plotinus. For example, Hubler is quite right to tie the fact that "the One is beauty in himself" with the fact that "it is complete and whole in itself and lacks nothing" (2002) 195.

[26]. Miles (1999) 159 seems to understand the phrase "a beauty which makes beauty," in lines 31-32, as referring to the production of sensible beauty by the intelligible universe, rather than as referring to the production of intelligible beauty by the One. Such a reading, however, is obviously incorrect.

[27]. On the seemingly strange notion of "shapeless form" (*amorphon eidos*) (33.4), see the illuminating paper by Schroeder (2004).

(32.34-39); then he goes on to show that, in order to reach transcendent beauty, we must go beyond every form, that we must strip ourselves of all forms, be they sensible or intelligible (33.1-12). Even when the soul is contemplating the beauty of the Intelligible World, he says, it is "still in need," still trying to discover "how it should contemplate that which is above," "that which it desires without saying why it longs for something like this" (33.10-12). Why is it so? It is because, explains Plotinus, that which is above the Intelligible Universe

> is what is really beautiful (*touto to ontôs*), since the nature of the best and the nature of the most lovable is in the altogether formless (*eiper en tôi pantê aneideôi hê tou aristou phusis kai hê tou erasmiôtaton*) (13-14).

It should not go unnoticed that, in this sentence, Plotinus reminds us expressly of the two principles that he has established in the first two parts of his argument, that is, once again, 1) the Good is formless and thereby infinite, 2) the most intense love will stem from an infinite object of love. He clearly does so in the part of the sentence that reads:

> the nature of the best and the nature of the *most lovable* is in the *altogether formless*.[28]

The explicitly stated conclusion that comes from these two principles is, as we can see, that the Good is the "really beautiful" (*to ontôs*). Furthermore, the exact same conclusion is restated — and hence corroborated — five lines later, where Plotinus, after explaining once again that the soul seeks what is formless or shapeless, writes that the beautiful things that are "mixed:"

> must be measured and limited, but not the really beautiful (*to ontôs*) or the super-beautiful (*to huperkalon*); but if this is so, it must not be shaped or be a form. Therefore, the primary beautiful (*to prôtôs*) and the first (*prôton*) is without form, and beauty (*hê kallonê*) is that, the nature of the good (*hê tou* ***agathou phusis*****) (19-22).**[29]

[28] This explicit reminder really underscores, in my view, the systematic and carefully-built character of the whole passage that runs from 32.1 to 33.22.

[29] As with the expression *kallos huper kallos* used in 32.29, the expression *to huperkalon* used in this passage has been quoted out of context to back up the contention that the Good was not really beautiful (see, for instances, Massagli [1981] 131 and Susanetti [1995] 136). But it goes without saying, as Armstrong saw, that the meaning of *to huperkalon* is here "the super-beautiful", i.e., as the text itself says, the "really beautiful." *Huperkalos* is used with a similar meaning in V.8[31].8.21.

It is of course true that the present paper, having merely proposed an analysis of the argument unfolded in *Ennead* VI.7[38].32-33, leaves open a number of fundamental questions. In particular, I have not addressed here the larger and key issue of Plotinus' conflicting remarks in the whole of the *Enneads*, which might lead one to consider that he was willing to accept "a variety of ways of expressing the relationship of beauty to the Good."[30] Nevertheless, it is my hope that, by shedding a brighter light on one small but important piece of the puzzle, I contributed to a better understanding of one facet of Plotinus' thought on beauty.

[30] Armstrong (1966 [vol. I]) 263.

PLOTINUS ON THE BEING OF THE ONE

John Bussanich

Plotinus' insistence that the One is beyond being and thought can encourage us to apply the negative dialectic dogmatically and to slip into the error, as John Findlay put it, of thinking of the One as "the irremovable blank background, the void logical space, of everything and anything" (1967, 108). Our search, he suggested, "is not best understood as a journey towards emptiness and negation" (138), but rather towards fullness and perfection. When Plotinus speaks of the One as luminous, formless beauty and as pure consciousness and actuality, he neither contradicts the negative theology by adopting a discursive, affirmative philosophy of being in the Aristotelian or Thomistic sense nor does he indulge in poetic metaphors that are neatly expunged by negative dialectic. Speech about the One utilizes two dialects: one metaphysical and one mystical. The first describes the One as absent and as nothing or as present and as everything, the second incorporates metaphysical and psychological terms within a performative discourse that escapes the limitations of both affirmative and negative language in order to evoke the experience of mystical presence. I shall argue that some later Neoplatonists and most modern scholars have mistakenly interpreted Plotinus' symbolic experiential language as positive theology. The standard reading has had the unfortunate effect, in my view, of privileging negative theology and thus blocking access to what is a higher mode of discourse.

The practice of negation maintains transcendence first by removing our discursive concepts and later by revealing the limitations of non-discursive intuitive thought. "How then do we ourselves speak about it? We do indeed say something about it, but we certainly do not speak it, and we have neither knowledge nor thought of it...For we say what it is not, but we do not say what it is" (V.5.14.1-6).[1] The One is not any one thing nor all things together, nor is it substantial being or any attribute (VI.9.3.35ff., V.5.12.47-50). Its perfection requires it to be non-composite, unlimited, and without internal distinction. By contrast, substantial being is limited, determinate, and intelligible. It is the same as and different from noetic thought (V.3.10) and it transcends both sensible being and ordinary dianoetic thought. It is here in the everyday world, which is constructed by perception and discursive thinking, that the practice of negative theology begins. Only through relentless purification and intellectual inquiry into the nature of intelligible being, by the mutually supportive exercise of negation and

[1] All translations are from A.H. Armstrong's Loeb edition, 1966-1988.

affirmation, can individual souls participate in νόησις, which is non-discursive, meditative "thinking."[2] Ontologically, the philosopher ascends from thinking about immanent, enmattered forms to communion with transcendent, paradigmatic forms. To refer to the ascended soul's meditative absorption in pure being requires a radical readjustment in perspective: what initially transcended sensible perception and dianoetic reason is now fully present, i.e. immanent, to the noetically active soul. When the soul "becomes Intellect," its awareness is identified with perfect thought and it experiences bliss, light etc (see Wallis 1976). Lloyd observes that "an individual who has exercised the faculty whose thoughts are those of Pure Intellect can give a phenomenological description of his experience—what Intellect or the life of eternity feels like and looks like" (Lloyd 1990, 125). He adds that ubiquitous accounts in mystical literature of these affective and visionary features substitute for a direct description of the object, viz. pure being, which is impossible (e.g. V.8.7, VI.7.31ff.). This substitution, if you will, signals the initial use of mystical language and marks the partial suspension of both negative and positive discursive accounts of Intellect. It cannot be stressed enough that entering fully into noetic activity transcends rationality.

When the soul that has become Intellect aims to touch the One it must practice a more intense form of negation and affirmation: positively, through meditative concentration on the One's presence to intelligible being, negatively, through removing otherness, sameness, and complexity. This movement beyond Intellect notoriously involves the activation of the erotic or inner intellect:

> We are not prevented from having it, even if we do not speak it. But just as those who have a god within them and are in the grip of divine possession may know this much, that they have something greater within them, even if they do not know what, and from the ways in which they are moved and the things they say get a certain awareness of the god who moves them...so we seem to be disposed to the One, divining, when we have our intellect pure that this is the inner intellect. (V.3.14.8-15)

This advanced degree of awareness is a precondition for the experience reported in *Ennead* VI.9:

> What then could the One be, and what nature could it have? There is nothing surprising in its being difficult to say, when it is not even

[2] See Lloyd 1986 and Bussanich 1997b on non-discursive thought in Plotinus. For detailed discussion of the experiential perspective see Bussanich 1988 ad loc. and on the theme of Plotinus' mysticism Bussanich 1994 and 1997a.

> easy to say what Being or Form is....But in proportion as the soul goes towards the formless, since it is utterly unable to comprehend it because it is not delimited and, so to speak, stamped by a richly varied stamp, it slides away and is afraid that it may have nothing at all. (VI.9.3.3.1-7)

This is not a mere conceptual *aporia* but an extreme existential agitation that is virtually unknown to modern thinkers:

> We run round it outside, in a way, and want to explain our own experiences of it, sometimes near it and sometimes falling away in our perplexities about it. The perplexity arises especially because our awareness of that One is not by way of reasoned knowledge or of intellectual perception, but by way of a presence superior to knowledge. (VI.9.3.52-4.4)

It is direct contact with the One in his soul that inspires Plotinus to speak figuratively of the One: "we speak and write impelling towards it and wakening from reasoning to the vision of it" (VI.9.4.13-14). Such speech is directed towards those who wish to see, who have an "awareness of the glory there" (18), who have an "erotic experience" of resting in the beloved One (19), and "who are able and prepared to receive it" (26-27). I contend that in these evocations of the experience of the One's presence Plotinus relies on a mode of discourse distinct from the negative and positive theologies.

The experiential perspective of these and many other passages in the *Enneads* contrasts sharply with the essentially intellectual character of the *aporia* as it is expressed in Proclus:

> I see here a great fuss being stirred up by those who think that these negations lead us into the absolute non-existent or something such, since by reason of the lack of definition our imagination does not have anything definite to grasp onto, inasmuch as nothing is proposed to it, but everything absolutely is removed from the One, and for this reason they are persuaded that one must establish some nature and characteristic for the One. (*In Parm.* 1105.32ff.)[3]

Proclus proceeds to criticize unnamed thinkers who in ascribing positive attributes to the One violate the strictures of the negative theology. Scholars disagree who Proclus' targets are, whether Porphyry, Plotinus, or others.

[3] The *APC* states a similar concern: "I can sense myself slipping back from (ἔξολισθάνω) the knowledge (γνῶσις) proper to Him, a knowledge which remains in simplicity and has no relation to what is known, and uttering in consequence unclear formulations because of my lack of ability to express these concepts properly." (Fr. 2 = VI.12ff.)

Before examining his critique in detail it will be useful to recall some of Plotinus' statements about the One which may have elicited Proclus' concern.

Plotinus' enigmatic descriptions of the One's activities in VI.8, are "for the sake of persuasion" (13.1-5, 47-50). In this treatise he refers to the One's existence (7.47: ἡ οἷον ὑπόστασις αὐτοῦ), actuality (16.15-18, 20.9), being (7.49-50: κατὰ τὸ εἶναι ἡ ἐνέργεια ἢ κατὰ τὴν ἐνέργειαν τὸ εἶναι, 20.9-16), substance (7.52), life (7.51), self-will (13.38), self-causation (14.41-2; 16.14-5, 21, 29; 20.2-6), free will (13.1-8, 16.38-9, 21.12-5), omnipresence (16.1-2; cf. III.8.9.25, III.9.4.1-7), looking to itself (16.20-21), as a non-intellectual νοῦς (16.16, 18.21-22), radiance (16.14), as love of itself, object of love, and love itself (15.1-8, 16.12-16). In this and other treatises he also ascribes some sort of awareness to the One: κατανόησις and συναίσθησις (V.4.2.17-19), ἐγρήγορσις καὶ ὑπερνόησις (VI.8.16.32-33), looking to itself (VI.8.16.12), being directed towards itself (νεῦσις αὐτοῦ, 6.8.16.24), and being τις ἐπιβολὴ πρὸς αὐτὸν (VI.7.39.1-2). These attributes and activities can be divided into at least six groups: (a) classical ontological terms and their derivatives; (b) classical and especially Aristotelian noetic terminology with some neologisms; (c) terms for consciousness; (d) the language of actuality and motion; (e) terms for desire and will (ἔρως, ἔφεσις, βούλησις); and, (f) concrete tactile terms. It has long been controversial how to construe these remarkable statements about the One. With Proclus most scholars believe that they represent only provisional attributes and that they are to be negated completely. I shall argue that Plotinus transforms them from univocal philosophical terms into evocative symbols.

The lynchpins of Plotinus' metaphysics of the One are Plato's assertions in *Republic* 509b that the Good is beyond οὐσία and in *Parmenides* 137cff. that the One is partless and without attributes.[4] The Platonic Good is the cause of being to the forms, the luminous source of their knowability, and the ultimate term of the soul's erotic ascent. Thus, the philosophical ambiguities in Plotinus' conception of the first principle reflect its provenance in both the Platonic Good and One. Consistent with the latter it must be unlimited, indeterminate, and beyond predication, but as the former it must also be fully real and creative. To refer to the One's reality he generally employs τὸ εἶναι and ὑπόστασις (VI.8.7.47-50), which are also applied to soul and Intellect (Cf. Gerson 1990, 304n23). Occasionally, however, he even

[4] See Gerson 1990, 64 and 1994, 231n5 on the difficulties of linking the first One of the *Parmenides* with the Good of the *Republic*.

refers to the One's οὐσία (VI.8.7.52, 12.34; V.6.2.13), but not, one assumes, in such a way as to abrogate its perfect, simple, and non-composite nature. These locutions are fully synonymous statements of the One's self-identity: it "is only itself and really itself, while every other thing is itself and something else" (VI.8.21.32-3; see also VI.8.13.56-7). The various activities and properties ascribed to the One consistently follow this principle. Its ἐνέργεια, its life, and so on are bespeak the One itself. They should not be conceived as essential attributes of a substance that qualify and differentiate it: the One's "substance" and its "attributes" are identical. Because the One's being is not the limited being of Intellect and it possesses the unlimited power to produce all things, it is reasonable to conceive of the One as infinite being, though in Intellect being is limited and determinate.[5]

This interpretation has been rejected by some scholars on the grounds that it endows the One with a determinate nature that violates its non-compositeness and simplicity.[6] These are legitimate worries and they are not easily answered. Perl (2002, 133) has argued strongly that conceiving the One as being is unacceptable:

> The central point of Plotinus' doctrine that being is not supreme…is that *anything whatsoever* is not and cannot be the ultimate ground…The One, therefore, as Plotinus repeatedly says, is not any thing, indeed is Nothing. No common term whatsoever can be applied to beings and the One. As Plotinus explains, 'It is not equal to the other units so as to be one of their company; otherwise, there will be something in common between it and those which are included in the count with it, and that something in common will be before the One itself' (V.5.4).

In response it should be noted that Plotinus does not say that the One is Nothing in the way that Dionysius and Eriugena do, i.e. that the One is nothing *tout court*.[7] What the *aporia* noted above indicates is that the One *appears* to be nothing. I take the point of this to be that negation, just as much

[5] See Rist, 1967, 25 and Gerson 1990, 204.

[6] See e.g. Gilson 1952, 22 and Perl 2002.

[7] Cf. Perl 138ff. for the comparison of Plotinus with Dionysius. Porphyry does state that the One is "not-being beyond Being" (*Sent.* 26) and the *APC* even employs "ignorance" (ἀγνωσία) as the cognitive state appropriate for apprehending the One (Fr. 4 = X.27). These formulations do anticipate developments in medieval Platonism, but they differ at least linguistically if not conceptually from Plotinus. It remains possible, however, that they are motivated by similar experiences.

affirmation, is an inherently limited mental operation. Plotinus typically says that the One is not a being or not one of the intelligible beings, e.g. VI.9.5.30, III.8.9.53-54, 10.28-35, and V.5.12.47-50. Nevertheless, if Plotinus does conceive of the One as some sort of being, doesn't he predicate something in common between the One and Intellect? Such a conception, in Perl's view, would amount to "situating the One...within the totality of being, and making it subject to a term more inclusive than, and hence prior to, itself" (ibid.). Perl is correct that Plotinus wants to reject this conclusion, but I am not convinced that he has formulated the problem correctly.

I think that Plotinus avoids this dilemma by investing his henology, albeit implicitly, with the Aristotelian principle of focal equivocity and the graded univocity of being. In *pros hen* equivocity things have a name in common, but they do not share the same definition, though the definitions are not unrelated. The definition applies primarily to one and derivatively to the other. Gradable univocity means that several subjects have more or less of the same attribute (see Gerson 1991, 333ff.). Admittedly, this is an imperfect solution since *strictu sensu* the One is indefinable and it is not a substance with attributes. Moreover, it would seriously misrepresent Plotinus' metaphysics to describe the One and Intellect as primary and secondary instances of being, respectively. Yet Plotinus provides some grounds for a kind of hyper-paradeigmatism in the relation between the One and Intellect when he says that limited, determinate, and intelligible being is a trace and image of the One (V.5.5.13, 23). He seems to have embedded the Platonic-Aristotelian notion of perfect being within the idea of an infinitely powerful and productive first principle. Thus, he paradoxically asserts both that the One's perfection derives from its οὐσία (V.6.2.13) and that its perfect activity is beyond οὐσία (VI.8.20.9-16). As supreme efficient cause it is responsible for the existence of each οὐσία (VI.6.13.50) and it preserves all things in existence (VI.7.23.22, III.8.10.1-2, VI.9.1.1-2). What complicates Plotinus' metaphysics of causation is the implication that the One's reality contains intelligible and other realities "within itself" in an indeterminate and ineffable manner.

> How is that One the principle of all things? It is because as principle it keeps them in being, making each one of them exist? Yes, and because it brought them into existence. But how did it do so? By possessing them beforehand. But it has been said that in this way it will be a multiplicity. But it had them in such a way as not to be distinct: they are distinguished on the second level. (V.3.15.27-31; cf. also V.4.2.16, VI.7.32.14, VI.8.21.24-5)

> It must be better than life and intellect; thus the other [i.e. intellect] will turn towards it both the life which is in it, a kind of image of

> the life in that in so far as this lives, and the intellect in it, a kind of representation (μίμημα) of what is in that, whatever this may be. (V.3.16.38-42).

To understand the relation between the One's quasi-being, life, and intellect and their intelligible images, I refer to A.C. Lloyd's analysis of the P-series. Neoplatonists saw procession and return as series, proceeding *ab uno* and returning *ad unum*, in which the first term, which is a whole prior to its parts, is neither synonymous nor homonymous with its derivatives (Lloyd 1990, 76-85). The first term of the series, what he calls the quasi-genus, unlike the standard genus, "is not the potentiality of the species but the power of them. This means that it is a whole which actually contains the species—but the species as a whole, 'silently'" (1990, 81). The "predicates" of the quasi-genus are not properties *of* a substance, rather they are activities, which are not attributes, but *identical* with the substance (91).[8] Lloyd's explanation of gradable univocity adds the important insight that the activities of the substance are identical with it and are not even logically distinct attributes. Each attribute or activity can be construed individually in a discursive or noetic manner, i.e. as parts of the lexicon of positive theology. When properly negated, i.e. when their limitations and complexity are removed, they can be redeployed as symbolic language in a distinct mystical mode of discourse.

If this analysis of the One's unlimited reality is correct, it raises the possibility that the One can be seen as an essential or formal cause of intelligible being, though in a manner quite different from intelligible being's formal causality with respect to sensible particulars.[9] Against this notion Gerson asserts that while the One is the cause of everything's existence, it "does not give essence to anything, including Intellect, the locus of eternal essence...Whatever has essence has it from Intellect which is identical with οὐσία." Thus, Plotinus refuses "to accept that virtuality in being entails eminence in being...Plotinus cannot just infer that the One is eminently whatever its effects are in an inferior way. To do so would compromise the

[8] Lloyd 1990, 80: "the terms of a P-series do not share an identical generic predicate; but the differences between them in respect of this predicate are equivalent to different degrees of participation in its primary form..., the first term of the series." I have appropriated Lloyd's analysis of intelligible being and applied it to the One. See also the invaluable remarks of Strange 1987, 967-968.

[9] VI.8.14.33-34: "that from which these come is like the things which have come to be much more originally (ἀρχετυπώτερον) and more truly and more than as it is on their level in that it is better."

simplicity of the One" (1994, 32, cf. also 65ff.). Yet, in commenting on our texts in V.3, he observes that they "seem to suggest eminence" (ibid. 33). Indeed. The only consideration restraining Gerson from acknowledging some sort of eminence view in Plotinus' metaphysics of causation is the non-temporal account of the derivation of intelligible being from the One. I don't understand the cogency of this reservation. In any case, I agree with Gerson that Aquinas' account of the eminence of being is far more developed than Plotinus'. I also emphasize more than he does the role of Plotinus' own experience of the One, which has the effect of casting logical precision to the wind in an attempt to describe in metaphysical language what cannot be expressed.[10]

Formulations of the eminence view in Plotinus and in the *APC* (Fr. 5 = XII.29-35) were also criticized by the later Neoplatonists. In the passage quoted above Proclus mentions unnamed thinkers who ascribe various attributes to the One lest the One be considered non-existent. Hadot claimed that the author of the *APC*, in his view Porphyry, is the target of Proclus' series of criticisms. Dillon later suggested that Plotinus may have been a secondary target. I agree with Dillon that Plotinus' views would also trouble Proclus. In fact, the phrasing of some of Proclus' criticisms suggest that Plotinus may be his primary target and not Porphyry or the author of the *APC*. The first group of thinkers he mentions attributes "intellectuality" (νοότης) to the One (*In Parm.* 1106.1-6) "as being simpler than Intellect, and as it were the condition of intelligising taking place" on the grounds that actualities are prior to essences (1106.6-10). Additionally, prior to this unitary "intellectuality" comes partless thought (τὸ νόημα). As we have seen, Plotinus often conceives of the One's existence as a self-identical ἐνέργεια ἄνευ οὐσίας (VI.8.20.9ff.). Dillon (1992, 363) cites a similar idea in the *APC*, which situates ἐνέργεια prior to οὐσία: "the One…is neither being, nor substance, nor act (ἐνέργεια), but rather is in act and is itself pure activity (τὸ ἐνεργεῖν καθαρόν), so that it is also the being before being (τὸ εἶναι τὸ πρὸ τοῦ εἶναι)" (Fr. 5 = XII.22ff. Dillon 363, cf. Bradshaw 2004, 103). The "being before being" is designated as "absolute being" (τοῦ εἶναι τὸ ἀπόλυτον) a few lines later (Fr. 5 = XII.33). It is perhaps worth noting that where Plotinus identifies the One with ἐνέργεια – and Proclus too uses the substantive in his critique–the *APC* uses ἐνεργεῖ and τὸ ἐνεργεῖν καθαρόν. (However, we do find ἐνέργεια in Fr. 6 = XIII.10.) Also, like the

[10] Strange 1987, 983 makes the crucial point that this is even true of applying ordinary language to the intelligible world.

author of the *APC*, Plotinus in VI.8 also links ἐνέργεια with being denoted by the infinitive: "its activity is according to its being" (7.49-50: κατὰ τὸ εἶναι ἡ ἐνέργεια) and "being and acting there are the same" (4.29: τὸ αὐτὸ τὸ εἶναι ἐκεῖ καὶ τὸ ἐνεργεῖν). Thus, although both Plotinus and the *APC* conceive of the One as pure activity and as being without any distinction between substance and attribute (cf. Bechtle 1999, 253-54 contra Hadot), the terminology employed by the *APC* differs slightly from Proclus'.

What of the first and the third examples cited by Proclus, νοότης and τὸ νόημα? Hadot and Dillon claim Porphyrian provenance for the first since it appears in Victorinus (Dillon 1987, 451n86), though neither term appears in the *APC*. In the third example, Plotinus' use of paronyms with -μα suffixes, probably of Stoic provenance (cf. Hadot 1968, I.361-64), may be significant. Especially noteworthy is the distinction Plotinus draws in VI.7.39 between Intellect's self-thinking and the One's ἁπλῆ τις ἐπιβολὴ αὐτῷ πρὸς αὑτὸν. The One's concentrated and indivisible self-awareness is contrasted with Intellect's differentiated intellectual motion through the cryptic remark that "that kind of movement (οἷον κίνημα), simple and all the same, if it is to be something like a touch, has nothing intelligent about it" (39.19-20). Elsewhere he notes that "the intellectual act is without parts" (IV.3.30.7: τὸ μὲν γὰρ νόημα ἀμερὲς), though here νόημα does not refer to the One. If this parallel has any relevance it would be in the sense that "the intellectual act," which in Intellect is logically distinct from νοῦς and νοητόν, is *identified* with the One. Consider the case where Plotinus characterizes the One's ἐνέργεια as οἷον νοῦς, specifically a νοῦς that is also ἐνέργημα of itself (VI.8.16.16-18); later he adds there is "something like Intellect in the One which is not Intellect" (18.20-21).[11] Add to these the various -νόησις compounds that specify the One's awareness (V.4.2.17, VI.8.16.32). In sum, whereas Plotinus employs νοῦς, νόημα, and νόησις (in compounds) in reference to the One, the *APC* Fr. 2 employs the cognitive terms γνῶσις and γιγνώσκειν to characterize God's knowledge, the simple transcendent knowledge prior to knowledge.[12] The latter text seems less relevant to Proclus' concerns than do the Plotinian passages with their richer and more

[11] It is important to note that in this passage in VI.8.16 these quasi-noetic attributions to the One apply to it as final cause, as "the most lovable object," not as efficient cause.

[12] V.19ff.; cf. Dillon 1992, 361 and Bechtle 1999, 50.

diverse noetic vocabulary. The terminological correlations among these passages in Proclus, Plotinus, and in the *APC* are inexact, but it is not unlikely that Plotinus' statements and even his language might have elicited greater concern in Proclus than those of Porphyry or the *APC*.

Another factor complicating efforts to identify Proclus' targets is the uncertainty both as to whether Proclus was even familiar with the *APC* and whether Porphyry is its author.[13] And if it was not written by Porphyry the *APC* may be pre-Plotinian, as Bechtle has suggested recently, or even by a pupil of Porphyry. In any case, the originality claimed for it by Hadot in formulating the concept of pure, absolute being prior to intelligible being is exaggerated in light of Plotinus' more extensive speculation on the One's being. Even if the *APC* were pre-Plotinian and Plotinus was familiar with it, his symbolic accounts of the inner life of the One go far beyond it in semantic richness.

Returning to Proclus' critique, the third authorities he cites argue that

> since the first principle is cause of all things, situated above Life, above Intellect, above Being itself, it possesses within itself in some way the causes of all these things unutterably and unimaginably and in the most unified way, and in a way unknowable to us but knowable to itself; and the hidden causes of all things in it are models prior to models. (1107.9-15)

Dillon suggests that this authority is probably Iamblichus (1987, 452n91), by reference to the Iamblichean phrase "unknown to us" (cf. Iamblichus, *In Tim.* Fr. 88 Dillon). However, that text insists that what is beyond human comprehension is how the cosmic gods create physical bodies, an activity far inferior to the One's reality. Iamblichus' own conception of the hyper-transcendent One is certainly not under attack here. To my mind, Proclus' objection would seem more relevant to Plotinus' bold connection of the One's ὑπερνόησις–echoing Proclus' "knowable to itself"–with the source and causes of νοῦς:

> For something like what is in Intellect, in many ways greater, is in that One; it is like a light dispersed far and wide from some one thing translucent in itself; what is dispersed is image, but that from which it comes is truth; though certainly the dispersed image, Intellect, is not of alien form...that One is cause of the cause. He is

[13] Dillon 1987, xxviii-xxx presents several cautionary notes, though his later 1992 essay expressed greater confidence in Hadot's identification of Porphyry as the author of the *APC*. For scepticism about Porphyry's authorship cf. Edwards 1990 and Bechtle *passim*. I continue to suspend judgment on this question.

> then in a greater degree something like the most causative and truest of causes, possessing all together the intellectual causes (νοερὰς αἰτίας) which are going to be from him and generative of what is not as it chanced but as he himself willed. (VI.8.18.32-41)

Once again we encounter the hyper-paradeigmatism of the One, also evident in the passages from V.3.15-16 quoted above, but here combined with the imagery of all-pervading light, a common motif in the *Enneads* and in the *APC*.[14]

Later in his Commentary on the *Parmenides* Proclus launches an attack against yet another triad of Platonist misconceptions about the One: that it is αὐθυπόστατον, αὐτοκίνητον, and superior to every cause. While αὐθυπόστατον does not appear in the *Enneads*, in VI.8 he often refers to the One as cause of itself (13.57, see also 16.15, 21). The second trouble-maker dares to assert that the One is "self-moved" (αὐτοκίνητον) (1150.2ff.; cf. also 1167.10ff.). As candidates for this deluded Platonist Dillon suggests Numenius and Porphyry (1992, 364-65). Since neither thinker specifically attributes motion to the supreme One, I suggest that we consider Plotinus' comment that the One "is, in a way, borne to its interior, in a way, loving itself" (ὁ δ' εἰς τὸ εἴσω οἷον φέρεται αὐτοῦ οἷον ἑαυτὸν ἀγαπήσας, VI.8.16.13-14). Since this is an ecstatic utterance that abandons philosophical precision,[15] it is difficult to construe the One's erotic self-penetration as synonymous with Proclus' αὐτοκίνητον. However, on the basis of the total synonymy of the One's quasi-attributes proposed earlier, this utterly paradoxical activity must be identical with the more prosaic "bringing itself into existence." Proclus in fact maintains that self-motion follows from self-constitution, and notes the "kinship between the two concepts" (1150.4-6). In *ET* prop. 42 he links self-constitution with self-reversion. The same cluster of activities is applied to the One in Plotinus, including perhaps even self-reversion, if we accept that in V.1.6-7 Plotinus finds an ἐπιστροφή in the One.[16] Dillon suggests that Victorinus' notion of divine self-motion (*Adv. Ar.* III.2.12-16, Dillon 1992, 365) probably depends on Porphyry though he provides no textual evidence. Possibly relevant here are passages in *APC* Fr. 6 = XIII.1ff. and XIV.1ff., which examine "movement into itself" (εἰσελθεῖν εἰς ἑαυτὸν), but it is not obvious to me that Proclus has this passage in mind.

[14] Cf. Fr. 2 = V.34ff. with Dillon 1992, 362.

[15] See my discussion of this passage in Bussanich 1988 ad loc.

[16] Most Plotinus scholars ascribe the ἐπιστροφή to the pre-Intellect. Cf. Gerson 1994, 244n12 and, contra, Bussanich 1988 ad loc.

Moreover, Victorinus could have discovered divine self-motion in the *Enneads* as easily as in Porphyry.

Consideration of Proclus' critique of his predecessors anticipates, as we have seen, some modern scholarly concerns, and it also provides intriguing clues for understanding the lexical creativity of those who envisioned the quasi-being of the One. Also echoed in much contemporary scholarship is Proclus' silence about the impact of Plotinus' own experience of the One on his metaphysical formulations. Negation preserves the One's transcendence, but it is inadequate to express the mystic's direct awareness around and "within" the One. Plotinus' mystically performative language breaks free from the discursive language of both positive and negative theologies in his statements that the formless is most beautiful (τὸ ὑπέρκαλον, VI.7.33.20-21), that the soul becomes formless (34.2ff.), and, that because of the One's infinite nature, the soul's eros for it is unlimited (32.24ff.). Entering the infinite reality of the One means that the soul becomes the unlimited eros that the One itself is. Significantly, in the mystical ascent eros is not removed by negation (Rist 1964a, 97). And when united with "our true love" (VI.9.9.44-45), the soul transcends all psychological states:

> It is not afraid, either, that anything may happen to it, since it does not even see it while it is with that; but if all the other things about it perished, it would even be pleased, that it might be alone with this: so great a degree of happiness (ἐυπαθεία) has it reached. (VI.7.34.35-38)

Supreme bliss is a striking feature of union with the One, but, just as remarkably, it is the nature of the One's being in itself. Here lies the experiential source of the evocations of the One's being. What speaks is the self of visionary experience within the luminous, blissful, pure being of the One. But these ecstatic and performative utterances cannot be translated into discursive theological language. Nor should they be taken simply as affirmations to be negated, as do his successors and modern readers.[17]

[17] His successors' inability to understand Plotinus' dialect of mystical presence may indicate that they lacked his level of experience, as is suggested by Dodds 1963, xxiii: "What for Plotinus was the living utterance of experience seems to be for him [Proclus] literary tradition." Similarly, Rist 1964b, 218: "Perhaps there is some connection between the fact that Proclus never claimed to have attained such union and his shadowy comments on the flower of the whole soul," "for where Plotinus is a mystic, Proclus seems to know only a theory of mysticism" (ibid. 220).

I am grateful to an anonymous referee whose comments improved an earlier draft of this paper.

CONSULTING THE ORACLE: THE MANTIC ART AND ITS CAUSATION IN IAMBLICHUS' *DE MYSTERIIS*

Crystal Addey

Iamblichus' *De Mysteriis* is the most extensive surviving treatise from the ancient world on divination, sacrifice and other polytheistic religious phenomena.[1] Composed between 280 and 305 AD as a reply to Porphyry's *Letter to Anebo*, this work is written under the assumed guise of the Egyptian priest "Abammon."[2] This paper will consider Iamblichean views of divination and its relationship with theurgy as discussed in *De Mysteriis*. Book III is devoted to divination (μαντική). As a response to Porphyry's request for a clear description of "what happens in predicting the future,"[3] Iamblichus' exposition centres on what causes divine inspiration and divination and their possible classification. I shall suggest that the framework of Aristotelian theories of causation can be applied to Iamblichus' comments on divination to clarify his views on the operation and function of inspired and inductive divination and theurgic ritual. This paper will utilise Iamblichus' comments in III.11 on oracles as a particular case study for his views of inspired divination. In connection with this, Iamblichus' conception of divination and theurgy as illumination from the gods will also be explored.

[1] P.T. Struck (2000), "Iamblichus, *De Mysteriis*, Book 1," in R.Valantasis (ed) (2000), *Religions of Late Antiquity in Practice*, 489.

[2] Scholars generally agree that the *De Mysteriis* was written within this specific period. For its assignation to c.300 AD see H.D. Saffrey (1971), "Abammon, Pseudonyme de Jamblique," in R.B. Palmer & R.G. Hamerton-Kelly (eds) (1971), *Philomathes: Studies and Essays in the Humanities in Memory of Philip Merlan*, 231-233; P. Athanassiadi (1993), "Dreams, Theurgy and Freelance Divination: The Testimony of Iamblichus," *JRS* 83, 116, n.13. For a suggestion of 280 AD see J. Dillon (ed & tr) (1973), *Iamblichi Chalcidensis In Platonis Dialogos Commentarium Fragmenta,* 13, 18. Cf. E.C. Clarke (2003), "Introduction," in E.C. Clarke, J.M. Dillon & J.P. Hershbell (eds & trs) (2003), *Iamblichus: On the Mysteries*, xxxi-xxxvii, for a comprehensive discussion on the pseudonym Abammon.

[3] Iamblichus, *De Mysteriis*, III.1 (99.9-10), trs & eds: E.C. Clarke, J.M. Dillon & J.P. Hershbell (2003), Atlanta. All quotations and translations are from this edition, unless otherwise specified.

1. Inspired and Inductive Divination

Within Book III, Iamblichus clearly distinguishes two types of divination. The first of these is inspired divination, which includes oracles and possession by the gods. The second type is inductive or 'human' divination, as Iamblichus calls it, divination by signs, which includes haruspicy and astrology. Iamblichus seems to distinguish these two types of divination by their proximity to the divine and the modes of causation governing them. As will be discussed, Iamblichus clearly considers inspired divination to be superior to inductive divination. It is worth noting here that the division of divination into these two types had a long history in the Graeco-Roman philosophical tradition.[4] The Platonists and Stoics always distinguished between these two types of divination, which they also refer to as 'natural' and 'artificial.'[5]

2. Inspired Divination and Aristotelian Modes of Causation

At the beginning of Book III, Iamblichus counters Porphyry's challenge that divination is purely a human achievement, a case of humans using the right equipment, location and techniques, and thereby a phenomenon that "comes into existence."[6] He does this by focusing on inspired divination and emphasising that the principle of this type of divination is divine and eternal, following the general methodology utilised within the Platonic tradition of locating the principle of a phenomenon before moving on to discuss its particular manifestations:

> Μέγιστον δὴ ουν ἀλεξιφάρμακον πρὸς ἅπαντα τὰ τοιαῦτα ἀπορήματα ἐκεῖνό ἐστι, γνῶναι τὴν ἀρχὴν τῆς μαντικῆς, ὡς οὔτε ἀπὸ σωμάτων ἐστὶν ὁρμωμένη οὔτε ἀπὸ τῶν περὶ τοῖς σώμασι παθημάτων...τὸ δὲ πᾶν κῦρος

[4] Cf. A.H. Armstrong, (1987), "Iamblichus and Egypt," *Les Etudes Philosophiques* 2-3, 179; A. Sheppard (1993), "Iamblichus on Inspiration: *De Mysteriis* 3.4-8," in H.J. Blumenthal & E.G. Clark (eds) (1993), *The Divine Iamblichus: Philosopher and Man of Gods*, 142, notes that Iamblichus' concept of inspiration is in line with Plato's concept of 'prophetic madness' and with traditional Greek ideas of prophetic inspiration and divine possession.

[5] Plato, *Phaedrus*, 244d2–5, ed: I. Burnet (1901, 1960), Oxford; *Ion*, 533e-534a; 533d; 534e; 536c-d; 542a, Plato, *Opera, Tomus III* (1903), Oxford; Cicero, *De Divinatione*, I.6.11-12; I.33.72; II.11.26–27, ed: R. Giomini (1975), Teubner. Translation is that of W.A. Falconer (1923), Loeb edn.

[6] Iamblichus, *De Mysteriis*, III.1 (99.9–100.6).

αὐτῆς ἀνήκει εἰς τοὺς θεοὺς καὶ ἀπὸ τῶν θεῶν ἐνδίδοται...Τὰ δ' ἄλλα πάντα ὡς ὄργανα ὑπόκειται τῇ ἐκ θεῶν καταπεμπομένῃ τῆς προγνώσεως δόσει...

The greatest talisman, then, against all such difficulties is this: to know the principle of divination, to know that it is activated neither by bodies nor by bodily conditions ...Rather, all of its supreme power belongs to the gods, and is bestowed by the gods...All else is subordinate, instrumental to the gift of foreknowledge sent down by the gods...[7]

Iamblichus specifically asserts that the supreme power of divination belongs to the gods and is given to humans by the gods, indicating their primary role in divination; everything else involved in divination is subordinate and instrumental to the gods. Following this, Iamblichus stresses the difference between primary and secondary causes in divination:

Εἰ δή τις ἀφέμενος τῶν πρωτουργῶν αἰτίων ἐπὶ τὰς δευτερουργοὺς ὑπουργίας ἀποφέροι τὸ τῆς μαντικῆς, οἷον κινήσεις σωμάτων ἢ παθῶν μεταβολὰς ἢ γενέσεις τινὰς ἑτέρας ἢ ζωῆς ἀνθρωπίνης ἐνεργείας ἢ λόγους ἐμψύχους ἢ φυσικοὺς τιθέμενος...ὑπολαμβάνοι τὴν ἀκρίβειαν ἀποδιδόναι περὶ αὐτῆς, τοῦ παντὸς διημάρτηκεν. 'Αλλ' εἷς ὅρος ὀρθὸς καὶ μία ἀρχὴ περὶ πάντων τοιούτων, μηδαμῶς ἀναιτίως παράγειν τὴν τοῦ μέλλοντος μαντείαν ἀπὸ τῶν μηδεμίαν ἐχόντων πρόγνωσιν ἐν ἑαυτοῖς, ἀπὸ δὲ τῶν θεῶν τῶν συνεχόντων ἐν αὑτοῖς τὰ πέρατα τῆς ὅλης εἰδήσεως τῶν ὄντων, ἀπὸ τούτων θεωρεῖν μεριζομένην τὴν μαντικὴν περὶ πάντα τὸν κόσμον...Ἡ γὰρ τοιάδε ἀρχηγική τέ ἐστιν αἰτία καὶ διαφερόντως κοινοτάτη, ἔχουσά τε ἐν ἑαυτῇ πρώτως ἃ δίδωσι τοῖς μετέχουσιν ἑαυτῆς, καὶ μάλιστα ἀλήθειαν παρεχομένη ἧς δεῖ τῇ μαντικῇ...

If someone, then, straying from the primary causes, downgrades the skill of divination to secondary operations – position, for example, bodily movements or changes of emotions, or other happenings, either activities of human life or other psychic or physical explanations...he has wholly erred in supposing that he has given an accurate account of divination. **There is one correct rule and one first principle concerning all these matters: that is, never to derive divination of the future from those things**

[7] Iamblichus, *De Mysteriis*, III.1 (100.8-101.3). Cf. also III.1 (100.6-7); III.1 (102.8-9); III.2 (104.12-105.2); III.3 (107.4-6); III.8 (117.1-5); III.26 (162.7-11).

> **that have no foreknowledge as such, but to derive it from the gods** who in themselves possess the limits of all knowledge of existing things, from which the mantic power is distributed throughout the whole cosmos...**For such a principal cause is not only primordial and eminently universal but contains primarily within itself whatever it gives to those sharing in it,** and especially furnishes the truth which divination needs...[my bold].[8]

Here Iamblichus emphasises that the divine is the principal cause of divination, contrasting this primary cause with the 'secondary operations' involved in divination, such as bodily movements and other physical and psychic human activities. These 'secondary operations' are lower causes necessary for the divinatory process. However Iamblichus chooses to stress the comparative unimportance of such lower causes in relation to the significant role of the gods. He asserts that the divine is the primary cause of divination because the eternal and universal nature of the gods is such that they possess all truth and knowledge, which informs μαντική, knowledge of the past, present and future. This accords with the Neoplatonist principle that all things are contained in potentiality in the eternal principles and causes from which they are derived. This principle is clearly elucidated in Proclus' *Elements of Theology*:

> Πᾶν τὸ τῷ εἱναι χορηγοῦν ἄλλοις αὐτὸ πρώτως ἐστὶ τοῦτο, οὗ μεταδίδωσι τοῖς χορηγουμένοις.
>
> Everything which by its existence bestows a character on others itself primitively possesses that character which it communicates to the recipients.[9]

According to Iamblichus, the principle and essential nature of divination is contained in potentiality within the gods; this explains to some extent Iamblichus' marked emphasis on the divine as the most significant cause of divination.

Iamblichus also comments on those who are divinely inspired:

> Η γὰρ ὁ θεὸς ἡμᾶς ἔχει, ἢ ἡμεῖς ὅλοι τοῦ θεοῦ γιγνόμεθα, ἢ κοινὴν ποιούμεθα πρὸς αὐτὸν τὴν ἐνέργειαν·
>
> For either the god possesses us, or we become wholly the god's property, or we exercise our activity in common with him.[10]

[8] Iamblichus, *De Mysteriis*, III.1 (101.7–102.6).

[9] Proclus, *Elements of Theology*, Proposition 18; tr: E.R. Dodds (1933), Oxford.

[10] Iamblichus, *De Mysteriis*, III.5 (111.7–9).

At first sight, the last assertion seems to contradict Iamblichus' view that the power of divination is derived from the gods. However, this apparent contradiction disappears if we view Iamblichus' comments through the lens of Aristotelian theories of causation. Throughout Book III, Iamblichus repeatedly asserts the necessity of finding the cause, especially the primary cause, of different types of divination and divine inspiration.[11] Iamblichus would have been thoroughly familiar with Aristotelian theories of causation: the study and exegesis of the works of Plato and Aristotle was a central activity in Iamblichus' philosophical school in Apamea.[12] Indeed Iamblichus himself wrote commentaries on various works of Aristotle.[13] Aristotle sets out his scheme of different levels of causation in his *Metaphysics,* claiming that there are four kinds of causes: the Formal, Material, Efficient and Final causes.[14] The Formal cause encapsulates the essence or essential nature of the thing; the Material cause is the matter from which a thing is formed and the Efficient cause is the source of motion, or in other words, the creator. The Final cause is the highest cause in the hierarchy of causation: it is the ultimate purpose or 'good.'[15] According to Aristotle, these causes operate simultaneously to produce any given effect and they function hierarchically, with the highest cause having the greatest effect.[16]

Viewed from this perspective Iamblichus' comments show an integrated conception of the causation of divination: the gods are the Final cause of divination, and Iamblichus emphasises this since without the gods, there would be no divination or inspiration. Iamblichus clearly envisages a hierarchical scheme of causation, similar to that of Aristotle, in his exposition

[11] Iamblichus, *De Mysteriis*, III.1 (101.7; 101.13; 102.3-4); III.3 (107.11-12); III.8 (117.1; 117.8); III.9 (118.1-2); III.10 (120.11-12; 122.9; 123.6-8); III.19 (146.5); III.20 (148.4); III.24 (156.5); III.31 (175.14).

[12] J. Dillon (ed & tr) (1973), *Iamblichi Chalcidensis In Platonis Dialogos Commentariorum Fragmenta*, 15, 21.

[13] J. Dillon (1973), Ibid, 21. Cf. also John Dillon's emended version of this Introduction, "Iamblichus of Chalcis (c.240–325 A.D.)," *ANRW* II.36.2 (1987), 876-878.

[14] Aristotle, *Metaphysics*, 1.3.1 (983a24-32), ed: W. Jaeger (1957, 1973), Oxford. All quotations are from this edition, unless otherwise specified. Translation is that of H. Tredennick (1933), Loeb edn.

[15] Aristotle, *Metaphysics*, 1.3.1-2 (983a24-b6).

[16] Aristotle, *Metaphysics*, 2.1.6-7 (993b23-31); 2.2.9 (994b9-16); 3.2.6-8 (996b5-18); *Physics*, 2.3 (194b16-195a8); 2.7 (198a14-24), ed: W.D. Ross (1950, 1973), Oxford.

of divination, since he accepts that human beings do play a part in inspired divination. From III.20 – 25, Iamblichus gives a detailed exposition on the causality of divination in answer to Porphyry's challenges concerning the sole possible causes of divination.[17] Iamblichus' central point is not to deny that these human facilities have a role in divination; rather he is arguing that they are not the *ultimate* cause, a role he reserves for the gods. They are subordinate, lower causes which have less importance than the Final cause; therefore one must view divination in terms of its ultimate causation in order to understand its complete nature. Iamblichus constantly reiterates this fundamental point with the examples of lesser causes.[18] For example, in III.7 he states that divine inspiration does not come solely from the daemons but from the gods and that it does not belong to the soul, intellect or one of their faculties, or to the body.[19] Although the human soul, intellect and body do have a role in divination, they are auxiliary, lower causes,[20] which need to be in a receptive, purified state in order to receive the inspiration of the god, who works through them. The soul and body of the prophet must not disturb, control or pervert the divine harmony which pervades them; otherwise the divine transmission or oracle will be distorted, misleading or even false. In this sense, Iamblichus emphasises the passivity that is necessary for the reception of the divine, as he deems the prophet's soul and body to be far lower causes in his hierarchical scheme of causation.

This comparative analysis of hierarchical levels of causation is particularly clear in Iamblichus' remark on the human race:

> μία δ' ἐστὶν ἐν αὐτῷ τῆς ἐνυπαρχούσης πλάνης καὶ ταραχῆς καὶ τῆς ἀστάτου μεταβολῆς ἰατρεία, εἴ τινα μετουσίαν θείου φωτὸς κατὰ τὸ δυνατὸν μεταλάβοι· ὁ δὲ ταύτην ἀποκλείων ταὐτὸν ποιεῖ τοῖς ἐξ ἀψύχων ψυχὴν παράγουσιν ἢ τοῖς ἀπὸ τῶν ἀνοήτων νοῦν ἀπογεννῶσι· καὶ

[17] Iamblichus, *De Mysteriis*, III.20 (147.12-149.3); III.21 (150.3-14); III.22 (152.10-153.1; 153.8-13); III.24 (156.5-11); III.25 (160.1-11). Cf. G. Shaw (1998), "Divination in the Neoplatonism of Iamblichus," in R.M. Berchman (ed) (1998), *Mediators of the Divine: Horizons of Prophecy, Divination, Dreams and Theurgy in Mediterranean Antiquity*, 236, n.42.

[18] Cf. For example, Iamblichus, *De Mysteriis*, III.7 (114.13–115.1).

[19] Iamblichus, *De Mysteriis*, III.7 (114.6-8; 114.13 – 115.2).

[20] Iamblichus, *De Mysteriis*, III.7 (115.4-11). Cf. Aristotle, *Metaphysics*, 1.2.5 (982a25-29); 1.3.1 (983a24-32); 2.1.7 (993b26-31), 2.2.8-9 (994b6-16).

> γὰρ αὐτὸς ἀπὸ τῶν μὴ θείων τὰ θεῖα ἔργα ἀναιτίως ὑφίστησιν.
>
> But there is one remedy for its inherent straying, confusion and unstable changing, and that is, if it participate as far as possible in some portion of the divine light. But whoever excludes this, does the same thing as they who produce a soul from things without a soul, or who would generate a mind from things mindless; for such a person postulates divine works without a cause from things not divine.[21]

This comment depends on the principle that the greater cannot be caused by that which is inferior to it, a vital principle which forms part of the foundation of Neoplatonist metaphysics.[22] Aristotle applied such a principle to his theory of causation: the higher a cause is, the greater its effect.[23] Iamblichus himself refers to this principle in his refutation of Porphyry's challenge that divine possession is the accomplishment of the human body or soul:

> ...οὐδὲ πέφυκεν ἀπὸ τῶν χειρόνων τὰ κρείττονα ἀπο γεννᾶσθαι.
>
> ...nor is it the nature of the greater to be generated from the inferior.[24]

Proclus also states this principle, specifically formulating it in terms of causation:

> Πᾶν τὸ παρακτικὸν ἄλλου κρεῖττόν ἐστι τῆς τοῦ παραγομένου φύσεως.
>
> Every productive cause is superior to that which it produces.[25]

Iamblichus' comment regarding the inherent straying of the human race is also based on the Neoplatonist principle that 'like produces like,' since μαντική consists of divine foreknowledge and so must ultimately be caused

[21] Iamblichus, *De Mysteriis*, III.18 (144.11-145.2).

[22] Cf. E.R. Dodds' comment on Proclus' Proposition 7 which states this principle, (1933) *Proclus: Elements of Theology*, 193: "This is the principle on which the whole structure of Neoplatonism is really founded."

[23] Aristotle, *Metaphysics*, 1.2.5 (982a25-29); 1.3.1 (983a24-32); 2.1.7 (993b26-31); 2.2.8-9 (994b6-16).

[24] Iamblichus, *De Mysteriis*, III.8 (116.13-14).

[25] Proclus, *Elements of Theology*, Proposition 7; tr: E.R. Dodds (1933), Oxford.

by divinity. Iamblichus specifically refers to this concept in connection with the causation of divination:

> πᾶν μὲν γὰρ τὸ γιγνόμενον ὑπ' αἰτίου τινὸς γίγνεται, καὶ τὸ συγγενὲς ὑπὸ τοῦ συγγενοῦς ἀποτελεῖται, τὸ δὲ θεῖον ἔργον οὔτε αὐτόματόν ἐστιν (ἀναίτιον γὰρ τὸ τοιοῦτον καὶ οὐ πάντως τεταγμένον), οὔτε ἀπ' ἀνθρωπίνης αἰτίας ἀπογεννᾶται· ἀλλότριον γὰρ καὶ τοῦτο καὶ ὑποδεέστερον, τὸ δὲ τελειότερον ὑπὸ τοῦ ἀτελοῦς οὐκ ἔχει δύναμιν παράγεσθαι. Πάντα ἄρα ἀπὸ θείας αἰτίας ἀποβλαστάνει τὰ προσόμοια αὐτῇ ἔργα φυόμενα.
>
> **For everything that happens arises from a specific cause, and what is kindred is produced by that which is kindred**, but the divine work is neither accidental (for such is without a cause, and not at all ordered) nor is it produced by a human cause…that which is more perfect has no ability to be produced by that which is imperfect. **All things, then, that spring from a divine cause are works that are naturally akin to it** [my bold].[26]

The principle that 'like produces like' also informs Iamblichus' idea that the gods can use the human being as an instrument in divination because the human soul contains something divine within it which it can recollect, or, as Iamblichus states, the human participates to some degree in the divine light.[27] This is clearly stated in III.9, which examines the different types of divine ecstasy and rituals to Cybele, Sabazios and the Korybantes, which included music to bring the initiate to a state of divine inspiration. Here Iamblichus explains the divine using the human being as an instrument with reference to the human soul's recollection of the divine harmony,[28] a clear echo of Plato's theory of recollection which describes the soul's original procession through divine Forms before its descent into the world of generation.[29]

[26] Iamblichus, *De Mysteriis*, III.20 (148.4 – 9); Cf. V.20 (227.13-228.2).

[27] Cf. Iamblichus' discussion of dreams at III.3 (106.11-14).

[28] Iamblichus, *De Mysteriis*, III.9 (120.2–10)

[29] Plato, *Phaedrus*, 250b5-251a7; cf. *Republic*, 401d5-402d4, ed: I.Burnet (1902, 1967), Oxford.

3. Inspired Divination: Oracles

Iamblichus' differentiation between levels of causation and firm emphasis on the primary cause of inspired divination are also apparent in his discussion of oracles, one of the most famous types of 'inspired divination' in antiquity.[30] Following the order of Porphyry's examples of prominent oracular shrines, Iamblichus first discusses the operation of Apollo's oracle at Claros, which prophesies by means of water. After performing many preliminary ceremonies and after drinking from the spring, the prophet delivers his oracles. Having described this practical operation Iamblichus concludes that the water has oracular power; his explanation of this fact concurs with his ideas about the ultimate causation of divination.[31] The divine exercises its power by a process of illumination or emanation, giving prophetic power to the water without any kind of fragmentation or detraction from itself, because of its eternal, unchanging and whole nature.[32] In his discussion of Iamblichean views of light and divine illumination, John Finamore has referred to this as, "an interpenetration of the immaterial with the material, with no contamination of the immaterial element."[33] According to Iamblichus, the illumination of the god needs a suitably prepared vehicle: all of the prophet's ritual preparations are merely required so that he will be receptive to the god's presence.[34] For example, he states that the water from the spring bestows the purification and receptivity on the prophet's soul so that it is able to receive the illumination from the god.[35] Iamblichus' statements concerning the oracle at Claros imply that the prophet himself is a lower cause of the oracle, since he utters the words of the oracle and therefore the divine transmission manifests itself through him, using him as an instrument. However, Iamblichus continues to emphasise the primacy of the role of the divine which ultimately causes the prophet's state of inspiration.

A similar pattern can be traced in Iamblichus' comments on the Pythia at Delphi:

[30] Cf. A. Sheppard (1993), "Iamblichus on Inspiration: *De Mysteriis* 3.4-8," in H.J. Blumenthal & E.G. Clark (eds) (1993), 140.

[31] Iamblichus, *De Mysteriis*, III.11 (124.13–125.6).

[32] Cf. Iamblichus, *De Mysteriis*, III.12 (129.1–4); III.19 (146.7–10).

[33] J. Finamore (1993), "Iamblichus on Light and the Transparent," in H.J. Blumenthal & E.G. Clark (eds) (1993), 59.

[34] Iamblichus, *De Mysteriis*, III.11 (125.6–126.3). Cf. II.11 (97.9-12).

[35] Iamblichus, *De Mysteriis*, III.11 (125.3-6).

> Η δ' ἐν Δελφοῖς προφῆτις, εἴτε ἀπὸ πνεύματος λεπτοῦ καὶ πυρώδους ἀναφερομένου ποθεν ἀπὸ στομίου θεμιστεύει τοῖς ἀνθρώποις, εἴτε ἐν τῷ ἀδύτῳ καθημένη ἐπὶ δίφρου χαλκοῦ τρεῖς πόδας ἔχοντος χρηματίζει, εἴτε καὶ ἐπὶ τοῦ τετράποδος δίφρου ὅς ἐστιν ἱερὸς τοῦ θεοῦ, πανταχῇ οὕτω δίδωσιν ἑαυτὴν τῷ θειῳ πνεύματι, ἀπό τε τῆς τοῦ θείου πυρὸς ἀκτῖνος καταυγάζεται...ὅταν δ' εἰς ἕδραν ἐνιδρυθῇ τοῦ θεοῦ, τῇ σταθερᾷ τοῦ θεοῦ μαντικῇ δυνάμει συναρμόζεται· ἐξ ἀμφοτέρων δὲ τῶν τοιούτων παρασκευῶν ὅλη γίγνεται τοῦ θεοῦ. Και τότε δὴ πάρεστιν αὐτῇ χωριστῶς ὁ θεὸς ἐπιλάμπων, ἕτερος ὢν καὶ τοῦ πυρὸς καὶ τοῦ πνεύματος καὶ τῆς ἰδίας ἕδρας καὶ πάσης τῆς περὶ τὸν τόπον φυσικῆς καὶ ἱερᾶς φαινομένης κατασκευῆς.
>
> The prophetess at Delphi, however, whether she gives oracles to human beings from a subtle and fiery spirit brought up from an aperture, or prophesies in the innermost sanctuary while seated on a bronze stool with three legs, or on a seat with four legs that is sacred to the god, she thus gives herself absolutely to the divine spirit, and is illuminated by the ray of divine fire…whenever she is found on the seat of the god, she is in harmony with the divine, unwavering oracular power. And as a result of both these preparations she becomes wholly the god's possession. Then, indeed, the god is present, shining on her separately, being himself other than the fire, the spirit, the particular abode, and all the physical and sacred trappings appearing in connection with the place.[36]

Iamblichus repeated use of the word εἴτε (*whether...or*) when discussing the ritual preparations undertaken by the Pythia serves to highlight their inferiority as a cause of oracles in comparison with the supreme power of the deity. As with the prophet at Claros, the divine causes the oracular inspiration itself; the prophetess' preparations are simply instrumental in causal terms, preparing her soul to be capable of receiving the inspiration and illumination of the divinity. Indeed as with the prophet at Claros, the prophetess at Delphi is implicitly viewed by Iamblichus as a secondary 'instrumental' cause of her oracular utterances, which are ultimately caused by the god using her as an instrument.

[36] Iamblichus, *De Mysteriis*, III.11 (126.4-9; 126.11–127.3).

4. Inductive Divination and Aristotelian Modes of Causation

Iamblichus' constant emphasis on the Final cause of divination also informs his definition of the two categories of divination: inspired and inductive divination; the latter of which is viewed as an inferior mode of divination. As we have seen, for Iamblichus, the principle of inspired divination is that it is ultimately caused by the supreme power of the gods. When Iamblichus discusses inductive divination, which comprises divination by signs, such as haruspicy and augury, he refers to this type of divination as 'artificial' and 'human':

> Φέρε δὴ ουν ἐπὶ τὸν διὰ τέχνης ἀνθρωπίνης ἐπιτελούμενον τρόπον μετέλθωμεν, ὅστις στοχασμοῦ καὶ οἰήσεως πλείονος εἴληφε·
>
> Come, then, let us turn to the mode of divination, accomplished by human skill, which partakes largely of guessing and supposition.[37]

According to Iamblichus, inductive divination operates via human 'guesswork'; in this sense it is a human skill (τέχνη). Iamblichus then discusses the workings of inductive divination:

> ...σημείοις τισὶ τοῦτο θείοις χρῆται ἐκ θεῶν ἐπιτελουμένοις κατὰ ποικίλους τρόπους. Ἀπὸ δὲ τῶν θείων τεκμηρίων κατὰ τὴν συγγένειαν τῶν πραγμάτων πρὸς τὰ δεικνύμενα σημεῖα συμβάλλει πως ἡ τέχνη καὶ στοχάζεται τὴν μαντείαν, ἐξ εἰκότων τινῶν αὐτὴν συλλογιζομένη. Τὰ μὲν ουν σημεῖα οἱ θεοὶ ποιοῦσι διὰ τῆς φύσεως...ἢ διὰ τῶν γενεσιουργῶν δαιμόνων οἵτινες τοῖς στοιχείοις τοῦ παντὸς καὶ τοῖς μερικοῖς σώμασι ζῴοις τε καὶ τοῖς ἐν τῷ κόσμῳ πᾶσιν ἐπιβεβηκότες ἄγουσι τὰ φαινόμενα μετὰ ῥᾳστώνης ὅπηπερ ἂν δοκῇ τοῖς θεοῖς. Συμβολικῶς δὲ τὴν γνώμην τοῦ θεοῦ ἐμφαίνουσι, καὶ τὴν τοῦ μέλλοντος προδήλωσιν....
>
> ...this kind uses divine signs that have been perfected by the gods in various ways. From divine signs, in virtue of the relationship of things to the signs shown, the technique somehow draws conclusions and guesses at the divination, inferring it from certain probabilities. The gods produce the signs either by means of nature...or through the agency of daemons concerned with creation, who, presiding over the elements of the universe and individual bodies, indeed over all living beings in the cosmos, guide the phenomena with ease in a

[37] Iamblichus, *De Mysteriis*, III.15 (135.1–2).

> manner pleasing to the gods. They reveal through symbols the purpose of the gods, even giving advance notice of the future...[38]

Iamblichus posits that inductive divination operates using signs which are implanted or illuminated by the gods through nature and also through the agency of daemons concerned with creation. His account implies that the signs implanted in the natural world, such as the entrails of the sacrificial animal in haruspicy, are the Material cause of this type of divination. The daemons, who implant the signs "in a manner pleasing to the gods" could be viewed as the Efficient cause of inductive divination, since they are responsible for placing such signs in the natural world. Iamblichus' explanation of the operation of inductive divination is clearly based on the concept of sympathy (συμπάθεια) as he himself states:

> Καὶ ἡ ἕνωσις δὲ καὶ ἡ συμπάθεια τοῦ παντὸς καὶ ἡ ὡς ἐφ' ἑνὸς ζῴου συγκίνησις τῶν πορρωτάτω μερῶν ὡς ἐγγὺς ὄντων, τὴν τῶν σημείων τούτων πομπὴν ἐκ θεῶν ἀνθρώποις καταπέμπει, διὰ τοῦ οὐρανοῦ μὲν πρώτως ἔπειτα διὰ τοῦ ἀέρος ἐκφαινομένην τοῖς ἀνθρώποις ὡς οἷόν τε μάλιστα λαμπρότατα.
>
> And the union and sympathy of the all and the simultaneous motion, as in a single living being, of parts farthest away as though they were near by, cause the sending down of these signs from the gods to human beings, first through the heaven and then through the air, with the greatest possible brightness.[39]

Given Iamblichus' comments, it seems that the inferiority of inductive divination stems from the human interpretation and supposition of the meaning of these signs rather than the nature of the signs themselves, which proceed from the divine.

Thus Iamblichus' distinction between these two categories of divination is based on his conception of their primary (Final) causes: inspired divination is ultimately caused by the gods whereas inductive divination, although utilising signs implanted by the gods through intermediaries such as daimones, depends upon human interpretation and skill. Thus human reason is the primary cause of this type of divination. Iamblichus clearly asserts that inspired divination has a much closer proximity to divine truth and knowledge whereas inductive divination is largely based on human skill (τέχνη). This is the fundamental distinction between the two types of divination as stressed in

[38] Iamblichus, *De Mysteriis*, III.15 (135.7–136.4).

[39] Iamblichus, *De Mysteriis*, III.16 (138.1–5).

Book III; they are distinguished by their proximity to the divine and the modes of causation governing them.

5. Inspired Divination and Theurgy

It remains to ask why Iamblichus so strongly emphasises the primary and Final cause of divination in Book III of *De Mysteriis*. A specific rationale can clearly be seen which relates to the purpose of the *De Mysteriis* as a whole: to clarify and justify theurgy (lit. 'god-working' or 'divine work') which relies ultimately on the divine. Inspired divination forms an important part of theurgic ritual. Thus, by showing the ultimate divine cause of inspired divination, Iamblichus explains the purpose of using divination in theurgic ritual and also emphasises the similarity between inspired divination and theurgy: both are caused by and derived from the gods; without the gods, humans would not be able to utilise divinatory or theurgic practices. Iamblichus concludes Book III with a comment on the nature of the true mantic art as a cause of both oracles and theurgic operations:

> Εν ουν τοῦτό ἐστι τὸ ἄχραντον καὶ ἱερατικὸν θεῖόν τε ὡς ἀληθῶς γένος τῆς μαντείας...ἀλλ' αὐτὸ ἐξῄρηται πάντων, ὑπερφυὲς ἀίδιον προυπάρχον, οὐδὲ παράθεσίν τινα ἐπιδεχόμενον οὔτε ὑπεροχήν τινος ἐν πολλοῖς προτεταγμένην· ἀλλ' ἀπολέλυται καὶ καθ' ἑαυτὸ μονοειδὲς πάντων προηγεῖται...ἐκ γὰρ τοῦ τοιούτου τρόπου παραγίγνεται ἅμα τε καὶ ἐν ταῖς μαντείαις ἡ ἄπταιστος ἀλήθεια καὶ ἐν ταῖς ψυχαῖς ἡ τελεία ἀρετή. Μετὰ τούτων δὲ ἀμφοτέρων δίδοται τοῖς θεουργοῖς ἡ πρὸς τὸ νοητὸν πῦρ ἄνοδος, ὃ δὴ καὶ τέλος δεῖ πάσης μὲν προγνώσεως πάσης δὲ θεουργικῆς πραγματείας προτίθεσθαι.
>
> This, then, is one kind of mantic, which is undefiled and sacerdotal, and truly divine...But it is itself entirely removed from all, supernatural, and eternally pre-existent, neither admitting any comparison nor pre-eminence among many; it is free from all this, and takes precedence over all according to its uniform self...For in such a fashion arises, at the same time, both infallible truth in oracles, and perfect virtue in souls. With both of these, ascent to the intelligible fire is granted to theurgists, a process which indeed must be proposed as the goal of all foreknowledge and of every theurgic operation.[40]

[40] Iamblichus, *De Mysteriis*, III.31 (178.13 –14; 178.15 – 179.3; 179.4 – 8).

The central agenda of the *De Mysteriis* is to justify the practice of theurgy: explaining the primary and central role of the gods in inspired divination, which in itself is an important element of theurgic ritual, seems to lend further weight to Iamblichus' argument for the significance of theurgy over merely theoretical philosophy. I would suggest that the main aim of Book III is to show how these theurgic and divinatory practices rely on divinity and to give a full account of their ultimate principles and causes in order to allow the reader a much more profound understanding of the 'gifts of the gods.'[41]

6. Conclusion

Iamblichus' conception of the hierarchical structure of the causation of divination informs his exposition of inspired and inductive categories of divination. The primary cause of inductive divination is human reason, that of inspired divination is the divine, which accounts for the similarity between inspired divination and theurgy. Iamblichus asserts that since the inductive mode of divination is entirely different from the inspired mode, it only has the power to predict everyday events, those directly concerned with generation.[42] This implies that for Iamblichus inspired modes of divination, such as oracles, contain philosophical truth and can bestow eternal and divine knowledge. This distinction may well have wider implications within the *De Mysteriis*. For instance, the pattern established here for the primacy of inspired divination could be viewed as a symbol for Iamblichus' wider claim of the superiority of theurgy above a merely rational philosophy.[43]

[41] Cf. Iamblichus, *De Mysteriis*, III.25 (160.1-11); Cf. Iamblichus' comments on the many benefits to humans of divine epiphanies, *De Mysteriis*, II.9 (87.11-88.14).

[42] Iamblichus, *De Mysteriis*, VI.4 (244.10–14).

[43] For a view of philosophy culminating in theurgy, see Proclus, *Commentary on Plato's Parmenides*, 74k, trs: G.R. Morrow & J.M. Dillon (1987), Princeton: "These dialectical operations are the preparation for the strain towards the One, but are not themselves the strain."

ASTROLOGY AS DIVINATION: IAMBLICHEAN THEORY AND ITS CONTEMPORARY PRACTICE

Gregory Shaw

The heavens in their entirety are within us.
-- Marsilio Ficino

Longing is what turns us inside out until we find the sun and the moon and stars inside..
-- Peter Kingsley

In *The Literal Meaning of Genesis* St. Augustine warns his readers about the dangers of astrology. He says:

> When astrologers tell the truth, it must be admitted that *this is due to an instinct that, unknown to man, lies hidden in his mind.* And since this happens through the action of unclean and lying spirits….a good Christian should beware of astrologers and of all impious diviners, especially of those who tell the truth, lest his soul become the dupe of demons and…enmesh itself in their company.[1]

As we are well aware, Augustine also fiercely condemned theurgy as a form of divination because it, too, invoked demons, led souls to their perdition, and perhaps more significantly, placed them outside his ecclesiastical control.[2]

Yet in this passage, Augustine is entirely in agreement with Iamblichus regarding astrology. For both men, true astrology relies on "an instinct that, unknown to man, lies hidden in his mind."[3] Of course, Iamblichus would have disagreed with Augustine's condemnation of the daimons who reveal this instinct, for it was precisely the purpose of theurgical rites to enmesh us in their divine company and thereby release us from the

[1] Edmund Hill, (2002), *Augustine On Genesis,* II, 17, introduction, translation and notes, Hyde Park, NY.

[2] Marcus Dods, (1950), *Augustine, The City of God*, 10.10, New York.

[3] " *instinctu quondam occultismo dici, quem nescientes humanae mentes patiuntur…." On Genesis,* II, 17, op. cit.

blindness of living under fate. Not surprisingly, Iamblichus' view of astrology is uniquely tied to his critique of the discursive methods that had taken hold among both Greek philosophers and astrologers. As a theurgist who aligned his soul with the stars and planets measured by the astrologers, Iamblichus drew from Platonic and Hermetic themes as well as from his own experience to distinguish the authentic and primordial rites of astral theurgy from the astrology practiced by the Greeks.

Iamblichus, therefore, rejects astrology as much as Augustine does but for vastly different reasons. In the hands of Greek intellectuals, with their charts and calculations, the ancient gods who traced luminous circles through the sky were reduced to causal ciphers placed within schemas that only astrologers were able to interpret. Porphyry assumed that our personal daimon could be discovered from these calculations and that, once determined, the soul could perform sacrifices to free itself from the rulers of fate.[4] Against this technical (*technikês*) approach to finding one's daimon, Iamblichus proposes a theurgical (*theourgikê*) method (*DM* 273.1-2) and denies that the daimon can be determined by celestial configurations. He says:

> ...the personal daimon never comes to us from the configuration prevailing at our birth, but there is a more primordial principle (*presbutera archê*) of him than this, which I will explain later...(*DM* 275.10-13).

Iamblichus' objection to Porphyry's approach is consistent with the entire polemic of the *De Mysteriis*. Porphyry presumes that access to divinity can be intellectually mapped out, that divine reality is something we can know, discuss, or even dispute (*DM* 7.10-13). Porphyry's approach to astrology, like his approach to all forms of divination, attempts to explain theurgical matters by considering them from a "technical and human perspective" (*DM* 279.14-15). In the case of astrology Porphyry's errors reflect those commonly held by Hellenic astrologers. Yet, despite this, Iamblichus says astrology (*mathematikê*) is a genuine theurgic practice. As he puts it:

> [I]n the case of astrology our response is that it itself is true but those who are wrongly informed about it fall into contradictions, since they know nothing of the truth. This situation, after all, is not particular to it alone but is true of all the sciences that have been handed down by the gods to men; for progressively, in the course of

[4] *DM* 275.1-3. All translations of the *De Mysteriis* are based on Emma C. Clark, John M. Dillon, and Jackson P. Hershbell (2003), *Iamblichus, On the Mysteries,* translated with introduction and notes, Atlanta. In several instances I have changed their translation slightly. All references to the *De Mysteriis* will be cited as *DM.*

> time, through the repeated admixture of much that is mortal, the divine character of the knowledge contained in them comes to be extinguished *(DM* 279.9-14).

The sciences that once brought souls to fullness and divine participation were distorted by our titanic self-love into discursive abstractions, mind games, that give us the illusion of control.[5] Astrology presents a perfect example. Since the movement of the planets and stars could be calculated and accurately predicted, and since these same celestial bodies revealed the patterns of fate—to which all mortals are bound—the knowledge of these patterns gave astrologers the sense that they could accurately predict the hand of fate in people's lives; thus, they came to possess the authority of spiritual guides, and many still do today. Yet, according to Iamblichus, astrologers "know nothing of the truth" (*DM* 277.10).

To give Porphyry a more appropriate context to understand astrology and the role of our personal daimon, Iamblichus refers to the Hermetic teaching that each human being "has two souls," one above fate, imbued with divine power, and the other created by, and subject to, the influences of the created cosmos. As he explains:

> [O]ne soul derives from the primary intelligible and shares in the power of the Demiurge while the other is given to us from the circuit of the heavenly bodies, *and into this there slips the soul that sees god.* This being the case, the soul which descends to us from the cosmic realms accommodates itself to the circuits of those realms, but that which is present to us intelligibly from the intelligible transcends the cycle of generation, and it is by virtue of this that we attain emancipation from fate and ascend to the intelligible gods (*DM* 269.3-9).

An intelligible and demiurgic presence remains with the embodied soul despite its absorption in generated life. A capacity to see god inexplicably "slips into" our fated life and through its divine eye we theurgically ascend to the gods.

The puzzle Iamblichus needed to address was how the cosmic gods that bind the soul to the cycles of generation also liberate us from these

[5] Damascius characterizes the fixation on our separate individuality as a consequence of titanic influence. He says: "The apparent self-determination (*to dokoun autexousian*) of wanting to belong to oneself alone, and neither to superior nor to inferior beings, is produced in us by the Titans." L. G. Westerink, (1977), *The Greek Commentaries on Plato's Phaedo*, Vol. II, *Damascius*, 9.5.8, text and translation, Amsterdam.

cycles.[6] It is a question that goes to the very heart of theurgy. For, on the one hand, the will of the Demiurge as expressed through the cosmic gods is to ensoul the world, to generate mortal life, including our own: in a word, to bind us to the fate of mortal existence.[7] Yet, on the other hand, the theurgist knows how to embrace embodied life in such a way as to awaken the "god-seeing" element, which allows him to step out of time by moving with it in a divine way. A theurgic ascent to the gods does not escape the body, nor is it in opposition to our descent and binding. Theurgy, rather, leads the soul even more deeply into the will of the Demiurge and discovers our liberation hidden within our bonds. Its rituals allow us to move from the periphery of embodied awareness to its divine center. Ultimately, it allows the gods to appear in embodied life, to reveal themselves in human form through our mortal existence.[8] This is clearly the implication of Iamblichus' remarks on the conformity of our binding and release. He explains:

> Nothing in such a process is accomplished contrary to the ordinance laid down from the beginning, so that the gods would change their plans in virtue of some subsequently performed theurgic ceremony, but rather from their first descent the Demiurge sent down souls for this purpose, that they should return again to him. There is no change at all in this sort of ascent, nor is there any conflict between the descents and ascents of souls.... Release from the cycles of generation is in harmony with the attention given to bring them into generation (*DM* 272.4-11).

Although Iamblichus speaks of two souls, the intelligible soul of Hermetic doctrine does not remain undescended but insinuates itself into our fated existence and is awakened by theurgy. Iamblichus says this higher presence in the soul is pre-established (*protetaktai*) as "a divine good more

[6] *DM* 271.1-3, Porphyry asks: "Well, then, is it possible to liberate oneself through the gods who revolve in the heavens, and at the same time think of them as the rulers of destiny and as binding down our lives with indissoluble bonds?"

[7] Iamblichus maintains that the embodying function of the cosmic gods and their attendant daimons fulfills the will of the Demiurge. See G. Shaw, (1995), *Theurgy and the Soul: the Neoplatonism of Iamblichus*, 40, University Park.

[8] See the view of the school of Calvenus Taurus, *Stob. I*, 379.3-6: "...the purpose of the soul's descent is to reveal the divine life, for this is the will of the gods: to be revealed through souls. For the gods come forth into bodily appearance and reveal themselves in the pure and faultless life of souls." This view is cited with approval by Iamblichus. Now see John Finamore and John M. Dillon, (2002), *Iamblichus: De Anima,* text, translation, and commentary, Leiden.

primordial (*presbuteron*) than our nature," and through it we engage the gods (*DM* 165.14). Like the soul's "innate *gnôsis* of the gods," it lies hidden in our essence, "superior to all judgment, choice, reasoning, and proof, and is united from the beginning to its own [divine] cause" (*DM* 7.12-14). Significantly, this presence cannot be known intellectually but is revealed in the soul's essential yearning for the Good.[9] As the Oracles put it, when souls descend into bodies, the Father fills them with a "deep eros" (*bathus erôs*) to return.[10] Despite its importance, this innate gnosis and longing remain unknown and invisible to the lens of discursive thinking. Therefore, it is not by our knowing, calculating, or predicting that we ascend to the gods but by the intensity and quality of our longing. The true astrology of Iamblichus had to engage this pre-ordained longing; it was not an attempt to overcome or to outthink fate but to penetrate to the essence of fate and recognize the presence of the liberating gods in their generative binding.[11] In this kind of "ascent," the soul discovers that in the midst of being a fated and temporal creature it participates in the order of time itself: although present in a body, it begins to hear the rushing sound (*rhoizos*) of the stars as it enters their eternal order.[12] Iamblichus says that the "time" reached in this experience "is different from

[9] *DM* 8.1. Since Iamblichus rejected the Plotinian view that the soul remains undescended, his theurgical Platonism required an element in the soul that could link us with the gods and thus serve as the functional equivalent of Plotinus' undescended soul. Iamblichus refers to this principle in a variety of ways, sometimes calling it "another principle (*hetera archê*) of the soul above all nature and generation" (270.6-7), an innate gnosis, a more primal divine good (described above). Even more vaguely, he states: "For that element in us which is divine (*theion*), and intellectual (*noeron*) and one (*hen*)—or, if you so wish to call it, intelligible (*noêton*)—is aroused, then, clearly in prayer, and when aroused, strives primarily towards what is like itself and joins itself to absolute perfection" (46.9-12). Iamblichus was more concerned to argue that there is a divine principle in us than he was in identifying it with precision. After all, it was not something we could *know* but only recognize through our yearning for the One. Therefore, in a theurgical context, precision about naming it was beside the point. It was present but entirely inaccessible to reason because it "precedes" reason and thus comes to our awareness "from outside" (*exôthen*). See my discussion of this principle in *Theurgy and the Soul: the Neoplatonism of Iamblichus*, op.cit., chapter 11: "Eros and the One of the Soul."

[10] *Chaldean Oracles* 43; see Ruth Majercik (1989), *The Chaldean Oracles*, text, translation and commentary, Leiden.

[11] *DM* 271.3-8.

[12] *DM* 104.1

the time which the physicists inquire into,"[13] and it is also different from the times and cycles studied by the astrologers. The soul taken into this primal dimension of time is no longer merely an "ordered" (*tattomenê*) creature but an "ordering" (*tattousan*) divinity.[14] It becomes a full participant in the demiurgy of the world.

Yet most of us, then as now, live on the periphery of ourselves, seeking to defend or acquire what our passions demand. As Plotinus so aptly put it, the soul feels perpetually threatened, "battered on all sides by the totality of things,"[15] and we live in a contracted posture we call "the self." Iamblichus maintained that even for the most gifted theurgists it takes an entire lifetime to release the soul from this contraction, and part of the discipline in achieving this release is to recognize those characteristics of soul that correspond to the rulers of destiny. In this light, astrology may help the soul recognize when it is participating in the gods in an unbalanced way, and Iamblichus provides a specific example. He says:

> That which is given in one manner [from above] is received in another by the things here below. For example, the emanation of Saturn tends to stabilize, while that of Mars tends to provoke motion; yet the passive and generative receptacle in material things receives the former as rigidity and coldness and the latter as exaggerated inflammation (*DM* 55.4-11).

The gods are blameless and collectively establish the perfection of the cosmos, yet because we have not learned to receive them, in our anger we might be described as struggling with Mars, or in our rigidity as suffering from the weight of Saturn. In contrast to astrological lore where gods such as Saturn and Mars are seen as maleficent influences, in theurgical astrology one would create a receptacle appropriate to these divinities so that their emanations might be properly received. This is why theurgists would gather specific stones, plants, or animals at specific times; for the objects and intervals employed in the rite were associated with the gods whose presence was invoked.[16] Recognizing our imbalances and performing the appropriate rites is the essence of the theurgic art, and in an astrological context, it requires a particular receptivity to the promptings of one's daimon. This entity, Iamblichus says, personifies the totality of celestial influences received

[13] Sambursky and Pines, *The Concept of Time in Later Platonism*, (1971), 40.28-29, text and translation, Jerusalem.

[14] *Ibid.* 42.4-6.

[15] A. H. Armstrong, (1984), *Plotinus, Enneads* IV. 8.4.18, Cambridge.

[16] *DM* 233.7-16.

by the soul,[17] and there is no progress in theurgy until this daimon becomes familiar, when he "reveals the mode of worship proper to him and his name, and communicates the particular manner in which he should be invoked" (*DM* 284.6-7). By fulfilling the promptings of this daimon, the soul enters the divine order.

Porphyry was therefore correct in focusing on the personal daimon, but he thought this being could be known discursively, through charts and other calculations of the horoscope. Not only did Porphyry misunderstand the liberating function of the daimon, he was looking for him everywhere but where he could be found, in what Augustine calls *an instinct unknown to man, lying hidden in the mind.* And the way to contact this daimon is not found in technical calculations but in our receptivity. From the most subtle contact with the divine, to the invocation of a cosmic god and its attendant daimons, the skill required of a theurgist is a kind of *negative capability*, the capacity to be still enough and aware enough to receive an ineffable presence regardless of the context.[18] As the Oracles put it: "know without straining; turn back the sacred eye of your soul and bring an empty mind into the intelligible until you comprehend it...."[19] Iamblichus certainly knew about astrological calculations, but without first awakening his sacred eye and learning to receive the divine directly, such calculations would only have led him astray with the vanity of controlling fate. To Porphyry's question about the difficulty of casting horoscopes, Iamblichus therefore replies:

> Irrespective of whether these arts are knowable or not, it is the emanation from the stars that allots us our daimon whether or not *we* comprehend it. God-given divination can teach us about the stars according to the truth itself, and we do not need computation tables or the technical skills of divination (*DM* 276.11-14).

Iamblichus was not breaking new ground. The capacity to receive the gods through receptive emptiness was already outlined by Plato in a cosmological context when he speaks of the mother (*mêter*) and receptacle

[17] Iamblichus says the personal daimon "stands as a model (*paradeigma*) for us even before souls descend into generation" (*DM* 280, 7-8); also see also footnote #475 in *Iamblichus On the Mysteries*, op. cit., 337.

[18] The poet John Keats intuited this capacity with remarkable insight. In a letter to his brothers in 1817 he writes: "... NEGATIVE CAPABILITY, that is, when a man is capable of being in uncertainties, mysteries, doubts, without any irritable reaching after fact and reason...." This sentiment is a virtual paraphrase of Fragment #1 of the *Chaldean Oracles*.

[19] Majercik, op. cit., translation modified slightly.

(*hupodochê*) of the generated world (*Timaeus* 51A). This principle of creation, he says, "receives all things, in some mysterious way partakes of the intelligible, and is completely incomprehensible" (51AB). Yet, despite being inaccessible to reason (52B), the creation of the cosmos depends on this emptiness, for only its sheer receptivity guarantees an undistorted transmission of the forms. In a theurgic context, Iamblichus refers to this receptive principle when he speaks of a "pure and divine form of matter" issued from the Father and Creator and used by theurgists "for the reception (*hupodochê*) of the gods" (*DM* 232.13-233.2). This kind of matter, he says, is "given by the gods during blessed visions" (*DM* 234.7-8) and is naturally united (*sumphuês*) with them,[20] just as we are, through our "innate cognition (*sumphutos katanoêsis*) of the gods."[21] The correspondence between the cosmogonic receptacle and the theurgic receptacle is significant: both reveal and are directly linked with the gods. The essential skill of a theurgic astrologer, therefore, is the capacity for this receptivity, to endure a condition of not-knowing and not "reaching after fact or reason,"[22] to be led by the soul's deep and primordial eros for the divine.

Yet after theurgists engage their daimon, the question remains how they would employ the schemas of astrology? For to bring the soul into accord with the gods, to receive each purely, would require knowledge of the planets, their cycles, and their correspondences in nature. Since Iamblichus provides few specifics about this practice, we will turn to the 15th century magus Marsilio Ficino and then to the work of contemporary astrologers who view their practice as a form of theurgic divination.

Ficino is well suited to continue our thesis for he is in complete agreement with Iamblichus concerning astrologers and particularly their impiety of blaming the stars for the evil actions of men.[23] Ficino also despises astrologers for their pretence of making predictions about future events. These are precisely Iamblichus' complaints against astrologers of his own time: attributing evils to the cosmic gods and presuming to make accurate predictions of the future. Both errors rest on the assumption that the stars are causes and function as a cosmic "machine of destiny" which astrologers have the skill to read and manage. Ficino wrote a treatise attacking astrologers and

[20] Iamblichus says this visionary matter is of like nature (*sumphuês*) with the gods who bestow it and ensures contact with them (*DM* 234.8-11).

[21] *DM* 9.8-11.

[22] Keats, op. cit.

[23] Marsilio Ficino, (1996), *Meditations on the Soul: Selected Letters of Marsilio Ficino*, #76, London.

contrasts their practices with those of philosopher-magicians. In a declaration of war, Ficino exhorts his fellow philosophers to oppose astrologers whom he characterizes as "petty ogres [who] presume to equate themselves with God."[24]

Yet Ficino himself practiced a kind of astral magic, as surely as did Iamblichus. He drew up charts, made continual reference to planetary alignments, and integrated his vast astrological knowledge into the third part of his *Book of Life*, entitled "On Making Your Life Agree with the Heavens."[25] Ficino refers to Plotinus' argument that the stars are not causes but living signs that reveal the qualities of the World Soul. "The stars," Plotinus wrote, "are like characters always being written on the heavens" and it takes "a wise man" to read them.[26] What he reads, Ficino says, are the qualities of his own soul. In a letter to Lorenzo de Medici, Ficino insists that true astrology is not a study of the stars existing in some distant realm; it is a study of the soul. He writes:

> For these celestial bodies are not to be sought by us outside in some other place; *for the heavens in their entirety are within us*, in whom the light of life and the origin of heaven dwell.[27]

The purpose of astrology for Ficino is to lead us within, to the origin of heaven that deifies the soul. The petty ogres of astrology focused only on the peripheral self, to predict or manipulate events. Such diviners, Ficino says, are "not divine but mightily profane" since they bind us to illusions.[28] True astrology was an art of transformation, not a science of prediction. Angela Voss, a contemporary astrologer and Ficino scholar explains his position. She writes:

> ...the use of astrology as a basis for divination was...upheld by Ficino as its most legitimate application. His attack fell on those who abused the transformative potential of the divinatory moment by wanting to reduce it to a pseudo-scientific rational norm.[29]

[24] *Ibid.*, 165.

[25] Charles Boer (1980), *Marsilio Ficino, The Book of Life*, Dallas.

[26] Armstrong, *Plotinus, Enneads*, op. cit., II.3.7.5-13.

[27] Ficino, *Letters*, op. cit., 167.

[28] *Ibid.*, 166.

[29] Angela Voss, (2003), *Magic, Astrology & Music: The Background to Marsilio Ficino's Music Therapy and his Role as a Renaissance Magus*, unpublished Ph.D. thesis, City University, London; cited by Geoffrey Cornelius, *The Moment of Astrology: Origins of Divination* (2003), 7, Bournemouth.

In effect, the astrologers of Ficino's time—and Iamblichus'—were the scientists of their age, reading the heavens as doctors today read blood charts and x-rays. Astrology for them was a material science, not a symbolic art. But for the magus, astrology draws the soul into a changed perception and participation in divinity. Again, Voss writes:

> ...this mode of perception will not regard stars and planets as causal agents, but as symbols which reflect back to the human soul its inextricable correspondence with the cosmos, [and one's] ... astrological insight...will depend on the ability, and desire, of the individual to "tune in."[30]

We may well ask how one "tunes in" to the stars? And if this results in knowledge of future events, how does this foreknowledge occur? Sounding very much like Iamblichus, Ficino addresses these questions, and says:

> Through whatever art future things may be investigated, they are foretold more completely out of a *certain gift of the soul* (*dos animae*) than through judgment. Here often those unlearned in the art judge more truthfully than those who are learned....the truthfulness of the judgment [is] not so much through scrutiny of the stars, as by a certain foreknowledge innate to you (*praesigium tibi naturale).*[31]

Ficino shares with Iamblichus an antipathy for astrologers yet practices astral theurgy and, like Iamblichus, he believes we are guided more by an innate gnosis and divine gift than by discursive intelligence.

In light of their respective cultures, we might find Ficino's and Iamblichus' views of astrology understandable, even admirable. After all, they were living in a pre-scientific age. In their geocentric cosmos the highest divinity, above the 8th sphere, generously emanates gradations of divine presence that culminate in the generative sway of the sub-lunary realm. It was a profoundly influential and an aesthetically appealing map of our universe, but we now know that it was mistaken. So, we might ask, how could astrologers continue to have influence today?

I cannot address this question in all its complexity but would simply suggest that for Iamblichus and other Platonists the cosmos was not seen primarily as an object that could be scientifically explained. It was firstly a manifestation of the gods, a vast being or, as Plato put it, a living statue, an

[30] Angela Voss, *The Astrology of Marsilio Ficino: Divination or Science?*, (2001), <http://cura.free.fr/decem/10voss.html> 5.

[31] Cited by Cornelius, op. cit., 324.

agalma of divinity.[32] The time and space in this cosmos are not the time and space that modern science explores but the elements of a breathing three dimensional icon in which we are participants. The cosmology and metaphysics of this tradition do not primarily describe levels of reality in some physical or abstract realm. They are articulations of profound personal experience written in the language of cosmology and metaphysics. We tend to forget that all these "sciences," as Iamblichus put it, are rooted in *revelatory experiences* given by the gods.[33] As A.C. Lloyd reminds us, the levels of reality in Neoplatonism "*are* experiences; they are types of consciousness...." "[P]ersonal experience," he says, "is needed to complement the non-empirical philosophic system."[34]

So, what happened? How did the cosmos as an *agalma* of the gods become a machine of destiny whose planetary cycles determined the fate of the soul? In a brilliant and original book, *The Moment of Astrology*, Geoffrey Cornelius maintains that astrology as a form of divination was transformed during the late Hellenistic era into the pseudo-science that Iamblichus and Ficino condemned. Ancient divinatory astrology, by contrast, was known as *katarchê*, in which a horoscope is constructed from "the moment a question is posed to or by an astrologer."[35] Cornelius says that etymologically *katarchê*'s earliest use had to do with initiating sacrificial rites and later with seeking auspicious signs from the gods and hence, was a consecrating activity. In fact, ancient astrology was more like the reading of omens and comparable to divination through augury or liver-reading. The significance of these forms of divination depended on the intent and desire of the practitioner or, in Iamblichus' terms, on the degree to which the practitioner became receptive to the gods invoked. Rather than answering a question of fate by referring to the objective truth of the heavens, katarchic astrology was more like consulting the *I Ching* or the Tarot.[36] It was a means by which individuals could enter a more intimate contact with the divine through meditating on a unique expression of astrological symbols that corresponded to the moment of their consultation.

Astrology as we know it today, however, reveals the influence of Aristotle's theories of celestial causation given definitive form in the 2nd

[32] Plato, *Timaeus* 37C.

[33] *DM* 279.9-14.

[34] A.C. Lloyd, (1990), *The Anatomy of Neoplatonism,* 126, Oxford..

[35] Cornelius, op. cit., 98.

[36] Geoffrey Cornelius, "Is Astrology Divination and Does it Matter?", (1999), <http://cura.free.fr/quinq/01gfcor.html,> 1-2.

century by Claudius Ptolemy's *Tetrabiblos,* often called the Bible of astrology. According to Cornelius, Ptolemy succeeded in providing a "convincing rational explanation for natal astrology [and thus] to permanently embed divinatory-horoscopic astrology in a natural scientific model."[37] His success, however, reduced all forms of astrology to finding the "moment of birth," the seed, as Ptolemy put it,[38] shaped by the precise moment in the heavens when a person comes into the world. This spells the end of astrology as a divinatory practice. As Cornelius puts it:

> Once the symbolism of astrology is bound to this great order, the loss of the old participatory consciousness of omen-reading creates a fateful conception of the cosmos, a Machine of Destiny.[39]

In such a model, a capacity for profound receptivity is no longer required, for against the objective and impersonal machinery of the heavens, our state of consciousness becomes irrelevant. In this model, astrology ceases to be spiritual or transformative for it can be practiced by anyone with an ephemeris, curiosity, and a taste for self-deception.

Although a practicing astrologer himself, Cornelius believes that all attempts to find "scientific proof" for it are misguided. He writes:

> It is disingenuous of astrologers to even hint at a scientific basis of the sort understood in physics or biology. We'd be on *so* much stronger ground if we said, "What we do is a type of symbolic imagination. We believe it has real effects and real results....What we do is actually about the remarkable powers of human imagination that imply something very extraordinary about the nature of reality and the nature of mind."[40]

Cornelius' notion of symbolic imagination requires that astrologer and client enter the horoscope as a psychotherapist enters a dream, to encounter the living depths of the psyche.[41] Cornelius presses even further and encourages an approach where each astrological reading has the status of a religious

[37] *Ibid.*, 176.

[38] *Ibid.,* 85-88.

[39] *Ibid.,* 171.

[40] Geoffrey Cornelius, "Is Astrology Divination," op. cit., 4

[41] Geoffrey Cornelius, "Psychoanalysis, Divination, Astrology," (1991), <http://coa.hubcom.net/wzpatalk.htm,> 6-8.

ritual[42] whose success depends on the astrologer's familiarity with his or her personal daimon.[43] Cornelius says:

> What is perhaps most difficult for the modern astrologer to grasp...is that this intimate genius, natural to us and closest to our innermost intuition, is at the same time *divinely moved and prompted.*[44]

In his deconstruction of the Ptolemaic model, Cornelius has recognized that it is through the astrologer's negative capability, through a profound receptivity that eludes discursive analysis that the astrologer taps into the "intimate genius" (the Iamblichean daimon) that transforms an astrological consultation into a rite of theurgic divination. I find it remarkable that Cornelius and his circle of astrologers may be rediscovering the true astrology that had already been lost at the time of Iamblichus.

[42] Cornelius, *The Moment*, op. cit., 135-136.

[43] *Ibid.*, 110-111; 116.

[44] *Ibid.*, 323.

THE ROLES OF APOLLO AND DIONYSUS IN NIETZSCHE'S BIRTH OF TRAGEDY AND IN THE EMPEROR JULIAN'S THEOLOGY.

Jay Bregman

I

In Renaissance Europe, the Greek gods were usually accommodated as metaphysical abstractions under the umbrella of the Florentine "pagan" neoplatonic revival, with its "Synesian" religious syncretism, and its idea of a universal "ancient theology"; in which all the different major religions were close in time and spirit to the Mosaic revelation, and therefore compatible with Christian theology. These included Hermetic, Orphic-Pythagorean-Platonic, Zoroastrian and Chaldaean traditions. These traditions, nevertheless, were also considered to be in error to the extent that they diverged from the teachings of the Church, largely because of their wandering from the true original revelation, hence their subsequent doctrinal innovations. The Cambridge Platonist Ralph Cudworth, e.g., in his *True Intellectual System of the Universe* carefully compares the Christian trinity with the Neoplatonic Hypostases & criticizes Plotinus when he diverges from Athanasian Orthodoxy.[1]

The post-Enlightenment world saw significant changes in this regard. But even then, notwithstanding exceptional cases, Romantic syncretists did not oppose "Paganism" to Christianity: Except for Thomas Taylor's unique isolated attempt to revive the religion of Julian, Iamblichus and Proclus, there was no basic challenge to irenic syncretism before Nietzsche's. From late antiquity till modern times, then, the gods were subsumed under Christian categories. They were no longer "enemies" of the Church, but neither were they really outside of its orbit. The ancient critique of Christianity, on the philosophical level, in the works of Celsus, Porphyry, Julian (and Proclus & co-for the most part tacitly) was based on a Neoplatonic metaphysic. Hypostatic metaphysical abstractions had been turned into the traditional gods, in order to revalorize Hellenism-in a philosophical/allegorical form far removed from that of Homer, Hesiod and Classical Greece. Specifically, Apollo and Dionysus became respectively the overseers of the realms of unity and diversity: the one and the many.

[1] On this see Bregman (1982) n 31, 85-6.

It is possible to harmonize these ideas to some extent with Romantic philosophy; even with Schopenhauer, though the basic thrust of his though was in an apparently different direction. The early Nietzsche, of course, was still under the formers' spell when he composed *The Birth of Tragedy*, a work in which Apollo and Dionysus became modern "art gods". They also retained a kind of categorical metaphysical existence, emphatically rejected by the later Nietzsche.

In the emperor Julian's thought, these gods became part of an anti-Christian soteriology; part of a complex hierarchy, and they could only function as aspects of a Solar theological cosmos. Historically Julian's ideas were expressed at the point of the Christianization of the west, whereas Nietzsche's were made possible by the modern phenomenon of (sometimes radical) secularization, to which he made a major contribution. It could be said that Julian's was a metaphysically revalorized traditional religion formed in opposition to Christianty; whereas Nietzsche's was a "religionless aesthetic religion" intended to de-valorize and eventually invalidate Christianity. Both viewed Hellenism as the perfect antidote to Christianity, but their conceptions of Hellenism were, on the surface at least, diametrically opposed.

II

If, then, we compare the most radical critique of Christianity in antiquity, the emperor Julian's, with the most radical critique of the same in modernity, Nietzsche's, we are struck by an immediate and more or less obvious contradiction: Nietzsche's anti-Christianity is also anti-Platonism; Julian's anti-Christianity is a form of late antique neoplatonic religious Hellenism: Theurgic Neoplatonism. Nietzsche apparently never read Julian or the Neoplatonists. If he had, he would have had to view Julian as part of the problem, rather than as part of the solution.

Friedrich Nietzsche began his career as a Classical Philologist. Although one of the most promising scholars of his generation, he almost immediately rebelled against the demands of a disciplined "scientific" approach to the Classics. His artistic impulses and his philosophical outlook were also important for the formation of his notions about Greek civilization. Before composing his first major work, *The Birth of Tragedy from the Spirit of Music* (*BT)*, he wrote: "Scholarship, art and philosophy are now growing inside me so much that I'll be giving birth to Centaurs one day".

Nietszche inherited the modern idea of the Dionysus/ Apollo antithesis from the Romantics. The way in which he developed this conception of the "Apollinian" and the "Dionysian" as antithetical artistic impulses have become part of our cultural vocabulary. The characteristic

Apollinian art is sculpture; and Dionysian, pure music, despite the designation of Apollo as the god of music.[2]

Apollo is the god of plastic form, lucidity, clarity, law and so on-he provides a dreamlike mask-an image of serenity, behind the repose of which lies a world of change, violence and fate: Apollinian serenity, the restrained classical form, all of these characteristically Hellenic things we associate with Apollo were, for the Greeks themselves, at bottom, a beautiful façade which made existence bearable. Only through art, the world itself justified as aesthetic phenomenon-could the Greeks go on living.

According to Nietzsche, the Greeks were *not* essentially serene. Winckelmann, Goethe and their followers were mistaken. Behind the mask of Apollo lurked the real Hellas: the Hellas of "irrational" mystery cults & Dionysus, the god of orgiastic frenzy. The Hellenes understood the fragility of the individual and the *principium individuationis*-as Nietzsche's "educator" Schopenhauer would say.[3] If Apollo represented this principle of individuation, then Dionysus represented the inner essence of Life, as it were, the core of reality, it's Oneness, Schopenhauer's metaphysical Will. Even to the point of the breakdown of boundaries. The result of this may be terror. But it may also be ecstasy. As when Dionysiac revelers let go their individual identities merged in the group *enthousiasmos* to experience the Unity of Life *from below.* [4]

Attic tragedy, thought Nietzsche, arose out of the conflict of the tendencies personified by the two gods. But also from their union: Apollo and Dionysus are complementary deities, who ultimately speak each other's language. Thus the precinct of Dionysus is at Delphi, where he rules in the winter when Apollo visits the land of the Hyperboreans.

By the Second Century c.e. Dionysus, had become a Hellenistic "mystery god", whose devotees primarily sought future immortality rather than present ecstasy, or ecstatic immersion in nature; ecstatic self-

[2] Nietzsche claims that "music was already known as an Apolline art, only because of its rhythm...Doric architecture transmuted into sounds", excluded was the overwhelming power of sound, "the unified low of melody and incomparable world of harmony", in the Dionysian dithyramb culminating in the "whole of the symbolism of the body", in the dance (*BT* 2, 20-1)

[3] *BT* 1,16, where he quotes a famous passage of Schopenhauer on this principle

[4] In his *Dionysus,* Kerenyi quotes at length the passages in *BT* on the ecstatic experiences described by Nietzsche; but he considers his account a "fairy tale" and his contribution "dubious", though influential. But might not Nietzsche's passages also suggest what Kerenyi calls the god:"the archetypal image of indestructible life"? Kerenyi, 1976, 134-38.

transcendence dissolving the boundaries between self and nature, rather than personal immortality.[5]

Certainly, the late Classical and Hellenistic ages emphasized Orphic-Platonic-Pythagorean notions of the "Dionysian". A sublimation, thought Nietzsche, brought on by "Orphic ascetic impulses as a result of exhaustion and disgust & the new Platonic "moralism". Thus the "Orphic" "decadent" reversal of Dionysian affirmation and the will to life-negating asceticism.[6] The god's mysteries retained their importance, but more and more emphasized the promise of *personal* immortality, in connection with the death and rebirth of the god. These ideas eventually were assimilated to Middle and Neoplatonic notions of the immortality of the soul. This was also true of the Orphic-Dionysiac as well as the other mysteries: Isis and Osiris-Sarapis, *Magna Mater,* Mithras, Eleusis & co. Such late Hellenistic religious ideas would of course coincide perfectly with Nietzschean notions of the onset of decadence in the Greek world.

[5] For a good summary of the early Dionysian experience according to Nietzsche, especially the Olympian/Chthonic dichotomy, see Hatab (2001), section III, 48-53.

[6] The "Orphic" movement was of course already present in the Archaic period and perhaps represented an ascetic "counter-movement"to the more "extravertive /worldly" Dionysian rites.

Nietzsche attributes the denaturing of tragedy to Socratic dialectical rationalism & it's influence on Euripides. But he also realized the *Bacchae* presented a problem and suggested that Euripides perhaps in the end rejected his psychological rationalism and returned to the true Dionysian.

In BT 7, 39 he describes an after-reaction to Dionysian ecstasy that can lead to an ascetic outlook: "...when one once more becomes aware of...everyday reality it becomes repellent; this leads to a mood of asceticism, of denial of the will."

In "Homer's Contest"(as *BT* written 1872) Nietzsche, following Burckhardt, discusses the highly competitive "agonistic ideal" of early Greece and the "Aeschylean" notion that "from murder and the expiation of murder that the conception of Greek law developed; so, too, the nobler culture takes its first wreath of victory from the altar of the expiation of murder. After the wave of that bloody age comes a trough that cuts deep into Hellenic history. The names of Orpheus, Musaeus, and their cults reveal the consequences to which the uninterrupted spectacle of a world of struggle and cruelty was pressing; toward a disgust with existence, toward the conception of this existence as a punishment and penance, toward the belief in the identity of existence and guilt." And again: "the Greek genius tolerated the terrible presence of this urge-[to struggle and victory]-and considered it *justified*; while the Orphic movement contained the idea that a life with such an urge at its root was not worth living." Kaufmann (1967), 34, 35.

In the Fourth Century c.e., Julian's neo-Hellenism[7] the revalorized Hellenic religion through which he finally made his stand against Christianity, was basically a combination of the mystery religions, more or less subsumed under the relatively new (as Julian was well aware) imperial cult of Sol Invictus, interpreted according to the Neoplatonic Solar theology; succinctly expressed in Praetextatus speech in the Fifth Century c.e. *Saturnalia* of Macrobius: that *omnes paene deos ,dumtaxat qui sub caelo sunt ad solem referrunt....* (Mac. *Sat.* 1.17.2). "What follows then is a series of discourses connecting gods with sun-worship. Apollo, Liber, Mars, Mercury, Aesculapius, Hercules, Sarapis, Isis, Adonis, Attis, Cybele, Osiris, Nemesis, Pan, Saturn, Jupiter"[8]

Apollo and Dionysus had been given new and different valuations and new and different meanings. This was certainly true of the religion of Julian. As Gilbert Murray pointed out a long time ago, what strikes us about the religious strife of the Fourth Century is how similar the sensibilities of the competing advocates seem from a modern perspective.[9] Indeed, the perspective provided by Florentine Renaissance inclusion of all of this material from both sides in a new & very neoplatonic, but still Christian religious horizon makes this easily understandable.

The modern critique of Christianity has been associated with the Victorian "discovery" of the body; and the reaction against all asceticism and metaphysics as being disguised forms of the hatred of life has been one of Nietzsche's legacies. Thus Nietzsche, who read Augustine's *Confessions* for entertainment, and who thoroughly despised Paul, would probably have categorized Julian's religion as a still Hellenic form of that Platonic decadence which ultimately led to Christianity: Platonism for the people.

Perhaps Nietzsche would have seen in Julian someone whose instincts were in part still sound-to the extent that he was a traditional Hellene, but whose theurgic & neoplatonic neo-Hellenism was, at bottom, simply another

[7] I am adopting J. Brodd's useful term for the religion of Julian. Paganism is a theology- laden term, and Hellenism means Greek culture to most readers and is also confusing; thus "neo-Hellenism": "Julian, Myth and Platonism", delivered at the AAR Platonism and Neoplatonism Group Atlanta, 2003.

[8] O'Donnell (1979) 45-83, 67

[9] "For if Julian and Sallustius, Gregory and John Chrysostom were to rise again and see the world as it now is, they would probably feel their personal differences melt away in comparison with the vast difference between their world and this. They fought to the death about this credo and that, but the same spirit was in all of them (and quoting Geffcken)...'the most inward man in these four contemporaries is the same. It is the Spirit of the Fourth Century'." Murray (1960) 187.

expression of the decadent poison that had enabled the rise of Christianity. Not the right medicine-and in any case too little and too late.

Still under the influence of Schopenhauer, the early Nietzsche's Greek gods in some sense represent his own speculations, rather more than the classical Greeks. His categories are not strictly speaking always applicable to Greek religious reality. Wilamowitz pointed out that . . . "Apolline and Dionysian are aesthetic abstractions... and the old gods only supply sonorous names for the contrast..: "[10] On the other hand, F.M. Cornford called *BT* "a work of profound imaginative insight, which left the scholarship of a generation toiling in the rear"; theories of cult, myth and ritual held by such important scholars as Jane Ellen Harrison, and Gilbert Murray were also influenced by Nietzsche, and E. R. Dodds work on the Dionysian religion follows the general lines he suggested.[11]

There is some evidence that the wild Dionysus was opposed to the serene Apollo, in the early Archaic age. But by the Fifth Century, the functions of the two gods overlapped to a certain extent. Sophocles has the Muses attendant on Dionysus (*Ant.* 965; in a fragment of Aeschylus, *fr.*86) Mette gives Apollo ivy and calls him Bacchus; Bacchylides at Delphi writes a Dithyramb to Apollo. There are also new musical switches in mode between the Apollinian 'nomos' and the Dionysian dithyramb.

This convergence culminated in Hellenistic syncretism. Around 100 c e, Dio Chrysostom, an influence on Julian says, "Some tell us that Apollo the sun, and Dionysus are one and the same" (*orat.* 31.11). But Plutarch, the Delphic priest emphasizes their contrasting functions at the sacred precinct: "Dionysus with his orgies and dithyrambs is the lord of winter, while the pure and stainless Apollo, to whom the regulated and chaste music of the paean is sung, reigns over the summer months (*Mor.* 388-89)". Even if *the sparagmos & omophagia* remained perhaps part of some Dionysian rituals into Hellenistic times, by late antiquity cult practice was in tune with the philosophical and spiritual outlook of the age. Thus Dodds: "Late Greek writers explained the *omophagia* as [similar to] Christian communion; it was merely a commemorative rite, in memory of the day when the infant Dionysus was himself torn to pieces and devoured (*Schol. Clem. Alex.* 92.) Late antique Neoplatonic allegory and religious syncretism led to a reinterpretation of the nature of both gods.

[10] For brief account of Wilamowitz' attack on Nietzsche and Erwin Rohde's defense of his friend and counterattack se 'Introduction" to *BT,* Tanner (1992), 7-8

[11] For a cogent critical review of the scholarly, literary and psychological ideas of Dionysus from Nietzsche to Dodds and the French "Anthropologists" see Henrichs (1984) *passim.*

There is some validity to Nock's notion that Julian's neo-Hellenism became a religion of "conversion" & even a unified entity a "church", "by opposition and contrast"[12] to its now powerful rival and the ongoing Christianization of the Roman world. It is also true, nevertheless, that the examples of Proclus in the Fifth Century and Damascius in the Sixth suggest that Theurgy is a religion in its own right. A worship that adherents could maintain in the face of Christian oppression, even after the destruction of the Alexandrian Sarapeum and the precinct of Eleusis in the "Theodosian" 390's. Proclus considered Christianity "the prevailing opinion" and serenely practiced the ancient rites; he followed his ascetic regimen confident that the old religion would soon return.[13] Damascius and the Sixth Century Athenian Theurgists, driven out of Athens in 529 CE, by the Orthodox emperor Justinian, possibly settled in Harran, following a failed attempt to win the favor of the shah, where their descendants (possibly) continued to practice neo-Hellenism for centuries, in an atmosphere of religious tolerance. [14]

Furthermore, it is misleading to think of Theurgic Neoplatonism as merely, or even primarily a theoretical position.[15] It is not; it is basically a religious outlook, driven by a religious *a priori*. (Just as Kabbalah is a way of looking at/practicing Torah/Judaism and Pseudo-Dionysius articulates a way of Christian Theurgy in which *Praxis* is primary and *Theoria* secondary (cf., e.g., Iamblichus, *DM* 2.11, 12; 5.23, 26; 10.1-3)[16]

Julian himself continued the recently valorized Roman Solar Cult, as a sort of official imperial religion (for the most part) from Aurelian to

[12] Nock (1969) 15

[13] For Proclus cultic activities and religious universalism see Marinus' *Life of Proclus*, 19, 22, 28 tr. L. J. Rosan in Uzdavinys (2004) with additional notes.

[14] Uzdaviniys (2004) 273, has recently been attempting to verify this hypothesis by archaeological research in the area of ancient Harran, under the auspices of the American Society for Oriental Research.

[15] R. Smith's idea that Julian would not have adhered to a theoretical position such as Theurgy, by itself, but only did so because there were still cults of the gods, is not a coherent position. Smith (1995), 219-223; on this see Bregman (1999), 342, n.13.

[16] Clarke, Hershbell, Dillon (2003) cite appropriate passages in their useful brief outline of the nature and contents of *DM*, xlviii-lii. O'Meara (2003) argues that that the primary goal of Theurgy is "divinization", making man god., 31 n1; 128-30. See also G. Shaw (1995), 231-33. Indeed, to such an extent is Theurgy a religion in its own right that in the Nineteenth Century Thomas Taylor and some of his N. American disciples adhered to a revived Neoplatonic Hellenism; this revival continued, at least in Occult circles, till well into the Twentieth Century. Hilary Armstrong's remark that W.B. Yeats was a Theurgic Neoplatonist is not to be taken lightly.

Constantine. He thought of it as the cult of his Second Flavian house. To subsume this and all the other cults under the rubric of Theurgy was not a serious problem. The Solar Theology referred to above validates a Henotheistic understanding of all the "old gods" as powers, subordinates, aspects of Sol.[17] Likewise the Oracles and all the other cults, especially the Mysteries; even Judaism was accommodated by Julian; and at that, in its pure form, it was a version of Theurgy![18]

Julian's monism is evident from his writings. His rather more Byzantine Hellenic church would somehow unify all this. But unification in the concrete is not the only important idea here. All rites, mysteries & co could be understood theurgically: Proclus' "Religions of the world".

Proclus biographer, Marinus called him the "hierophant of the whole world".[19] Iamblichus is not specific concerning the exact theurgic rites of other religions-a few seem to be known. Babylonian, Egyptian & Iranian & the rest comprise an important part of the picture. Furthermore, Theurgists like Maximus of Ephesus, Julian's guru, "worked on" statues of Hecate and the Greek gods (Eun. *VS* 475) Hermetic and Isiac ideas were considered (rightly) Hellenized versions of originally Egyptian formulations. Iamblichus accepted this. He even faulted the Greeks for losing touch with these true rites[20]. He never says that the Chaldaean Oracles are the only theurgic texts. Nor does he, for the most part, say much about concrete positive practices of any sort. Thus it is incoherent to think of Julian as too eclectic to be a true Iamblichean. Iamblichus gave him the approach, the method, not the content of worship: without (non-trivial) problems, any of these could be attuned to the worship of all but *one* religious tradition. At bottom, they were all divine foundations, with one exception: for the emperor Christianity was a bastardized form of Hellenized Judaism (that combined the worst from both

[17] Muslims critical of what they perceived as compromised forms of monotheism in the late antique/early medieval Meditteranean inscribed on coins in Latin abbr. For 1) there is no God but God and he has no associates; i.e., the Christian Trinity; 2) there is no God but God and he has no subordinates; i.e., the revalorised gods of the Solar theology!

[18] Bregman (1995) for a discussion of the significance of this idea for Julian's program.

[19] *Life of Proclus*, 19

[20] Shaw (1995) 3, points out that unlike Julian and his followers, Iamblichus, following Plato, censures the Greeks for their innovations that have brought about the present de-sacralization of religious traditions; on the other hand, he praises the Egyptians and others for rigorously maintaining the ancient traditions.

groups); and that actually had come to threaten the Theurgic underpinnings of the divine world order.[21]

Julian's take on Hellenism is perhaps somewhat too emphatic and cloying at times; but his willingness to combine gods over wide spectrum makes possible a certain inclusiveness. He hoped that his mystical Iamblichean approach would prove efficacious on the esoteric as well as the popular level of cult practice. Perhaps this was too little and too late and not really practical. On the other hand, if there was a time by which Christianity inevitably became the majority religion, to paraphrase Hilary Armstrong, a long reign of Julian and a successor with a long reign might have prevented the establishment of the "Theodosian" State Church and its dire long term historical consequences.

Julian follows the late Neoplatonic tendency to present the gods as metaphysical entities. His tutelary god Helios is not only the visible sun and its Platonic analogue, "the good" or the intelligible sun. He is the central mediating cosmic power of the intellectual (*noeric*-gods as thoughts)-to distribute the Platonic ideas and thereby order matter.(133d-134a, these gods are distinguished from the intelligible or *noetic,* gods as objects of thought) It is Helios who enables us to perceive the intelligibility of things as well as their unity. He is the center of the intellectual causes, which guarantee the unity and perfection of the cosmos; he acts as its principle of coherence: he connects the unity of the intelligible realm with the unity of the visible. (138d-139a) His nature, powers, substance and activities are one; he is what he wills and does. He does not will what is not, nor does he lack the power to do what he wills. He does not want to actualize what he cannot. Such neoplatonic conceptions of god, shared by Christians, Julian presents as notions of *neo-Hellenism.* After all, what other philosophically coherent ideas of god were available to late antique religious thinkers?

Helios comprises with Zeus, the absolute causes, with Apollo, unified thoughts, with Dionysus, divided substance (144a-c). Athena as his forethought (*pronoia*) fills Selene with wisdom, so that she (Selene) can adorn the realm of matter (149b-150a). Aphrodite his cosmic generative power is "the love that moves the sun and other stars."(150b-c) On Earth, he is the guarantor of Greco-Roman civilization. In Julian's Solar syncretism all the gods are around the sun (*peri ton helion*) as powers, aspects and expressions of a deeper reality, which Helios symbolizes.

Given the metaphysical thrust of his thought, Julian accepted the allegorization of myth. His Dionysus is not only tame, he bears little

[21] Bregman (1995) 133 ff

resemblance to his archaic counterpart, although the Orphic tradition so popular among the Neoplatonists, provides a potential bridge between these two disparate figures.

In *Against the Galileans (CG)*, Julian discusses the incongruity of Hellenic as well as Christian myths. He uses Dionysus for an example: "then too there is the legend that Dionysus was rent asunder and his limbs joined together again. This is the sort of things described in the myths of the Hellenes…" *(CG* 44b) The emperor believed that philosophical allegory was necessary for the correct interpretation of myth. He presents his rationale in *orat.* 7, "to the Cynic Herakleios": "Whenever myths on sacred subjects are incongruous in thought, by that very fact they cry aloud, as it were, and summon us not to believe them literally but to study and track down their hidden meaning. (222d)".

The apparent amorality, brutality and incoherence of the myths represent a divine enigma behind which lies the truth. In Plato's time such myths would not only be allegorized, but criticized on the grounds that they presented a false view of divinity, which could only be entirely good, immutable and pure. But Juian's was a different age. The myths had to be re-valorized in order to save the "old gods", lest the wrong "opinion" become "the prevailing opinion".

To look more closely at Julian's conceptions of the two gods, in light of the imperative to protect the sacred Olympians: the starry spirits of a new more pious neo-Hellenism. The Delphic god proclaims the unity of all the gods. "…let us summon to witness Apollo, who sits in council with our god Helios)" Apollo's witness is the celebrated unity of Zeus, Hades, Sarapis, Helios (136a)-since he was identified with Dionysus, Sarapis' unity here also implies the unity of Apollo and Dionysus.[22] As Apollo is the god of unity, limit, sameness, Dionysus is the god of otherness, division, the unlimited, which he presides over as the unity-of-multiplicity. Both gods are still antipodal, but there functions are now understood *Platonice.*

For Julian Apollo still embodies the old Hellenic values in the new setting: the god and leader of all Greece, lawgiver and king, who resides at Delphi (*ho tees Ellados koinos heegemwn kai nomothetees kai basileus, ho en delphois theos*.) As a god of philosophy he is the *exegeetees* of the fairest thoughts and the intelligent purposes of Helios. He follows his own advice, *to gnwthi sauton,* through his knowledge of his own nature, which is that of Helios-and he is the colleague of the sun god by reason of his simple noetic intuitions (*haplotees noeesewn*), the stability of his substance (*monimos ousias)* and the consistency of his activity (*energeia)*. Syncretistically, Apollo

[22] This oracular verse is attributed to the Orphics in Macrobius, *Sat.* 1.18.18.

and Athena share his throne. The goddess is also the complete intelligence of Apollo. Behind Julian's belief in the Delphic god, and his hope to revive the Oracle, was his sense that the austere god of classical form had become a Neoplatonist.

By contrast Dionysus is needed to perfect life in our current diremptive state: "...in whomsoever the abundance of life has not been perfected (*teleesiourgeetheeei)* by the essential nature (*ousiai)*) of Dionysus-perfected by the Bacchic and divine frenzy of the god, (he)risks that his life flow into many- *epi polla rueenai ten zween*-and as it flows be torn to shreds. *(orat.* 7, 222a-b) Thus to suffer the fate of Pentheus is to lose spiritual coherence, meaning, and a life with unified purpose. Here multiplicity is on al levels that centrifugal force which pulls us away from the Good or the One in our souls. Since this world is involved by its nature in multiplicity we need Dionysus, who is the personification of the metaphysical principle that rules the cosmos in its multiple aspect. His nature is uniform (*henoeidees)* wholly indivisible (*pantelws adiaretees)*-in the divisible world *(meristwi)* and pre-existing whole and unmixed in all things. These words are to be understood not literally, say Julian, but in the sense used by Plato, Plotinus, Porphyry and the inspired (*daimonios)* Iamblichos.

Damascius clearly distinguishes the Dionysiac from the Titanic modes of life."The Titanic mode of life is the irrational mode, by which rational life is torn asunder. It is better to acknowledge its existence everywhere, since in any case at its source there are Gods; then also on the plane of rational life, this apparent self-determination, which seems to aim at belonging to itself alone and neither to the superior nor to the inferior, is wrought in us by the Titans; through it we tear asunder the Dionysus in ourselves, breaking up the natural continuity of our being and our partnership, so to speak, with the superior and the inferior. While in this condition, we are Titans; but when we recover our lost unity, we become Dionysus and we attain completeness." (*In Phaed.* 9.)[23]

III

The early Nietzsche remained a metaphysician of art; in *BT* he is rather an "upbeat" Schopenhauer. The Symbolists in Paris (where he expected to be "understood") combined ideas in ways that perhaps make the sharp

[23] For the relevant texts on Dionysus in Damascius (tr Westerink) with additional notes on Dionysus, Neoplatonic monad/triads, and comparisons with Porphyry and the Platonic tradition see Uzdaviniys (2004) 274-76 (Damascius *In Phaed.*. 3-19; *Phaed.* 61c2-62c4)

distinction between the early Nietzsche and the Neoplatonists "fuzzy". "We made a singular mixture of Plotinus, of Edgar Poe and of Schopenhauer", wrote M. Denis. Both believes the soul gives the realm of sense something of its own; art can redeem nature by discovering in phenomena positive links with the Idea.[24] Schelling developed what he called "Dionysiology" in order to determine man's relationship to the absolute spirit (see below). In a further progression, Nietzsche's Dionysus, no longer conceived as separate or above man, became "the Dionysian", an abstract metaphor for the state of higher intoxication. And the Dionysian experience brought union with the "primal oneness".[25] The Will of Schopenhauer at the center of reality.

Nietzsche perhaps intended to indicate the oneness of Nature; the purely "immanent" unity of "this world". Yet Nietzsche is not always clear *and* the ecstatic states he discusses and the ideas behind them may be interpreted in diametrically opposite ways. Or at least suggest a "coincidence of opposites". The "urgrund", "primal ground" of Medieval/Reformation German mystics, of interest to Schopenhauer, may also be conceived as "the One from below", the "Ground of Being". A phrase made famous in modern theology by Tillich, whose "God beyond God" also implies a form of Neoplatonic apophatic theology. . Schopenhauer's Will is noumenal and transcends the Kantian phenomenal categories of time, space and causality. Given such ambiguity New England Transcendentalists and French Symbolists might well play down differences.

[24] Bregman, "Neoplatonism and American Aesthetics" in Alexandrakis and Moutafakis (2002) 177-92, 179; Bergson's "life spark'(elan vital) informs matter and body and is connected with his study of Plotinus' immanent "Soul"

[25] Henrichs (1984) 218, who reviews all the theories of Dionysus and sees Nietzche as following Schelling in the further interiorization of the god, but from a different metaphysical angle. For Holderlin the god is a brother of Jesus and they are identified rather that opposed. Nietzche's Dionysus became "the Dionysian", a metaphor for the state of higher intoxication. (A discussion of Schelling is in section III below.)

Henrichs discusses the Nietzchean Zagreus myth: "...Dionysus Zagreus represents "nature" as the "primal unity" which is the ultimate source of all existence, and his dismemberment typifies the division primordial oneness into individuals. Nietzsche interprets the rebirth of the god as the end of individuation and as man's fusion with the primal unity"(222).such an idea is at least anlogous to the somewhat similar conception of Julian and the theurgic Neoplatonists.

Thus the "moment" of dismemberment also represents individuation and in this sense is analogous to the Neoplatonic notion of Dionysus, who rules over divided substance:"Creation is twofold, either indivisible or divided, the latter...is ruled by Dionysus", Damascius *In Phaed.* 3, Uzdavinys (2004) 274.

Nietzsche's description of the Dionysian ecstatic union with the supra-individual primal unity in or behind Nature is also an example of "extrovert" mysticism.[26] Perhaps, rather than metaphysics, his major difference with mainstream Neoplatonism (and Schopenhauer), was with it's often "introvert" emphasis. The early Nietzsche had not yet arrived at his violent opposition to any metaphysical palliatives. (But Paul A. Swift suggests that even before he wrote BT, Nietzsche had revised his view of Schopenhauer; and perhaps he really believed the Dionysian frenzy was rooted in the causal phenomenal order, rather than beyond it: by "timelessness" he simply meant a type of common experience shared by many people in different times and places.)[27]

This having been said, the direction and thrust of Nietzsche's thought, even at this early stage would surely put him at odds with a Neoplatonic camp that could still lead to a Christian metaphysic: the usually anti-Christian Romantic advocate of Julian's religion Thomas Taylor, for example, had no quarrel with the Christian Pseudo-Dionsysius the Areopagite; he thought that he had merely "changed the names" and that his Christianity was a veneer for a truly theurgic Neoplatonic world-view.

Gerhardt Ladner, remarked that rather than going from Hellenism to Christianty, as Synesius had done, the Florentines had moved in exactly the opposite direction, from Christianity back to neoplatonized Hellenism; and that Holderlin made the last *great* attempt to combine the two traditions.

For the "German Plotinus" Schelling, Dionysus[28] represents a crucial "moment" in the history of spiritual evolution on the way to the highest religious consciousness; only knowable through "revelation"; i.e., Christianity.

The Greeks' mystery teaching allowed them already to stand "right on the threshold of an explicit formulation of absolute monotheism" (Beach (1994) 242). Schelling's "neo-Neoplatonism", then, belongs with those

[26] For an up to date, interesting and thorough discussion of "extrovert" mysticism and the natural world see Marshall (2005).

[27] Swift (2005) discusses the possibility that Nietzsche moved away from Schopenhauer's will before he wrote *BT*, and began to see the "primal unity" as still phenomenal; either he went back to an earlier view in *BT* or he meant to interpret the primordial unity in a different way, though he expressed it "as if" it were a metaphysical reality to give the reader a sense of the power of such experiences, 47-48, 62-63. But the evidence here seems rather thin and ambiguous. And the "Dionysian" reveler would laugh at these distinctions.

[28] The following discussion of Schelling and the Greek gods is based on the analysis offered by Beach (1994) 205-30, 238-44.

syncretistic attempts to combine Christianity with other traditions, especially Greek, but to maintain Christianity's primacy.

In the final analysis the "absolutely transcendent" of the ascetic Proclus and Thomas Taylor under which Apollo tends toward pure unity and Dionysius plays the role of the unified ruler of divided substance; and their essentially Christian analogues in Renaissance Neoplatonism and German Romanticism are not easy to reconcile with the Dionysian primal oneness of Nietzsche. And Perhaps more important than these conceptions of the divinity are the stances toward existence that they imply. Stances which Nietzsche attempted to oppose despite Schopenhauer's influence. Art for Nietzsche is the opponent of the life negating ascetic ideal.[29] The nineteenth century attempt to combine of Plotinus and Schopenhauer, might strike us as artificial. Yet, to the extent that Nietzsche was still under the spell of Schopenhauer when he wrote the "Birth of Tragedy", some connection (or at least analogy) remains possible between Dionysus as the undifferentiated oneness of nature and existence as such (the Will) and "the unified ruler over divided substance", Dionysus as a neoplatonic abstraction.

Nietzsche was only beginning to create a new mental world, radically post-Enlightenment and post-Romantic. His revived Dionysus was at first the harbinger new "mytho-aesthetic" sensibility; in no way an analogue to Christ, whose opponent and antipode he was to become. Thomas Taylor's "paganism", on the other hand, was idiosyncratic, like that of a Renaissance Neoplatonist who *actually* did become a religious Hellene in the tradition of Julian.

The emperor Julian lived in an entirely different intellectual milieu. Biblical based religion was transforming the Classical civilization, while Julian was involved in the "rearguard action" of an innovative but dogmatic revalorization of Hellenism. His "revival" of Dionysus made the god one of several "savior figures", who fit into a complex hierarchic structure, functionally metaphysical opponents of Christ.

Nietzsche never discussed and apparently never read Julian and the great Neoplatonist critics of Christianity. If he had, it is safe to conclude that he would have found them to be inhabitants of a strange twilight world in which their attempt to save Hellenism, could at best only lead to another Platonic religion of negation, not altogether different from its putative opponent.

[29] See Young (1993) 119, quoting Nietzsche: "art far from serving the ascetic ideal is its fundamental opponent. And Schopenhauer's "maliciously ingenious" attempt to reverse truth...in favor of a nihilistic life-view. Art (is) precisely the great self-affirmation of the will to live.

AUGUSTINE, PROUST AND THE RHETORIC OF TIME AND CREATION

Burcht Pranger

This article is part of a long term research project about rhetoric and temporality in Augustine.[1] A tension appears to exist between Augustine's Neo-Platonism and basic Augustinian tenets and aporias such as the status of time and creation, the role of language and rhetoric including questions about predestination and the gift of perseverance. Roughly speaking, the problems arising from this tension might be roughly formulated as follows. Given the fact that Augustine's thought before but also after his conversion is underpinned by a basically Platonic tendency to turn inward in search for ideas and ideal being, how can such idealism be squared with another essentially Augustinian maxim of the temporal and irreducible status of time and creation and, subsequently, the status of language in general and rhetoric in particular as expressing the facts of life? Of course, there is the Augustinian system of signs whose referential nature would seem to fit in nicely with the underlying ideal structure of reality, and, as such, with the Platonic mode. But frankly, such a parallelism will not do. For that to be the case the revelatory power of time and creation, driven by eternity and the celestial city, is too forceful a presence in Augustine. So, if Augustine's thought is in one way or another to be labelled as Platonic, it will by necessity be a Platonism of a very special kind.

The idiosyncratic nature of Augustinian Platonism can be illustrated by briefly mentioning the vision at Ostia. It is generally known that this passage in which Augustine describes how he and his mother are lifted up out of the tumultuous world of multiplicity to the unspeakable heights of mystical silence to be touched for one single moment by the divine, abounds with Neo-Platonic references and connotations. However, the problem here is not so much the question as to how to reconcile this Neo-Platonic substrate with more biblical-Christian notions which, sooner or later, went into the making of "Augustine the bishop." The problem is rather the fact that, for Augustine, this unspeakable and indivisible moment represents reality; it is *res*. Questions are hereby raised with regard to the status of the non-divine rest of reality, creation, for instance, and, more specifically, with regard to the interaction between the two. How does eternity, the indivisible moment of divine reality manifest itself in time? For Augustine, the rhetorician, establishing this

[1] Cf. Pranger (1995, 2001, 2002).

integrity of reality is a matter of voice, of saying the word or even the Word, - and, thus, at the same time, of revelation. Consequently, saying the word, appropriating voice, to use a phrase coined by Stanley Cavell, means being given grace and illumination.[2] It is sheer epiphany that here does the trick. Once more I want to emphasise that saying the word does not emerge out of a diffuse realm of opportunities found in human experience. As far as Augustine is concerned, it is the other way around: *da quod iubes, iube quod vis.*[3]

In this paper I propose to discuss the following problem: if for Augustine the way of saying or remembering things comes down to being a matter op epiphany, how does that epiphany work? As a gift it is bound to go against the grain of natural, linguistic utterances. Being more than - and different from - Platonic ideas pure and simple, "voice" as the revelatory moment in action cannot hide behind an idealistic structure or status nor is it to be seen as a revelation or epiphany of something other than voice. In other words, although the inner recesses of the mind are opened up in remembering and speaking, they are not shelters from which revelation springs forth or to which it returns. In this respect the later Augustine is true to himself when he continues to present predestination as the divine reality that, however hidden and incomprehensible for the human mind, does not cease to emerge and to establish itself as *res*, reality without a shadow.

The first obstacle we face in approaching the arrogation of voice as encapsulated in *da quod iubes* is language itself. In the *Confessions*, the ultimate appropriation of voice manifests itself as the performative of action the one moment during which Augustine is seen to have himself possessed by the divine Word by "putting on the Lord Jesus."[4] However, the sustainability of that possession has proven to be problematic. At first glance, Augustine seems to have addressed this problem quite successfully by extending, in the *Confessions*, the moment produced by the *tolle lege* - both backward and forward - as one protracted cry toward God who in a sense can be said, in his turn, to have rewarded this sustained prayer by causing to rain down on the head of the supplicant biblical words and images as ever so many epiphanic moments. The revelatory moment *par excellence* at which Augustine, guided by the *tolle lege*, has wrapped himself in the cloths of Christ would seem both as radiantly beautiful and frightening as the way in which Proust sums up his

[2] See in particular Cavell (1994).

[3] Cf. its threefold appearance in book 10 of the *Confessiones*, twice in chapter 29 and once in chapter 31.

[4] *Confessiones* 8, 29; Cf. Romans 13:13-14.

hero's discovery of life and love in the closing lines of *A l'ombre des jeunes filles en fleurs/Within a Budding Grove*:

> And after Françoise [the maid servant] had removed her pins from the mouldings of the windowframe, taken down her various cloths, and drawn back the curtains, the summer day which she disclosed seemed as dead, as immemorially ancient as would have been a sumptuously attired dynastic mummy from which our old servant had done no more than precautionally unwind the linen wrappings before displaying it to my gaze, embalmed in its vesture of gold.[5]

What is so reminiscent here of the Augustinian rhythm in the *Confessions*, is the sheer suspense included in the moment of seeing the mummy "embalmed in its vesture of gold." This Proustian epiphany finding his hero on doctors' orders, in bed in the mornings "with the room darkened," recalls the novel's famous beginning: "*Longtemps je me suis couché de bonne heure*/For a long time I used to go to bed early;" both the *longtemps* and the *de bonne heure* are somehow reminiscent of the "late" of the *sero te amavi* (*Confessions* 10, 38). This beginning is, in its turn, resumed in the opening sentence of *Within a Budding Grove II* about the orders of the Balbec doctor to spend the mornings in the darkened room from which the daylight was to be resolutely shut out. It is from that darkness spanning the half-dream, half-sleep train of thought then of the young boy and of the adult author now that musings invade his mind about the bright sunshine outside on the beach where he had first been watching and, subsequently, been meeting, and getting acquainted with the group of young girls on holiday. But, just as for Augustine writing the *Confessions* was not primarily about reconstructing the past but, rather, about restoring memory in its efforts to hold on to the moment of voice, so Proust's hero, in search for lost time, records his fight to hold on to the duration of images (as the representation of time). Thus the incredible lightness and magical touch of the episode *Within a Budding Grove*, are counterpointed by decay and death, by unsustainability. Not only does it appear hard if not impossible initially to distinguish the distinct features of the young girls's faces. The rapidly approaching moment of a consciously personal identity (coinciding with the developing focus of the male hero on a "single" girl and imagined to culminate in bodily possession) also contains the contours of old age, decay and death. In the episode itself no clue is given as to the moment the two - the blossom of youth and the decay of old age - meet. As the

[5] Proust (1971) 355.

proposed encounter with the favourite girl of the moment, Albertine, ends in failure due to her refusal of physical rapprochement, no intermediary between past and future is offered that would enable the hero as well as the reader to pinpoint the fullness of time. The holiday season nearing its end, the girls gone, the hotel (at Balbec) about to be closed down for the winter, Augustine's *distentio animi*, the spreading out of the soul in the *regio dissimilitudinis*, can, as it were, be seen on its way back: the immensity of light, the sea and the world at large emerging out of the unfolding of the curtains highlight the "undressing" of the mummy in order to reveal its splendour *as if* opening up a future of unlimited dimensions. Yet at the same time the epiphany of the late summer day refolds the entire scene back and turns it, for all its brightness, into a mummified monument of *temps perdu*, "dead, dead, dead."

The following problem now presents itself. The evanescent course of Proustian imagery as representing the elusive presence of the past is firmly embedded inside the flow of his language proper. The very elusiveness is both produced and restrained, so to speak, by the verbal waves of Proustian discourse. In contrast, Augustine's reconstruction of temporality seems to resort, not only to motionless notions of authority—whose effects would appear to be threatening enough in themselves. Those notions are also expressed in terms of voice; a voice, however, that cannot avoid being frozen in the timeless authority of scriptural speech. How, then, can that speech still be "epiphanic" if that which it represents is absorbed by the fixedness - or call it eternity - which the Augustinian soul had been searching for so desperately? Not surprisingly, this aporia is most keenly felt when we confront the problem of predestination as the epitome of eternity's presence: "What have you that you did not receive?" It is this Scriptural question that somehow has to be made operational by being scrutinised, not only as to its being spoken *apud deum*, but, rather, with regard to its effectiveness and its intelligibility here and now.

Whatever changes may have occurred in the course of Augustine's intellectual career, he was constant throughout to the principle of the instrumental meaning of rhetoric and reflection. Tied up as language - including the language of Scripture - is with the memorial process of remembering, willing and understanding, as sketched out in the *Confessions* and pursued as well as elaborated in *De trinitate*, it is never to be viewed as an independent entity for its own sake, as are neither the instruments of rhetoric and intellectual scrutiny. In the case of reading and understanding Scripture, however, those instruments are not to be used for improving the delivery of speech or the writing of books. Rather, they are employed by the Christian reader in order to "crack" the speech and writing that as such are perfect. The fact, then, that *da quod iubes* is linguistically enshrined in the perfect gift of Scripture accounts for Augustine's extraordinarily relaxed attitude toward the use of the rules of (pagan) rhetoric and interpretation with regard to the understanding of Scripture. In his defence in the prologue to *De doctrina christiana*,[6] the use of interpretative rules and of rhetoric (the *modus inveniendi*/the discovery of the material and the *modus proferendi*/the presentation of the material) against those who, claiming direct access to Scripture, boast they can do without them, he firmly shifts the focus of the "possessed" interpreter to the arrogation of voice in space and time rather than to timeless inspiration to be derived without any intermediary from the divine.[7] Paul on the road to Damascus may have been "enlightened by a divine voice from heaven." Yet he "was sent to a human being to receive the sacrament of baptism and be joined to the church." The same applies to the centurion, Cornelius, who was told by an angel that his prayers had been heard, but was nonetheless to be tutored by Peter in the subjects of "faith, hope and love" (Acts 10). Likewise the Ethiopian eunuch in the story from Acts 8, who was reading the prophet Isaiah in his chariot needed the help of Philip "to understand what he was reading." "How can I [understand] except some man should guide me?"[8] "All this could certainly have been done through an angel, but the human condition would be really forlorn if God appeared unwilling to minister his word to human beings through human agency (*si per homines hominibus deus verbum suum ministrare nolle videtur*)."

Now one can easily be misled by the firmness of the rules (such as the rules of Tyconius which Augustine discusses in *De doctrina christiana*) as well as the educational toughness of the *modus inveniendi* and the *modus proferendi*, and mistake them for the solidity of (the content of) Christian teaching. That, however, would be a serious distortion of *De doctrina*'s tenor. The book is shot through with elements of shakiness and fragility resulting from either the drive of love or the gaps of inadequacy which have to do with frictions between signs and the signified. As for the latter, Augustine's famous theory of signs as presented in the first book of *De doctrina* pervades the rest of it. The very fact that signs refer to one *res*, one entity, God or the Trinity, which is the only part of reality to be enjoyed for its own sake, injects

[6] *De doctrina christiana*, preface. Green (1995) 6-9.

[7] For a discussion of the identity of the potential opponents (in the ascetic circles) mentioned in this passage, see Pollman (1996) 76-80.

[8] Acts 8:31.

unrest into all the rest of reality and turns the discussion of signs and the technical ways of dealing with them into the hectic business of referentiality. The resulting urgency of referentiality as the teaching how to return "home" as quickly as possible is further enhanced by the other pervading feature, the drive of love. Following up on a dramatic evocation of the Old Testament fathers "who were found (*inventio*!) by Christian liberty to be on the brink of interpreting the useful signs to which they were subjected - Old Testament rites and ceremonies - to the level of the things of which these were signs," Augustine is able to reduce the tiresome number of many signs to the splendid economy of a *praesens praesentis*:

> But at the present time (*hoc tempore*), when a brilliant demonstration of our freedom has been revealed in the resurrection of our Lord, we are not oppressed by the tiresome necessity of attending to signs, even the signs we now understand. Instead of many signs there are now but a few signs, simple when performed, inspiring when understood, and holy when practised, given to us by the teaching of our Lord himself, and the apostles, such as the sacrament of baptism and the celebration of the Lord's body and blood.[9]

This self same economy regarding signs can now be extended to the one and only instrument that is capable of breathing life into them and of bringing them back to the one and only *res* to which they refer: God to be loved and enjoyed for his own sake.

> But scripture enjoins nothing but love, and censures nothing but lust, and moulds men's minds accordingly. Similarly, if their minds are taken over by a particular prejudice, people consider as figurative anything that scripture asserts to the contrary. But it asserts nothing except the catholic faith, in time past, present, and future. It narrates the past, foretells the future, and demonstrates the present, but all these things serve to nourish and strengthen this love, and to overcome and annihilate lust.[10]

Here it becomes clear that a fine line is being drawn between Scripture and the reading of Scripture, teaching and the carrying out of teaching. What is more, underlying the reading and teaching of Scripture is a drive toward their becoming superfluous. Out of the future and the past a present is being produced which is nothing but eternity's shadow as reflected in the contraction of *hodie* - the times in which we live - in the moment of

[9] *De doctrina christiana* III, X, 14; 33; Green (1995) 144-7.

[10] *De doctrina christiana* III, X, 15; 35; Green (1995) 148-9.

resurrection. In terms of the *Confessions*, this moment consists of "putting on the Lord Jesus and making no provision for the flesh in its lusts," a moment that is echoed in the link established in the *De doctrina* quote between love and the annihilation of lust. In other words, it is the moment at which the toilsome story of signs is being abridged, "a shorthand of the facts" established; it is the moment of the arrogation of voice.

> Therefore a person strengthened by faith, hope, and love, and who steadfastly holds on to them, has no need of the scriptures except to instruct others. That is why many people, relying on these three things, actually live in solitude without any texts of the scriptures. They are, I think, a fulfilment of the saying: "If there are prophecies, they will lose their meaning; if there are tongues, they will cease; if there is knowledge that too will lose its meaning."[11]

Temporality as the challenge to live out a *praesens praesentis* concerns all. Being taught to read properly is nothing but to learn to catch the moment at which voice can be arrogated. That voice, in turn, rather than being absorbed by mystical silence detached from any articulation and focus, pinpoints the explosive effect of time in the guise of full possession as the moment at which language and knowledge have run their course and, as on the command of the *tolle lege*, are being abridged and condensed to continence as the holding on to (*tenere*) a word that is no longer spoken and taught but lived to the full, transformed into a love that, having done away with past and future, faith and hope, will prevail; "for when one reaches eternity the other two will pass away and love will remain in an enhanced and a more certain form." As accomplished readers who have appropriated and fulfilled the scriptural sayings to the point of the latter losing their meaning, the desert fathers have indeed turned into Scripture themselves.

Regardless how attached, through subterranean links, to eternity - and the eternal Word - the Christian faith may be, it remains at the same time an intrinsic part of creation, and, consequently, of temporality. Conversely, the eternal Word, motionless in its (Neo-platonic) ideal state, is firmly rooted in language and reality itself. Thus we can observe Augustine solving a problem that had been haunting him during his protracted quest for wisdom: the beauty and eloquence—which, once upon a time, had looked like the ugliness and

[11] *De doctrina christiana* I, XXXIX, 43; 93; Green (1995) 52-3. Cf. 1 Cor. 13:8. Notice the contradiction in terms between the solitary existence of those people on the one hand and their being in the position to teach others, on the other.

barbaric nature—of Scriptural speech. Not only is he able to demonstrate, in *De doctrina*, the Hellenistic respectability of Scriptural (mainly Paulinian) language in terms of tropes and figures. He also manages to present it, for all its authority and divine inspiration, in its guise of temporal fragility, bringing to the surface the beauty of epiphanic speech, that is, speech, that has been perfectly effective and revealing then and there, and, for that reason, and for that reason alone, is capable of being effective and revealing here and now.

> At this point someone may be asking whether the Christian authors whose divinely inspired writings have created for us the canon of scripture with its most beneficial authority should be pronounced just wise, or eloquent as well. In my experience, and the experience of people who feel as I do on this matter, the question is a very easy one to answer. For when I understand these authors, not only can I conceive of nothing wiser; I can conceive of nothing more eloquent. Indeed, I venture to say that all who correctly understand what these writers are saying realize at the same time that it would not have been right for them to express it in any other way. For just as there is one kind of eloquence appropriate to the young, and another kind appropriate to the old—and we should not call it eloquence if it does not match the status of the speaker—so there is a kind of eloquence appropriate to writers who enjoy the highest authority and a full measure of divine inspiration. They spoke in their own particular style, and it would be inappropriate for them to have used any other style, or for others to have used theirs (*nec ipsos decet alia nec alios ipsa*). It is appropriate to them, and the humbler it seems, the more thoroughly it transcends that of others, not in grandiloquence but in substance. When I fail to understand them, their eloquence is less clear, but I have no doubt that it is of the same standard as that which appears clearly when I do understand them.[12]

Although there is no denying that the authors of Scripture used rhetorical devices when appropriate, it is the pinpointing of the right moment in the right words as the true reflection of reality that was paramount. The result looks like a seamless coincidence of time, circumstances, literary expression, and, it should be added, eternity as the performative of time then and there. It is the intensity of this performative moment that is responsible for the epiphanic power and effect of Scriptural language—even when the going gets rough and the eloquence and beauty of certain Scriptural passages look utterly obscure to

[12] *De doctrina christiana* IV, VI, 9; 25, 26; Green (1995) 205-7.

the Hellenistic reader. Beauty and eloquence do reappear, however, when stylistic obscurity has proven to be in the service of better understanding and greater clarity.

The efficiency of biblical language as the intensity of focus (*nec ipsos decet alia nec alios ipsa*) which does not allow for any mixture between different styles and speakers but highlights their unity in one particular sacred author at one particular time, seems somehow reminiscent of the problem of predestination, without, it should be added, solving any of it aporias. If we leave the breadth of eternity aside momentarily and concentrate instead on its effects in and on time, the temporality of punctuated moments comes to the fore. These moments have been expressed so adequately then and there that they could not have been said differently. Admittedly, things become more complicated if we shift our focus to the divine planning activities that have always been in the forefront of the official dealings with the problem of predestination. And even though there is no denying that in the later Augustinian treatises, repetitive attention is given to the divine "yes" and "no," yet, in one way or another, it seems impossible to detach both the circularity and the accomplished nature or, rather, the "ideal" state of those who will be saved because they are predestined to be saved from the sacred words that have been said as they have been said. It is up to the reader to appropriate the gift of text in the same way as he is to appropriate the gift of life. He has, in other words, to meet the challenge of acquiring perseverance and sustainability of voice to the extent, rarely achievable in this life, that, "if there are tongues, they will cease, if there is knowledge that too will lose its meaning." This very epiphany of Scripture will occur at the moment the illuminating truth reveals itself in the guise of *words* once spoken and now read, reread and re-enacted.

To return once more to the Proustian image, the voice that heeds the divine vocation is a dead body, a mummy to be un- and refolded. The mystery of it all is that we are not presented here with a romantic story of our incidental return from the dead as if there were life outside the unwrapping of the mummified body, or, for that matter, brightness of light and vastness of air and sea outside the epiphanic folding or unfolding of Proust's curtains. As a result, the intermittences of temporality are not governed from outside nor are they in any way bridged and smoothed over by divine providence or, philosophically speaking, by an infrastructure of ideas which look independently behind the screen. Constituting a universe of weak and strong voices, those intermittent moments are left to themselves only to be sustained by mental hardware disguised as the gift of grace, life *wie es gewesen*.

MONOPHYSITISM AND THE EVOLUTION OF THEOLOGICAL DISCOURSE IN CHRISTIAN NEOPLATONISM

Edward Moore

I.

Christian Neoplatonism began with the work of Origen of Alexandria, notably his seminal treatise *De Principiis* ("On First Principles"). In this text, we find Origen in dialogue with the Hellenic philosophical tradition, specifically Platonism and Stoicism. Although Origen was critical of these schools, one finds in the pages of *De Principiis* a concerted effort to synthesize these traditions. The most prominent example is his conception of the Trinity, which is essentially a basic Middle Platonic triadic emanation schema inserted into a Christian theological context.[1]

The Father, according to Origen, is the One, the single ungenerated and eternal source of all Being, and therefore, Himself beyond Being. The Son is the Logos (Intellect, or Mind) containing the eternal thought-forms of the Father; and yet while the Son is not, strictly speaking, *un*generated, He is said to be *eternally* generated, and therefore coeval with the Father. From the Father and Son emanates the Spirit, which is not quite equivalent to the World-Soul of Middle Platonism,[2] though it comes close, to the extent that it pervades the cosmos, and is described as the immaterial well-spring of God's grace infusing the material realm with the divine presence. One notes here a strict hierarchy, as Origen puts it plainly: the Father is greater than the Son, and the Holy Spirit is inferior to both, yet still fully divine and worthy of veneration.[3]

Origen's speculative philosophical theology did not raise the question of the essence (*ousia*) of the Godhead, or whether the Father, Son, and Spirit share a single nature (*phusis*), etc.; for Origen was utilizing the basic conceptual schema of Middle Platonism, though in a markedly Christian theological framework. While he does use the term *hupostasis* in reference to the persons of the Trinity,[4] he is not utilizing that term in the very strict, carefully determined manner of the later Church Fathers, for whom it meant

[1] See, for example, Berchman (1984), and Moore (2003).

[2] See Dillon (1982).

[3] Origen, *De Principiis*, fragment 9 (Koetschau), in Butterworth (1966), pp. 33-34.

[4] Origen, *Against Celsus* 8.12; *Commentary on the Gospel of John* 2.10.75.

three distinct persons sharing a single essence or nature.[5] Rather, Origen understood the Godhead as an eternally unfolding process in which the Father is always the creator, the Son always the only-begotten (*monogenês*) Logos, and the Spirit the eternal presence of God amidst His creation.[6] However, this rather neat Platonic-Christian schema was quickly distorted and twisted into a maze of increasingly complex theological difficulties by the sophist-logician-theologian *Arius of Alexandria* (c. 280-336 A.D.), resulting in what has been described as the archetypal Christian heresy: that the Logos is "the Son and Servant of God, but in no way God in the same sense as the Father [is] God."[7]

According to Arius, only the Father is unbegotten, for He is the source of all things; however, the Son is still defined as a creature, and therefore essentially distinct from God.[8] Arius did not believe that the Father and Son share the same essence or nature; rather, he believed that the Son is not only absolutely different from God the Father, but that the Son is incapable of comprehending the Father's divine intelligence. The task of the Son, according to Arius, is to initiate the flowing-forth of the Father's incomprehensible mind in the created realm, without ever reflecting upon the source of His (the Son's) activity. For this reason, Arius describes the Son as the greatest of God's creatures, but a *creature* nonetheless – for the Son's knowledge of the Father is limited to the activities that He accomplishes through His Father's Will.[9]

A very clear articulation of Arius' triadic schema is preserved by St. Athanasius, in his treatise *On the Synods of Ariminum and Seleucia*, displaying a marked Neoplatonic influence (I quote the words of Arius himself, as preserved by his opponent):

> ... there is a Triad, not in similar glories. Not intermingling with each other are their subsistences [*hupostaseis*]. One is more glorious than the other in glories to infinity. Foreign from the Son in essence [*ousia*] is the Father, for He is without beginning [*anarkhos*]. Understand that the Monad was; but the Dyad was not,

[5] See, for example, Gregory Nazianzen, *Letter 101 to Cledonius*.

[6] Origen, *De Principiis*, fragment 9 (Koetschau), in Butterworth (1966), pp. 33-34.

[7] McGuckin (2004), p. 29.

[8] The primary source for this doctrine is the "Letter of Arius to Alexander, Bishop of Alexandria," *c.* 320, recorded in Athanasius, *On the Synods of Ariminum and Seleucia*, 16.

[9] See Gregg and Groh (1981).

> before it was in existence [*huparxê*].[10] It follows at once that though the Son was not, the Father was God. Hence the Son, not being (for He existed at the will of the Father), is God Only-begotten [*monogenês*]; and He is alien from either. Wisdom existed as Wisdom by the will of the Wise God. Hence he is conceived in numberless conceptions: Spirit, Power, Wisdom, God's glory, Truth, Image and Word.[11]

We see here that Arius is not using the term *hupostasis* to refer to persons, but rather to metaphysical properties or powers exclusive to each entity comprising the divine triad. While Arius paid little attention to the Holy Spirit (for the status of the Son was a much more pressing issue at this period of Christian theological development),[12] the above-quoted passage shows that he was attuned to the problem of God's active power in the created realm. Yet it was left to his most brilliant pupil, the sophist-rhetorician-philosopher *Eunomius of Cyzicus* (c. 325-395 A.D.), to overcome the logical impasse that arises when one considers Arius' statement that the Son does not know God as well as He knows Himself, alongside the concept of the Son as the most perfect creation of the Father.

According to Eunomius, Christ the Logos is the creative force of the Father, revealing Himself through acts occurring in the sensible realm. Admitting that Arius was correct in his statement that the Son does not comprehend the Father as well as He comprehends Himself, Eunomius makes the radical claim that humanity is capable of knowing the Father as well as He knows Himself.[13] Does this mean that created humanity is superior to the Son of God? Not at all. It simply means that there are at least two modes of

[10] The Father = Monad, the Son = Dyad. This is a more philosophical version of the oft-repeated slogan of Arianism: 'there was when the Son was not.' We find here a Christianization of the Platonic-Pythagorean concept of a primordial One that limits and gives form to the unruly Dyad, thereby producing the sequence of numbers (culminating in the Decad) that are responsible for producing the material (sensible) realm. In short, the Dyad only becomes a source when it is limited and controlled by the Monad; – this is the principle of Monarchianism ('single source') which had a long and influential career in Patristic thought. – E.M.

[11] Arius, *Thalia* (fr.), in Athanasius, *De synodis Arimini* 15.3 – tr. modified; originally tr. in Stevenson (1957), p. 346.

[12] However, it should be noted that Arius' pupils, Aetius and Eunomius, attempted to formulate a doctrine of the Spirit based on the notion that it is the first and most perfect of the creations wrought by the Son through the will of the Father (Eunomius, *Apol*. 25; 28; Basil, *Contra Eunom*. 2, 33; Kelly (1978), pp. 255-256.

[13] See Mar Gregorios (1988), p. 34.

knowing God: the active and the passive. Christ the Logos knows God through His (the Son's) continual act of carrying out the creation envisioned ideally within His (God's) mind;[14] human beings know God through the contemplation of the symbolic terminology of Holy Scripture.[15]

Eunomius taught that the words describing God in the Old and New Testaments are not mere correspondences, but actual symbols relating directly to the divine essence.[16] Therefore, to understand the terminology is to understand the Godhead. This is the persuasive thesis of one of the greatest Christian Neoplatonists of the Late-Hellenistic/Early Byzantine era: *that language and linguistic concepts are a surer path to knowledge of the Godhead than imitation of the active, creative intimacy of the Father with His own Son.* It required the philosophical and theological brilliance of the greatest Eastern Church Father (beside Origen) to counter this thesis of Eunomius, and thereby bring a new dimension to Christian thought. I am speaking of *St. Gregory of Nyssa* (*c.* 331-395 A.D.), to a discussion of whom we now turn.

II.

The eminent historian of Christian dogma, Adolf von Harnack, remarked that Gregory of Nyssa's *Catechetical Orations* is the only treatise of the fourth century worthy of being classed with Origen's *De Principiis*.[17] This is no small praise, and when one reads Gregory's work, it becomes clear that the praise is warranted.

After an initial, failed attempt at refuting Eunomius, Gregory went back to the drawing board. Not to be daunted by Eunomius' pristine logic, Gregory developed a purely *Christian* logic, based on his original notion of the *diastêma*, i.e., a gap or fissure (in French, *enspacement*)[18] separating God from His creation. According to Gregory, there are two types of existents: the atemporal and infinitely unknowable Trinity, and the created order, comprising all of nature, with humanity as the most perfect expression of

[14] Here we find the distinction between *logos endiathetos* and *logos prophorikos*; see, for example, Olympiodorus, *In Aristotelis categorias commentarium* 80.35-37.

[15] St. Gregory Nazianzen, *Fifth Theological Oration – On the Spirit*, 5.

[16] Kelly (1978), p. 249.

[17] Harnack (1898), p. 334.

[18] This French translation, first proposed by H. Urs von Balthasar, adequately captures the idea that the separation between God and Humanity is not mutual – God continues to commune with His creation, though His creation does not necessarily remain aware of this fact. See Balthasar (1995), Chapter I, "The Concept of Spacing."

God's love and grace, for humanity has the special status as the created image of God.

Gregory's distinction does not render God absolutely ineffable, but simply reminds us that we can only know God to the extent that He reveals Himself to us through His activities (*energeiai*) – language is not up to the task of revealing the divine essence, it can only explain divine acts.[19]

With Gregory's theology a new concept comes into play: **yearning** (*epektasis*, an infinite "stretching" out toward God). Since we are separated from God by an unbridgeable gap or fissure (*diastêma*), our desire to unite with Him will remain eternally unfulfilled. The infinite richness of God's mind will continually be poured out for those who seek Him, yet with no possibility of a final repose or *stasis*. The essence of God, argues Gregory, is the essence of a *creator*, and in this he is following Origen, who declared that there never was a time when God was not Father – and, consequently, never a time when the Son was not the Son.[20]

Here Gregory posits an atemporal ontological modality of the Godhead, i.e., the Trinity. We find Gregory abandoning the Monarchianism[21] of the Arians in favor of a dynamic conception of an eternally creative Trinity. Now if the triune Godhead is eternally creative, it must follow that its greatest creation, Humanity, is eternally changeable, for creation implies a continual process of growth and development. And so we arrive at the unavoidable reality of human existence: that humanity is both spirit and flesh. As C. Stavropoulos writes:

> The fact that human beings are not only spirit, but also flesh is one more reason which gives them the possibility of returning to God. For if people were only spirit and consequently sinned as spirits, they could not be redeemed since the spirit cannot change, but

[19] See Balthasar (1995), Chapter 7, "Desire and Knowledge."

[20] Prestige (1977).

[21] "Monarchianism" indicates a theological conception of the Father as the *single source* (hence the name) or First Principle of the Trinity, and was usually taken as implying subordinationism, i.e., the doctrine that the Son and Spirit are of lesser divinity than the Father. This is a prime example of Middle/Neo-Platonic thought entering into Christianity; for just as the Platonists argued that the Dyad is subjected to the controlling power of the One, so did the Monarchians make a similar argument regarding the Trinity, specifically the relation of the Son to the Father. See McGuckin (2004), pp. 225-227. It should be noted, however, that Monarchianism took on many forms, mostly related to the status of Christ. For a set of translated extracts from primary texts regarding this phenomenon, see Stevenson (ed.) (1957), pp. 157-160, etc.

> remains unchangeable because of its simplicity. But human beings also have bodies. And they are changeable and can be transformed because they are complex.[22]

At this point we encounter the Orthodox Christian concept of a distinction between "image" (*eikona*) and "likeness" (*homoiôsin*) in human beings (Gen. 1:26 LXX). As "spirit" or mind (*nous*) humanity bears always the image of God; this image can be partially effaced or obscured (like the sea-god Glaucus in Plato's allegory)[23] but never completely removed from the human being. The likeness, however, is not something given to humanity upon their creation by God, but rather something toward which they must strive – indeed *yearn* – if they are to achieve salvation. Gregory of Nyssa thereby affirms the profoundly historical character of human existence, as he insists upon the necessity and reality of the continuous striving of the *image* for its *likeness*.

> 'Never will the soul reach its final perfection, for it will never encounter a limit ... it will always be transformed into a better thing.' The reason for this infinite becoming is the very infinity of the source, which the creature seeks to be reunited with: 'Since the First Good is infinite in nature, communion with it on the part of the one whose thirst is quenched by it will have to be infinite as well, capable of being enlarged forever.'[24]

The problem immediately arose (from the Arian camp) that if Christ is both divine and human (this was the position of the defenders of Nicene Orthodoxy) then it follows (according to the Arian logic) that He (Christ) is also changeable, for changeability is implied in the formula that the image is innate, while the likeness is something attainable. If Christ is in any way changeable (i.e., capable of attaining something that He lacks) – so the Arians argued – then our salvation is not guaranteed, for Christ may become corrupted, turned to evil, etc.[25]

Gregory of Nyssa's argument, in response, was that Christ's activity was not two-fold, but unified, for Christ was perfectly aligned with the activity (*energeia*) of the Father. This argument stems from the Biblical insistence that Jesus Christ was without sin. So what we find in Gregory is the idea that Christ and His salvific activity stems wholly from the *energeia* of the Father – in fact is a direct, historical manifestation of the Father's

[22] C. Stavropoulos (1995), p. 187.

[23] Plato, *Republic* 10.611d.

[24] Balthasar (1995), p. 38, quoting Gregory (*Contra Eunomium* 1.2.340d).

[25] See, for example, Placher (1983), Chapter 6, "Truly Human, Truly Divine."

activity.[26] It will be useful to note here the statement of St. Athanasius, regarding the disconnect between the triune God and His creation:

> ... His being in everything does not mean that He shares the nature of everything, only that He gives all things their being and sustains them in it (*De incarnatione Verbi Dei* 17).[27]

The doctrine of the transference of natures (i.e., the Athanasian/Apollinarian formula that "God became man so that man may become God")[28] clearly does not apply to all of God's creation, only to humanity. Yet the fact that Christ has a special, unmediated connection with the *energeia* of the Father, while humanity is separated (according to Gregory) from God by an unbridgeable gap (*diastêma*), implies that there is a single activity (*energeia*) of God, and a two-fold activity of humanity, as it seeks to unite with God – i.e., to overcome the dichotomy of flesh and spirit in a union of *inherent* image and *potential* likeness. So here we bump up against Gregory's unwitting positing of a *Monenergistic* theology.[29] We will now turn to the final portion of this paper, which is concerned with the *Monothelite* (single will) theology of Maximus the Confessor – the last of the great Christian Neoplatonists.[30]

Before proceeding, however, it will be helpful to briefly discuss the importance and implications of the *mono*-predicate theology that was

[26] St. Gregory of Nyssa, *Address on Religious Instruction*, 6.

[27] From an anonymous translation (1996) Crestwood, NY: St. Vladimir's Seminary Press.

[28] It is not clear whether Athanasius himself coined this theological formula, or if it is the product of the 'heretic' Apollinaris. Regardless, this onto-theological formulation became a major source of doctrine in the Eastern Church. See McGuckin (2004), pp. 21-22.

[29] Monenergism is intimately connected with Monarchianism and subordinationism, for its premise rests on the assumption that there is a single power or activity (*energeia*) flowing from the Godhead, originating with the Father, and to which the subordinate divine beings – the Son and Spirit – are completely beholden, as agents of the Will (*thelêma*) of the Father. This naturally results in Monothelite (single will) doctrine.

[30] St. John of Damascus utilized extensively the Neoplatonic thought of his era, as he sought to synthesize the diverse opinions of the earlier Church Fathers, in the service of a unified Christian catechism. This is not to say that John was not original – he composed a treatise "On Dragons and Phantasms" – but he did not possess the brilliant mind of a speculative theologian like Maximus. His talent resided more in compilation than in original thought. For more on the Damascene, see Tatakis (2003), p. 82 ff.

prevalent in the Eastern Church during this era.[31] While many Church Fathers objected to the Neoplatonic-derived monism of thinkers like Arius and his pupil Eunomius, for example, it must be noted that these objections arose from an attempt to formulate a concept of Christ as the Divine Logos, the second person of the Trinity, and His relation to humanity.

The main reason why Orthodox Fathers objected to Monophysitism is that it degraded human nature to something changeable and therefore not of inherent value in God's created schema. In other words, if God could bring about the Incarnation of the Logos, for the purpose of uniting – and, indeed, equating – the human nature with the divine (as formulated so succinctly in the Athanasian/Apollinarian statement quoted above), it follows that there was really no purpose for creating human nature in the first place! God should simply have created divine beings from the beginning, and saved Himself the trouble of historical intervention, and all the theological problems it produced.

Monenergism, however, is a more delicate issue. Gregory of Nyssa sought to circumvent the debate over the number of natures in Christ by introducing a logic based upon the radical discontinuity between the respective divine and human ontologies, arguing that God's activity is unified in respect to both His will and the actions of human beings, yet the effects of the divine activity and the human response are radically disconnected, due to the *diastêma*.[32] The only factor uniting humanity and divinity is the principle of 'single activity' (*monenergeia*), a concept not directly attributed to Gregory of Nyssa but one which, I posit, is implicit in his theological works.[33] This concept allowed Gregory to affirm the distinction between the human and divine natures, while at the same time maintaining the primacy of the divine

[31] Conspicuous by his absence in my paper is likely Pseudo-Dionysius the Areopagite. I am not downplaying or denying his immense importance in Christian Neoplatonic theology; rather, I am devoting more space to a discussion of lesser-known Christian Neoplatonists. For those who are unfamiliar with Ps.-Dionysius, I would recommend the following works: Jones (tr.) (1980); Luibheid (tr.) (1987); Lossky (1995).

[32] In other words, human beings are free to respond to God in any manner they see fit. The cosmological implications of these responses will not necessarily be favorable – but they will express a freedom of will and a sense of independency that is largely alien to Western conceptions of Christianity, where God is usually regarded as a despot, rather than a benevolent king.

[33] Specifically, in his treatise "To Ablabius: On 'Not Three Gods" (*Ad Ablabium quod non sint tres dei*), where he writes that "'Godhead' signifies an operation and not a nature ..." Tr. in Richardson and Hardy (ed.) (1954), p. 261. Ablabius was a younger contemporary of Gregory, to whom the Saint wrote several letters, including the one I have cited.

act over the human contribution to historical existence. If God's act is the sole act affecting human history, then human activity effectively counts for nought, and we arrive at a veiled version of Monophysitism – i.e., a theology of a primordial and all-pervasive Godhead, in which human nature plays little or no part (this is connected intimately with the *monotheletism* of Maximus, as we will now explore).

Maximus the Confessor sought to correct this problem by thinking not in metaphysical terms (Monophysitism), nor, like Gregory, in an ontological manner (resulting in *monenergism*), but rather in an **existential** manner, resulting in the Neoplatonic *monotheletism* of his advanced Christological and eschatological works.[34] For Maximus, the Christian profession of faith – that Truth is a *Person*, **Christ** – took on cosmological implications and effectively placed the Divine Logos at the center of the universe, as the guiding principle of human existence. Stoicism returns with a vengeance. By this I mean that the guiding power of the cosmos, according to Maximus, is the all-pervasive Logos (Christ), whose Will (*thelêma*), derived from the Father, is the over-arching determining force in the created realm. Once again, humanity is given short shrift. While Maximus does not deny that the will of humanity is important, he nevertheless affirms that it is only *God's* Will that shapes the fate of the cosmos. *Monotheletism* finds a home in the work of the last great Eastern dogmatic theologian.

The reason for this, I posit, is the prevalence of a mystical tradition of asceticism, self-denial, which flourished for centuries among the Eastern monastics. This tradition taught the necessity of a complete negation of one's personal, egocentric will, and the absolute reception of the Will of Christ, as the prerequisite for *theôsis*, or divinization. In Maximus, however, this reception was not couched in terms of a transference of natures (as it had been for Athanasius/Apollinaris and Chalcedonian Orthodoxy in general); rather, the controlling idea was that the individual human being, the person, had to relinquish his or her autonomy, and yield place to the over-powering Will of God.

[34] I consider Monophysitism to be a distinctly metaphysical position, since it makes a general claim about the role of Christ the Logos in the created realm – i.e., that He is the source and sustenance of this realm. The ontological aspect of St. Gregory of Nyssa's concept of the *diastêma* resides in the notion that God's being is revealed through His energies or activities (*energeiai*). Finally, the existentialism of St. Maximus the Confessor resides in his insistence upon the presence of God's Will in the world, which makes the cosmos a personal arena in which God acts for the purpose of saving His Creation.

Referring to the salvific state, Maximus writes, in his *Chapters on Knowledge* (2.88G): "In this state only God shines forth through body and soul when their natural features are transcended in overwhelming glory."[35] The contemporary theologian Lars Thunberg correctly comments on this passage, remarking that, according to Maximus, the soul receives God as "a substitute for [its] own ego."[36] This anti-humanist theological attitude was to have an immense influence on the development of Byzantine thought, eventually resulting in the re-emergence of humanism in the work of early cosmopolites such as Photius and Michael Psellus, culminating in the seminal work of the father of the Renaissance, Gemistus Plethon.

In the case of Maximus, however, we see the problem of Monophysitism and its offshoots coming 'full circle,' as it were. The 'transference of natures' doctrine of St. Athanasius and company – *that God became man so that man may become God* – was gradually removed from the soteriological sphere of early Christian kerygma, and transplanted in, or grafted upon, the pagan Hellenic tradition, resulting in Monophysitism, which declared that Christ's Incarnation was a metaphysical event affecting human nature in a cosmological – rather than a personal – manner.[37] The response of Gregory of Nyssa sought to differentiate Christ's activities (*energeiai*) from His ontological status as the Son of God (the Dyad, Logos, etc.). Gregory's approach was primarily ontological, insofar as he sought the being of God not in a metaphysical construct (as did Eunomius) but in an active participation of God in His created realm. The problem with Gregory's theology, however, was that it over-emphasized the transcendence of God, and downplayed (likely in opposition to Eunomius) the ability of humanity to grasp at least a small portion of the mysteries of the Godhead. The end result is that all humanity is left with – according to Gregory – is a naturalistic theology that does not fully account for revelation.[38]

Maximus, however, elevates revelation to the only possible access of the human being to God. According to Maximus, human beings have a mission from God – and it is a noble one – i.e., to elevate all of nature to communion with the Deity. But the catch is this: while the effort is on the

[35] Berthold (tr.) (1985).

[36] Thunberg (1985), p. 89.

[37] This is most marked in the theology of Eutyches, who taught that Christ had two natures before His Incarnation, and only one nature afterward! See Davis (1983), p. 171.

[38] On the topic of natural theology in the work of Gregory of Nyssa (and the Cappadocians in general), see Pelikan (1993).

part of humanity, the **will** *emanates* from God (the Neoplatonic flavor of the term "emanates" here is not unintentional). According to Maximus – and here, it seems to me, he is over-extending the 'transference of natures' doctrine of Athanasius and company – the Incarnation of Christ the Logos would have occurred whether or not humanity fell into sin.[39] In other words, the purpose of God's creation was/is to manifest Himself objectively, in the Hegelian sense of *thought thinking itself.* Maximus believed that human existence is merely a function of the divine mind; theories of fate, determinism, astrology, etc., are given free reign here, as we find in later Byzantine intellectuals such as Photius, Psellus, and others, who in their various ways sought to correct Maximus (and his monastic successors), but succeeded instead in planting the seeds of the Renaissance.[40]

[39] Thunberg (1985), p. 74; also, Moore (2005), pp. 153-154.

[40] On this topic, consult Tatakis (2003), Chapters 3 and 4; and Woodhouse (1986).

ERIUGENA, EMERSON AND THE POETICS OF UNIVERSAL NATURE

Willemien Otten

I. Nature and Creation in Eriugena

I A. Christian Creation or Platonic Cosmos

In reading the early-medieval, Christian-Neoplatonic author John Scottus Eriugena (approx. 810-877 CE) we seem to encounter a mind that at first sight falls more into the Greek than into the Latin Christian tradition, as an integral part of which his thought is most often considered.[1] Clustered around nature as an overarching theme, the complex of Eriugena's ideas interrupts the steady flow of Latin medieval Christian thought developing from Augustine to Thomas Aquinas. With regard to the Christian nature of Eriugena's thought, the situation is obviously different from these more Christologically oriented thinkers, but the question is on what point exactly does he differ?

Among the aspects in which Eriugena's thinking stands out most, is the way in which God as creator moves and acts in and through creation. Whereas the act of *creatio ex nihilo* has also provided classic theological thinkers like Augustine and Thomas Aquinas with the firm underpinnings of their own concept of God as a transcendent divinity reigning supreme over the created world,[2] in Eriugena *natura* displays quite a different character. Its most striking feature is undoubtedly that being transcendent and immanent alike Eriugena's nature poses as a clear rival to God.

The priority of nature obviously causes serious problems when one attempts to assess Eriugena's thought as inherently or even predominantly Christian. Most scholars studying Eriugena detect a clear discrepancy between the Platonic and the Christian aspects of his work, which comes out most

[1] The difficult position of Eriugena is keenly reflected in the bifurcated analysis of his thought in Armstrong (1967). Here Eriugena is treated both under Part VI 'The Greek Christian Platonist Tradition from the Cappadocians to Maximus and Eriugena' and also under Part VII 'Western Christian Thought from Boethius to Anselm'.

[2] As an example one may point to Dupré (1991) 15-41, esp. 29-41, where Eriugena is surprisingly absent in a specific chapter on 'Classical and Medieval Antecedents'.

clearly in their analysis of creation.[3] The way in which the coming-into-being of Eriugena's system is most often found described is as follows. Through his reading of Greek patristic authors, Eriugena underwent the influence of Platonism, allowing it slowly but surely to encroach on his basic western (read: Augustinian) Christian tenets.[4] Adding substantial philosophical nuance and complexity to his thought, this influence brought him at the same time on the verge of heresy.

As an example we can point to the fact that his thought has long been seen as a kind of pantheism.[5] This charge, which rests on the supposition of a kind of convergence of nature and God, deprives Eriugena's nature of its dynamic outlook. As an inevitable result of this type of analysis, underneath and despite its bouncing jumble of images the Irishman's concept of *natura* cannot but make in the end for an entirely static whole.

The tradition of critical historical scholarship on Eriugena, which started in the 1930s with the seminal study of the Belgian scholar Maïeul Cappuyns, has clearly helped to lay such charges to rest. As a side effect that may not have been entirely unintended, he brought Eriugena back within the fold of non-heretical Christian thinkers or philosophers.[6] But there was a price to be paid as well. With the charges of pantheism having been neutralized, however, Eriugena's elaborate vision of nature became typecast instead as a conceptual monism, projecting an aura of 'natural' stiffness.[7]

I B. Eriugena's Idealism

In a move to focus more on nature's self-propelling development, philosophers have lately steered their researches on Eriugena in a different direction. They have been inspired in this by contemporary discussions about the end of western metaphysics and/or onto-theology as well as by the philosophy of postmodernism. In conjunction with these and other debates,

[3] A classic publication in this regard is Allard (1982). Allard argues that Eriugena has an interesting perspective on being as existence (as we can know that God is, *quia est*) by which he forges an idiosyncratic synthesis of Christianity and Neoplatonism and anticipates the later interest of Aquinas.

[4] For an appraisal of this genealogical approach, see Otten (1994).

[5] On the charge of pantheism, see Moran (1989) 84-89.

[6] See Cappuyns (1969). Critical scholarship on Eriugena has long been impeded by the fact that he was listed on the Index.

[7] Cappuyns (1969) 385 rejects the idea of an idealist or substantialist monism or of pantheist tendencies.

Eriugena has been branded before all as an idealist. The work of Dermot Moran has been especially important in furthering the idealist approach to Eriugena in a specific, post-Heideggerian way.[8] Here I want to draw attention to two different aspects concerning Eriugena's position as an idealist thinker.

The first aspect involves the definition of idealism itself. In contrast to modern philosophers like Bernard Williams and Miles Burnyeat, who claimed that idealism never emerged in antiquity, Moran follows scholars like Richard Sorabji and Werner Beierwaltes in holding that it did. We can indeed speak about idealism in antiquity and by extension also about idealism in the early Middle Ages, as in the case of Eriugena.

Moran's view can be summarized as follows.[9] As unfolding in the *Periphyseon* -for that *opus magnum* remains the centerpiece of any contemporary analysis of our Irish author- Eriugena's system reflects a kind of intellectualist immaterialism. Differing from modern idealism in a Berkeleyan sense, Eriugena's thought revolves around a theological consideration of the consequences of the doctrine of divine creation. Moran argues that the Greek patristic tradition, influenced by Middle and Neoplatonism, was inspired by a different sense of creation than the standard imposition of form on matter. Operative principle in Greek patristics was a sense of creation as theophany, an appearance of the divine, according to the underlying principle that "like comes from like". Having adopted and absorbed this theophanic tradition from the Greeks, Eriugena communicated it to the Latin West, elaborating divine creation as a kind of self-creation which should be understood as a kind of eternal self-intellection or self-thinking.

For Moran, then, Eriugena's thought presents us with a clear form of idealism:

> "Eriugena's extreme intellectualist immaterialism differs from modern idealism in that it is motivated not so much by *epistemological* consideration of skeptical arguments concerning the existence of the external world, but by *theological* consideration of the consequences of the doctrine of divine creation. ... [T]his Neoplatonic Christian idealism expressly emphasizes the paradigm of self-knowing or self-awareness as the founding, thetic, cosmic act. God's self-understanding is the prime mover in the creation of the universe, and in this sense, intellection precedes being. The result is a system far removed from the supposed realism of the ancients."[10]

[8] See Moran (1989) 282-287.

[9] See Moran (1999). See also Otten (2002) esp. 373-376.

[10] See Moran (1999) 54-55.

God apparently creates by understanding himself, a creative act of which humanity as *imago dei* is likewise capable. Against Burnyeat's view of monism as either materialism or atomism, Moran sees Eriugena's idealism pointing to an expression of unity-in-plurality.[11] In this way Moran subtly opens the door for an understanding of the cosmic process as profoundly dialectical, even though the universe reflects the movement of 'thinking the one'[12].

My second point involves Moran's attempt to insert Eriugena back into the philosophical tradition in which he had not fully been integrated before. Already in his important study *The Philosophy of John Scottus Eriugena*, Moran had considerably updated the Hegelian position of Eriugena as the beginning of true philosophy.[13] It was his achievement to argue that Eriugena's philosophy should not be interpreted solely as a hierarchical metaphysics of order.[14] Moving beyond Eriugena as a mere forerunner of German idealism,[15] however, be it of a Hegelian or a Heideggerian variety, Moran attempted to highlight the originality of Eriugena's specific brand of idealism. In his view Eriugena is ultimately a thinker whose reflections on the metaphysics of creation depart from what is conventionally viewed as onto-theological tradition. When discussing Eriugena's view of nature, his study thus adequately presents his concept of *natura* as a form of difference-in-identity, in the way I have commented on above.[16]

Moran's analysis of Eriugena's philosophical contribution represents a big step forward that should be duly appreciated, even if one does not agree on all counts.[17] In outstanding fashion Moran has made the transition from seeing Eriugena as an isolated episode in early medieval thought to showing his relevance for contemporary philosophical views and discussions.

Naturally there is always something to be desired. What I still find missing is a set of guidelines by which to draw in more structural fashion on Eriugena's own comments on and definition of of nature as a more direct way to help us in unlocking the *Periphyseon*'s entire dynamic system. I may

[11] See Moran (1999) 60. The wording here is a slight change from Moran (1989) 285, where he uses difference-in-identity. See below n. 16.

[12] Cf the title of Beierwaltes (1985), *Denken des Einen*.

[13] Cf. Moran (1989) 79-102 (chapter 6: Eriugena as philosopher).

[14] See Moran (1989) 282.

[15] On the connection between German idealism and Eriugena, see Beierwaltes (1994b) esp. 313-320.

[16] See Moran (1989) 285. See also above n. 11.

[17] See Otten (2002).

disagree with Moran on whether idealism is the most important notion to discuss in Eriugena, but that his ideas are deeply relevant is a conviction that Moran and I share. To highlight Eriugena's contemporary relevance, I will try to focus once again on his concept of nature. I will do so through the work of Stanley Cavell. After all, he has engaged in conversation with another historical thinker whose focus on nature has rightly become famous, namely Ralph Waldo Emerson.[18]

II. Cavell and Emerson

II A. Emerson's Attraction for Cavell

What attracts Cavell in Emerson is "his music," an ear for which he developed when he was listening to the *Etudes* of his contemporary Franz Liszt even though he was still unable to read the notes. Yet Cavell's decision to devote a study to Emerson springs from a far deeper, underlying philosophical desire. In an attempt to contravene the flatness of modern philosophical practice and engage the full human being, Cavell is eager to 'listen for Emerson's text.'[19] Cavell's respect for and attraction to Emerson's use of daily and ordinary language is indeed striking, as it seems rather anti-philosophical. But Cavell precisely wants to escape from routine professional philosophizing, as he attempts instead to create the terms and conditions for the doing of good philosophy. Cavell finds the key to both these goals, the critical and the constructive, in a deep and lasting sense of ordinariness, the ordinariness of life. Emerson represents to him the supreme master of seeing life as art. His grasp of the ordinary is exemplary in that his texts match life's very spirit.

Both Emerson and Thoreau are unique to Cavell in possessing what he comes to call an intimacy with existence, that 'nearness' that is lost and can only be retrieved by 'sitting at the feet of the ordinary and the low' as one's gurus. Question and answer are very close together, as Emerson's inquisitiveness about the ordinary is as striking as the answers it might possibly contain. "Give me insight into today, and you may have the antique and future worlds", he provocatively stated in *The American Scholar*. Elsewhere, in the earlier *Nature*, he said:

[18] See Cavell (2003).

[19] This is an allusion to a collection of historiographical essays entitled *Listening for the Text. On the Uses of the Past*, see Stock (1990).

> "Give me health and a day, and I will make the pomp of emperors ridiculous. The dawn is my Assyria; the sunset and moonrise my Paphos, and unimaginable realms of faerie; broad noon shall be my England of the senses and the understanding; the night shall be my Germany of mystic philosophy and dreams."[20]

Here Emerson seems to ridicule the value and validity of antiquarian knowledge *per se*, in much the same way as Nietzsche could relish in the art of forgetting, as marking the third and most critical form of doing history.[21] But Emerson pushes in fact even further than Nietzsche, who ultimately wants to alternate between all three forms, by seizing on the ephemeral more radically and more consistently. 'No education beyond a natural education,' seems to be Emerson's motto in this last quotation, that is, an education with Nature as one's guide. The role of Nature is very close to that of a conduit or a midwife here, aiding and assisting the self in being born. From this first step other steps bringing the human self to greater wisdom and maturity follow as a matter of course, but not without constantly drawing and building on the first. Elsewhere in *Self-Reliance*, Emerson succinctly but powerfully states, "We denote this primary wisdom as Intuition, whilst all later teachings are tuitions".[22] It is this intuition that Cavell wishes to uncover and understand in his close reading of Emerson.

It is especially the way in which Emerson thinks and the phraseology he uses that appear to be of key importance to Cavell. In explaining his own position, Cavell throws us subtle clues, indicating that Emerson's prose aspires to the self-containment known best from poetry.[23] The emphasis on this aspect of self-containment can also offer us a more precise insight into Cavell's admiration for Emerson. He appears to admire Emerson most for making the ordinary a vehicle for the full meaning of life. In line with this, Cavell's interest in how Emerson connects what happens casually to what creates a casualty can be seen as another way of his pointing out how drama for the latter is not revealed as dramatic but taken in as part and parcel of the ordinary.[24] This observation of a relation between casual occurrence and casualty compensates in part for the charge that Emerson lacks a sense of the

[20] See the essay *Nature* in Emerson (1903-04) 1: 17. Quoted in Cavell (2003) 21 and 25.

[21] Nietzsche ranks the critical form of doing history after the monumental and antiquarian forms, advocating the uses of all three. See Nietzsche (1967b).

[22] Quoted in Cavell (2003) 99. On self-reliance in Emerson, see Buell (2003) 59-106.

[23] See Buell (2003) 107-57 ('Emerson's Poetics').

[24] See Cavell (2003) 6; 201.

tragic, which his continental admirer Friedrich Nietzsche possessed in such abundance.

It is clear that Cavell is not interested in distinguishing between Emerson the transcendentalist and Emerson the pragmatist. Such a distinction lacks the subtlety to express the dynamism of the latter's thought. It is this dynamism, emanating from an ebullient sense of the ordinary, which so fascinates Cavell in Emerson. By broadening the interest in Emerson beyond the questions of transcendentalism and/or pragmatism, however, Cavell considerably broadens the matter of his philosophical importance. He not only reconnects him to history, in the vivid way evinced by Nietzsche's first impressions, but he also seems to want to bring him back to life.

To underscore the relevance of Emerson to Eriugena, I want to highlight two Emersonian features, both coming out of my reading of Cavell. The first of these involves the notion of "a certain intimacy with existence,"[25] with which Cavell accounts for the self-containment and self-reliance found in Emerson's texts. Rather than discrediting Emerson's descriptions of Nature for their supposed lack of philosophical abstraction, as their unusual concreteness may strike one as embarrassing, Cavell sees them as an attempt to trump philosophy's proclivity for abstraction. We may take a brief look at the following Emersonian statement:

> "The sun shines and warms and lights us and we have no curiosity to know why this is so; but we ask the reason of all evil, of pain, and hunger, and mosquitoes and silly people" (Journal Entry, August 18, 1831).[26]

The lightness and all-pervasiveness of Nature here, oscillating between deep theodicy and the daily dosage of ephemeral sunlight, to which the absurdity of silly people is added in Becket-like fashion, displays a remarkable upward mobility. Yet it is nonetheless true that the origin of Nature's dynamic self-manifestation to which it refers remains deftly hidden in the folds of her own robe. Underlying Emerson's self-containment is a deep paradox, whereby Nature constantly invites us to throw our curious and incidental glances at her, even as she herself hides as much as reveals her full self through these. It is as if Emerson only whets our appetite for the full self of Nature or life, which we can wholly savour but never actually taste.

[25] See Cavell (2003) 23, where he deems it fundamental to the experience of ordinary language philosophy.

[26] Emerson (1958) 46. Quoted in Cavell (2003) 7.

The second Emersonian feature that I wish to draw from Cavell's analysis is the idea of writing as "a dialogue with oneself".[27] While Emerson invites us throughout his writings to be in tune with ourselves, he also beckons us to be sensitive to Nature, thereby bestowing an authentic cosmic ring on the notion of the human self. Interaction with self and interaction with nature are intertwined for Emerson, while at the same time nature and self are truly opposite entities or modes of being. As a climactic result of this structural tension nature for Emerson appears at times to be endowed with near-divine authority, as in this rhetorical and elliptical statement in his essay on *Nature*, "All things with which we deal preach to us. What is a farm but a mute gospel?" Just as the gospel proclaims our salvation, in the same way Nature contains salvation within her own recesses. She merely needs a human ear to awaken her voice, after which she can reap her harvest by reeling us in.

As a philosophical process, or rather the process of doing philosophy, Cavell cannot fail to see the 'attunement' with Nature in Emerson as running ultimately parallel with the dialogue with oneself. The synchronicity of the inward turn needed for both forms a precondition for the joint redemption of nature and self, just as the landscape and its viewer can only exist side by side by admitting to their mutually dependence.

II B. Emerson's Relevance for Eriugena

The dialogue with oneself is apparently what Cavell deems contemporary philosophy to be in want of, judging a good reading of Emerson as most apposite. A deep interest in the common, the familiar, the near and the low attracts Cavell most in Emerson's philosophy. In a way this interpretation puts Emerson in the company of Wittgenstein and Austin, criticizing metaphysics as too speculative and engaging instead in the firm knowing of what can be known and should be embraced. What is important to Emerson – and as such appreciated by Cavell–, bringing him at the same time in a curious but interesting relationship of resemblance to the early Augustine, is the question of how to ward off skepticism.[28] Just as the early Augustine was so threatened by skepticism that he wrote his *Contra Academicos* to refute it

[27] What I mean by this dialogue is intimated by Cavell (2003) 46, where he speaks of Socrates' speaking as opposed to Plato's writing, and comments that…"philosophy begins only when there are no further texts to read, when the truth you seek has already been missed, as if it lies behind you. In the myth of totality, philosophy has still not found itself, at least until it has found you."

[28] On his affinity with Austin and Wittgenstein in his defence of proceeding in philosophy from ordinary language, see Cavell (2003) 21-22.

before being able fully to embrace the truth of Christianity, in the same way Cavell's Emerson is constantly on guard. In contrast to Augustine and closer to Eriugena, Emerson's fear is not the wholesale loss of truth but how to prevent life's dissipation or dissolution into artificial meaning and monumental truth.

In Eriugena, the idealism so appreciated by Moran can also be seen as a reflex against skepticism. By providing the vastness of nature with a firm foundation in the human mind rather than in a forensic act of divine creation, Eriugena forces himself to be on constant guard against illusions, including those about the world's transcendent origin. Perhaps Eriugena's idealism had better be called hyper-rationalism, as it is ultimately more about method than content. The same razor of dialectical rationalism also inspires his use of negative theology, as this method likewise allows him to criticize the production of idolatrous truths, including idealist truths. When for Eriugena Nature that does not create (*natura non creans*) outweighs in the end Nature that creates (*natura creans*), his aim is not to deny the reality of either nature or God. Putting it in Cavellian-Emersonian terms, one might say that such statements propel Eriugena in the direction of self-creation, as he is forced to engage in an ever-greater intimacy with self. The power to do so is such, that there is no escape from it once the dialogue is begun; the only route open to those who have set out on the path to God and to Nature is a firmer embrace of self. In my opinion it is the anthropological horizon of their conversation with nature and God that in the end unites Emerson and Eriugena.

In pursuing this comparison I want to take Cavell's comment seriously that Emerson internalizes the division between theology and philosophy into his building of edification by incorporating both in his idea of Man Thinking, issuing the drive for the concept of Onward Thinking.[29] In this way Emerson guarantees that a certain progress of the dialogue with oneself is made. Still, a few questions related to the insight into nature relevant for Eriugena and Emerson need to be answered. They relate to what Emerson calls 'self-reliance' and 'intimacy with the self' and what in Eriugena are seen as the 'omneity' or 'universality' of nature. If, as in Emerson's notion of self-reliance, there is an intuition of wisdom, then the tuitions that follow are mere applications, not deserving a central status and not helping one along in the dialogue. The sought-after intimacy with existence is thus at risk of being endlessly deferred, and self-reliance can mask therapeutic self-deception. In Eriugena, the omneity of nature is equally at risk of turning into a self-

[29] See Cavell (2003) 17 for a comparison with Heidegger's idea of thinking as a matter of getting ourselves "on the way".

defeating concept. For if it is true that God is present in all of nature, without assuming a pantheist thinning of his presence, there arises a real problem as to the 'own' essence or identity of Nature. Is it a creator-dependent object, is it an illusory reflection of divine power, or an idealist projection of the mind?

The answer to such questions brings us back to the Augustinian fear of skepticism, but also to the formative influence of Christianity on both Eriugena's and Emerson's thought. I will start with some comments about Cavell and Emerson, on my way to gain more insight into the early medieval Christian Platonism of Eriugena.

III. Eriugena and Emerson on the Poetic Universality of Nature

The difficulty with Eriugena's concept of nature is how to perceive it as non-static, non-monolithic, but equally a non-pantheist whole. Moran's answer is to see Eriugena's concept of nature as an idealist system in which the act of self-knowing is thetic, and God's creation is ultimately nothing but his self-manifestation through self-knowledge. Because of the importance of the viewer's perspective in all this, Moran regards Eriugena's ontology, derived as it is from a perceived idealist epistemology, ultimately as a *me-ontology*.

Seeing Eriugena's idealism likewise as a reflex against skepticism, but seeing this reflex more as a matter of method than content, I am not entirely satisfied with Moran's idealist labeling. In my view, the best option is to try and bring out the dynamism of Eriugena's concept of nature. It can give us the Intuition needed, to speak in Emersonian language, subsequently to understand the *Periphyseon*'s various ontological and epistemological forays. To illustrate where this might lead us, I will conclude this article by giving my own interpretation of Eriugena's deeply puzzling five modes of being and non-being found in the opening section of his major work. Let me first summarize the five modes of being and non-being, with comments added from Moran on each one. After that I will reflect on them from a Cavellian-Emersonian perspective.

III A. Eriugena's Five Modes of Being and Non-Being

At the beginning of the *Periphyseon* Eriugena divides nature into being and non-being; this is the first and central division of universal nature. In a further comment he explains that being is that what can be seen and understood by the human mind, while non-being is what transcends the human mind.[30] From this division of nature it is clear that God falls under the rubric of non-being for him, with non-being taken in a superessential rather than a privative sense, as he adheres to the Dionysian logic of negation due to divine excellence. Eriugena then gives us his fourfold division of nature as a *genus* into four *species*, for which he has become best known and which has overshadowed the importance of his earlier division into being and non-being. Nature proceeds from God as its origin (*natura creans et non creata*) through the primordial causes (*natura creans et creata*) and material creation (*natura non creans et creata*), only to return to God as its final goal (*natura non creans et non creata*).[31] After the fourfold division Eriugena then resumes his first and foremost division by explaining the phrase 'being and non-being', which serves as a synonym for the omneity of nature, in more detail. He does so by enumerating five different modes of interpretation of this division.

He explains these five modes of being and non-being in the following way. (1) The first mode of being and non-being roughly resumes the primary division mentioned above, with being more or less synonymous with being understood and non-being with transcendence of the understanding.[32] (2) The second division into being and non-being takes its point of departure in a hierarchical vision of reality, as the lower can be called non-being compared to the being of the higher and vice-versa.[33] (3) The third division makes a distinction between manifest, visible creation, indicated as being, and nature's invisible reasons and causes that are called non-being, because they have not yet been called forth to existence.[34] (4) The fourth mode, which he calls a

[30] See Eriugena, *Periphyseon* (PP) I, CCCM 161: 3 (441A): As I frequently ponder and, so far as my talents allow, ever more carefully investigate the fact that the first and fundamental division of all things which either can be grasped by the mind or lie beyond its grasp is into those that are and those that are not, there comes to mind as a general term for them all what in Greek is called *Physis* and in Latin *Natura*. NB. The English translation here and in the following notes is that of Sheldon-Williams in Eriugena (1978) 37-45.

[31] See PP I, CCCM 161: 3-4 (441B).

[32] See PP I, CCCM 161: 5 (443A).

[33] See PP I, CCCM 161: 6 (444A). For an affirmation concerning the lower (order) is a negation concerning the higher, and so too a negation concerning the lower (order) is an affirmation concerning the higher.

[34] See PP I, CCCM 161: 7 (444C-445A): The third mode can suitably be seen in those things of which the visible plenitude of this world is made up, and in their causes in the most secret folds of nature, which precede them. For whatsoever of these causes through generation is known as to matter and form, as to times and places, is by a certain human convention said to be, while whatsoever is still held in those folds of nature and is not manifest as to form or matter, place or time, and the other accidents, by the same convention referred to is said not to be.

philosophical one, seems to turn this third mode more or less upside down. Invisible nature is now seen as true being and spatio-temporal creation is referred to as non-being.[35] (5) The fifth mode, finally, seems to stand apart as it applies only to human beings. Humans have lost the dignity of being on account of their sin, Eriugena states in Pauline terms, as a result of which they are more truly said not to be than to be. Through the grace of Christ, however, they can be called back to being.[36]

Moran's analysis of these five modes is relatively clear and straightforward.[37] The first mode of interpretation of being and non-being is central as it reiterates the ontological primacy of knowing over being. Based as it is on epistemological criteria, it can hence be interpreted in an idealist way. The second mode of interpretation is of a hierarchical character and is confined to the realm of created being. Again, following Moran, we seem to be dealing with a perspectival approach to being here, even though it is one that destabilizes Eriugena's famous idealist definition of humanity as an eternal notion in the divine mind (*notio quaedam intellectualis in mente diuina aeternaliter facta*).[38] According to this second mode, one could say from the perspective of created being that humanity only is, as long as it is lodged as an idea in the divine mind, whereas from a divine perspective one would precisely then have to say that it is not, or vice versa. The third mode based on distinguishing actual from potential things seems close to the second. This mode also has an interesting side effect, on which Moran likewise does not comment. According to this mode universal human nature, insofar as it has not been totally realized, actually is not. This can bring it into conflict with the second mode, as according to this third mode only created human beings truly are, so that humanity as an eternal notion in the divine

[35] See PP I, CCCM 161: 7 (445BC): The fourth mode is that which, not improbably according to the philosophers, declares that only those things which are contemplated by the intellect alone truly are, while those things which in generation....are changed...are said not to be truly....

[36] See PP I, CCCM 161: 8 (445C): The fifth mode is that which reason observes only in human nature, which, when through sin it renounced the honour of the divine image in which it was properly substantiated, deservedly lost its being and therefore is said not to be; but when, restored by the grace of the only-begotten Son of God, it is brought back to the former condition of its substance in which it was made after the image of God, it begins to be, and in him who has been made in the image of God begins to live.

[37] See Moran (1989) 217-228.

[38] See Moran (1989) 208-11. See also Moran (1999) 77. The passage is found in PP IV, CCCM 164: 40 (768B).

mind is not. The fourth mode lends itself best for an idealist interpretation; it is explicitly called 'philosophical'. Only intelligible things are seen as totally real and temporary existence is considered the equivalent to non-being. Finally, the fifth mode is entirely anthropological and subscribes to a more theological or moral interpretation of being.[39]

III B. An Emersonian Reading of the Five Modes of Being and Non-Being

From the above descriptions it is clear that it is quite a task to make an ordered and rational whole from these different modes of interpretation and Moran's idealist, *me-ontological* approach seems only partially successful. The problem that I have with Moran's position is that not all Eriugena's modes of interpretation can be used as instances of an idealist reading. As an alternative, I here want to put forth the thesis that these five modes of interpretation are to be read as a symphonic, non-exhaustive way of 'listening' to nature, seen somehow as the sum total of being and non-being. I will try to demonstrate below in a Cavellian-Emersonian way how I think one can see the five modes as different musical chords. Striking these chords makes us each time hear the whole of nature, or rather, makes us each time hear nature as a whole, thereby enriching rather than exhausting the very polyphony of this concept. The main difference between my Emersonian reading and Moran's idealist reading lies in the fact that the former puts the emphasis squarely on nature itself, rather than on the matter of its being understood. In my reading I deliberately approach nature as an open-ended and dynamic concept, a principle almost *sui generis*, the inexhaustibility and self-generative character of which is ultimately not a product of the human mind but gives birth to both mind and reason. This is what I see signified by the five modes of interpretation in which the collective whole of being and non-being can be divided.

Rather than following Moran in seeing intellection as preceding being, therefore, leading us into the quandary of nature's seeming contradictions, I am struck by the fact how the tension between being and non-being becomes totally elevated in nature. In the same way the division between God and mind is sacrificed, without causing nature to relapse into pantheism. What remains is nature's functionality as a dynamic principle, a principle of onwardness, as the dialectic between being and non-being, and between creation and non-creation, is ultimately that which makes time pass by for us.

[39] See Moran (1989) 225-26.

In my reading then the *first* mode of being and non-being is what sets God and humanity apart as co-creators and co-interpreters of nature, putting both in a separate category on account of their excellence of understanding. Thus negative theology and negative anthropology join hands indeed. Consequently, all being other than God and humanity must be shadowy being, not by being inferior but rather by being translucent, i.e., receptive to rational understanding. For me the *second* mode does not bring out the aspect of hierarchy as much as it reflects an affirmation and incorporation of the lower orders of nature by the higher ones, and vice versa. Affirmation and negation are thus found locked in a mutual embrace, one that brings on their intimacy with existence in an ever-tighter way. The *third* mode celebrates creation as a temporal manifestation of the divine, using nature's growth towards plenitude as a way to gain divine *pleroma*. This remarkable stress on the need for nature to unfold is understated in any idealist reading of Eriugena and has consequently given rise to the claim that he lacks a serious interest in history. Seen as creation, however, nature must be regarded as the historical self-manifestation of the divine. The *fourth* or philosophical mode draws on the distinction between Intuition and tuition, with the primordial insight separated from its material elaborations and applications.

The *fifth* mode, finally, brings the entire development of nature full circle, in a manner comparable to the unfolding of the fourfold division of nature into species ending with the supreme negativity of *natura non creans et non creata* (nature that does not create and is not created). Here it is not the movement of God but that of humanity that is emphasized. Whereas Moran puts this last division aside as moral and theological, as I myself did in *The Anthropology of Johannes Scottus Eriugena*,[40] I now tend to see it more in agreement with the other modes. Being the mirror image of the 'natural' understanding whereby the first mode characterizes divine and human forms of control, what is at issue in this final mode is the loss of dignity if our conversation with existence should fail. In that case we are forced to resort to the mediation and distance produced by rational forms of understanding, seen here as given to us by the grace of God. "It is very unhappy, but too late to be helped, the discovery we have made that we exist. That discovery is called the Fall of Man.",[41] so Emerson exclaims in Exp 3.75.20. Eriugena could have said the same. He definitely seems to have hinted at something similar, as the development of nature that had started with the first mode comes full circle with this fifth mode of being and non-being.

[40] See Otten (1991) 13.

[41] See *Experience* in Emerson (1903-04) 3, 75; cited in Cavell (2003) 120.

Further analysis may well help us to make the comparison between Eriugena and Emerson bear fruit also in other ways. Thus I hope that what has long been regarded as a far-away and distant Neoplatonic interlude in an otherwise considered stable tradition of orthodox Christianity[42] can through Emerson suddenly be brought to bear on the dynamics of the low and the ordinary, as applied to the Christian idea of creation. The chief contribution of the *Periphyseon*'s elaboration of creation does in my opinion not lie in its idealist perspective, but in the rich insight it gives us into Nature as God's way to help us with the passing of time, as that is after all what marks the existential human condition.

To conclude with a final Emersonian quote:

> "The secret of the illusoriness is in the necessity of a succession of moods or objects. Gladly we would anchor, but the anchorage is quicksand. This onward trick of nature is too strong for us: *Pero si muove*".[43]

[42] See also Otten (2006) (forthcoming).

[43] See *Experience* in Emerson (1903-04) 3, 55. Quoted in Cavell (2003) 12.

MARSILIO FICINO'S PLATONISM ON HUMAN-DIVINE KINSHIP AND ASSIMILATION

Mary Lenzi

The challenging and perennial problems of Platonism—*polypsychism* of cosmic and divine souls and gods; *polymorphous* metaphysics, religion, and cosmology; *tripartition* of the human soul; and *mind-body-soul triad* of the human being persisted well into the Italian Renaissance. Neoplatonists like Marsilio Ficino (1433-1499) clearly picked up the gauntlet for their times and worked through them in creating their Christian yet humanistic worldview and theology of the Florentine Renaissance. As inevitably for Ficino, the Neoplatonist, as for Plato (427-348 BC), faith in God, qua perfect Mind and Soul must save reason from its lifelessness, mortality, and ignorance. For reason cannot suffice to save humanity from itself, or from the throes of evil and injustice in the world and society.

Despite this religious resolution, requiring human virtues of faith, hope, and charity, Christian belief and practice must be founded upon the grace, justice, and mercy of God. These, combined with good works, purified wills and hearts (and the salvation afforded by Christ's death) provide the release and redemption that human souls necessarily desire, and for which humans live and bear all things in their earthly life. Human ensouled selves endure life-long change, motion, and activities to experience enjoining of their immortal souls with the heavenly unchanging divine in an afterlife.

First, this analysis of the cross-fertilization between Plato and Ficino manifests prominent common themes that require demonstration. These are their respective theories of the cosmos and the divine; divine and human virtues and happiness; human mortality and immortality of the soul; and divine transcendence of God's eternal soul and being. Second, through processes of assimilation—learning, mentoring, and modeling, both Plato's philosophy and Ficino's theology illustrate how humans may become more god-like and immortal in earthly life. Through communal life and shared beliefs in God, humans re-present communion with all souls in order to attain enlightenment and salvation in their afterlife. This analysis demonstrates that Ficino is truly a Neoplatonist. Ficino, following Plato, maintains that living a life devoted to philosophy and religion necessarily transforms humans, turning them from mortal embodied being to the personal immortality and happiness of their souls.

1 Kinship of all souls

For Ficino, theology is the *prisca* science and art of the divine in relation to the human, and for Plato metaphysics is the first philosophy of all being, human and divine. This classic Athenian philosopher-mentor and Florentine Renaissance philosopher-priest remarkably share the fundamental tenets of how human beings learn virtue and wisdom to achieve immortality and happiness of their human soul.[1] Due to a gift from the ruling Medici family, Ficino established a Platonic-like Academia in Florence beginning in 1462. In 1469, Ficino completed the first complete Latin version of Plato's dialogues in any Western language.[2] His chief philosophic work is *Theologia Platonica* (*Platonic Theology*, 1469-1474). Here Ficino examines the moral psychology and spirituality of the immortal soul in terms of Plato's philosophy on behalf of explaining Christian theology.

Natural human awe and wonder about divine immortality is nourished and perfected by communal living, education, and social, moral support. Such community leads the soul to higher truths and greater faith in the pure, absolute objects of philosophy and theology. These objects are divine, unchanging Being, the sun-like Being of all beings, called the "One," "Good," or "God." For Plato such truth is informed by reason, and a supporting faith in the rational process of philosophy itself. For Ficino, reason must be framed within the Christian faith, God's supernatural revelation brought to humanity through the life and teachings of Jesus Christ. Humans come to know truth through their reason. Reason is like "a divine light" that God implants in the human soul when it is created:

> In things, it is the nature or Form of each thing.... Truth is ...
> both a physical condition and a mental image.[3]

Ficino adopts Plato's analogy of the Sun and the Good from the *Republic*, yet he must alter this relation for Christianity. Reasoning reveals certain divine truths, without direct religious revelation:

> The *ratio* can find no Truth in the ... mutability of humanity,
> but only in divine essence.[4]

Reason alone is an insufficient human instrument to approach divine essence. Additionally, greater insight and intuition must accompany human reason, and these comprise the divine gifts from God to human beings, which lead them to ascend to god-like personal immortality in their afterlife.

[1] See Copenhaver and Schmitt (2002); Allen (2002).
[2] In 1473, Ficino was ordained as a Dominican priest.
[3] Rice (1958): 83.
[4] *Ibid.*, 83-84.

Ficino compares God and the Sun to the mind and the eye, and in *Platonic Theology* he calls "the Good" "Creator," that is, the "Shaper of the soul."[5] But how so? Perhaps if generally conceived, the divine mind, and its essences, forms, and ideas are the shapers of matter, which, in turn, are moved and made moveable by Soul, and countless, particular souls. Only when taken together and set in motion by souls may these general abstractions mirror all being in the universe and hence in humanity.

To understand how human-divine kinship of souls can exert such significant influence over one's personal internalization of reason and virtues, again, Ficino follows Plato: Both are firm believer in the power of images and of the human imagination in shaping human character and virtues. They find the image of the cosmos unfolding the different layers of the divine before the human eyes and mind. Significantly, the Greek word "cosmos" indicates both the beauty ('adornment') and rational order of the cosmos, and beauty and order naturally attract humans.

Love of 'Beauty' and 'Goodness,' and 'Love of God' are the intertwining motivations causing the human soul to make the ascent from its mortal life to immortality. Human admiration of the beauty of the cosmos can further lead to either (a) increasing admiration of the source of its beauty and rational order, as in the divine activity of Plato's Rational World Soul in *Laws X*, or (b) increasing personal internalization of the God of Christianity and divine Ideas. Ultimately, such admiration and internalization lead to the emulation of their divine activity in one's particular soul.

Ficino's hierarchy of beings is, however, unique in distinction from his predecessors, including Plato. Ficino's system presents five basic beings: (1) God; (2) Angels (Minds); (3) Rational Soul(s), namely, human; (4) Quality; (5) Body or Matter, divisible and extended in space and time. Soul is the greatest or most important being, because it is an "Intermediary" placed in the center of all being, and combining all things.[6] Hence, soul encompasses powers and moving forces, though in different degrees and proportions, in and through all reality.

Most novel, then, is Ficino's overturning of the typical Neoplatonist hierarchy, by his making humanity (rational souls) the center of the whole scheme of being. God is at the top, supreme in the genus of Being, full of infinite Goodness. With God at the top, the descending order (of beings) would be angels; souls; celestial spheres; species of animals; plants; minerals, down to shapeless prime matter.[7]

[5] Allen and Rees (2002): 215.

[6] Copenhaver and Schmitt (2002): 149-150.

[7] Allen and Rees (2002): 215.

In close agreement with the late dialectic and theology of Plato, Ficino maintains that the cosmos and the whole must be a dynamic, living unity, as an ensouled being. Ficino revived the Platonic doctrine of a World Soul in *Timaeus* and *Laws*. Ficino conceived the World Soul as an "Idol" or Image, which projects itself onto the World Body as onto a mirror.[8] Ficino's cosmology and philosophy are derived from Platonic theses of the soul's immortality and its centrality in the universe. Soul is the only being in the middle between the abstract realm of Ideas and the physical world. Being so makes soul the intermediary between human and divine being and realities. All things beneath God are but single, particular things, but the soul can truly be said to be all things.[9] Thus, soul can be considered the center of creation, the middle term of all things in the universe, and above all, the binding, joining center of the universe.

This special centrality of soul in the universe made humanity the most dignified of all objects of God's creation. Ficino's unique emphasis on such human dignity was drawn more from Renaissance Humanism than from Platonic religious views of the human person. Ficino believed and taught that the purpose of human life was contemplation, and active, loving engagement with truth, immortality, and God. The ultimate goal of human life was to be reunited with God in the immortal afterlife of the human soul. To realize this goal, according to Ficino, one must contemplate divine essences and God in a monastic life style.

At first, the human mind removes itself from its attachments, and from the externalities of the physical world, in order to reflect upon abstract ideas concerning knowledge and the inner being of soul. As one's mind and soul ascend toward such increasing abstraction, knowledge, and insight, a human being eventually reaches a point where it can arrive at an unmediated vision of God. However, this last stage could occur only after death, in the immortality that only the morally deserving soul would enjoy in the beatific vision of God.

2 Human-divine assimilation processes: platonic love; Christian community

The idea and processes of assimilation lie at the core of Ficino's philosophy and of human spiritual life. In articulating how human beings may assimilate to the divine, Ficino revived and newly envisioned Plato's

[8] *Ibid.*, 72.

[9] *Platonic Theology: Volume 2* (2002-2003): Bk. V.

vision of love. In fact, Ficino coined the term 'Platonic love,' and believed he perfected Plato's vision of the erotic love of philosophy through love (*philia* and *agape*) in Renaissance Christianity. In a word, 'friendship' united the members of Ficino's *Academia*, in the spiritual, contemplative community of like-minded '*complatonici*.'

At the social and interpersonal level, God is the bond uniting two or more humans in love and friendship as much as their souls' ascent toward God unifies any individual human (rational and willing) soul. Through the community and society of church and state, Ficino struggled with the paradox of contemplation: An individual is not merely in a personal search of prayerful solitude, but necessarily also an active participant in a social community of learners and believers. His resolution appears to be that the spiritual relationship between God and the human individual is forged through contemplation, being re-presented and co-created in friendship or love with other persons and the broader society. This relationship, for Ficino, constituted authentic spiritual, 'Platonic' love. When interpersonal love and spiritual relationships in friendship mirror the love of God, then friends attain the highest type of loving human friendship. Again like Plato, Ficino did not reject human sexuality and erotic love, but instead insisted 'Platonic love' was to be found in non-sexual, spiritual relations of friendship.

Overall, to comprehend Ficino's Neoplatonist resolution for Christianity, one must recall that Plato's philosophy investigated the *psyche*, the *polis*, and the gods. Platonic gods were the measure of humanity, and the soul immortal, but society, by means of its government and system of education vitally enables humans to interrelate and participate in the divine, immortal life and virtues of the gods. The soul's transformation and assimilation from human embodiment to its pure divine immortality is achievable through Platonic and Christian love and friendship (*agape*). One forges this friendship in a community of seekers and believers whose central motivation is provided by relations of likeness and kinship with others. Further, through images, representations, and microcosma (concerning psyche, polis, and the heavens), one may find increasing understanding of the macrocosmic reality that reflects divine beauty, love, goodness, and God.

Above all, the modeling and mentoring of human learners and believers occur by means of human and divine intermediaries. These are prophets, angels, saints, heroes, and great teachers. Socrates, Plato, Jesus, and Ficino himself are indispensable, because they represent messengers of the Gods. Through such mentors, together with the person's inner guide (*daimonion*, guardian angel, or one's conscience), humans can increasingly participate in the truths of reason and faith, and in the goodness and justice of God.

In training the soul for virtuous immortality and happiness, three frameworks for mentor-pupil relationships of kinship and assimilation are paramount: 1. Platonic philosophy; 2. Christian theology; 3. Theurgy (divination, prophecy, rituals, and even magic). These three also indicate paths that turn and enlighten the human soul toward the divine. All entail social, moral education of the mind, body, and soul through abstract reasoning, dialectical dialogue, symbolism, and ritualistic practices in community. As such learners and acolytes, humans develop and extend their souls toward enlightenment and immortality.

1. Philosophy serves to loosen, and eventually free the bonds of the human soul (psyche) from its body. Through training the mind and human motions, the soul approaches enduring forms and ideas. It accomplishes its purpose by increasingly abstracting from the embodiment of divine forms in particular, divisible, things of matter—extended in space and time, toward increasing participation in the unchanging divine and divine beings. This assimilation process of learning, for Plato, gradually abstracts and purifies the mind and soul from its bodily existence through the disciplines of mathematics, astronomy, cosmology, music, logic, and dialectic. The person eventually learns how to live for immortality—the soul's condition and value of loving truth forever.

2. Theology aims to instill greater faith and understanding of God through religious practice and devotion. For Ficino, the conversion and transformation of the human soul toward immortality (eternal happiness and goodness) occur through rituals, prayers, beliefs, and active practice of God's revealed words, Christ's teachings, and Church doctrines. These teachings and methods rechannel the soul's experience from lower to higher states of consciousness, purifying the human soul from sin (ignorance and weakness) in its sensible embodiment, to purer light, wisdom, and greater strength of mind, character, and soul.

3. Theurgy—magic, charms, ritualistic cures, astrology, and divination were widely practiced in Ficino's Renaissance times and society as much as in Plato's classical Greek world. The human soul, according to Ficino, possesses prophetic powers. These must be trained and harnessed in "doing divine work" (*theurgia*) in the soul's ascent from its mortal to immortal life:

> Platonic philosophy concealed an [esoteric] theology; that Plato used allegory [poetic expression] to hide theological mysteries.[10]

[10] Copenhaver and Schmitt (2002): 156.

Only special interpreters (lovers, poets, priests, and prophets) rapt in an ecstasy, and made divine through direct inspiration can commune with God. Ficino's belief and teaching of divination conveys this humanist paradox of joining scholastic, monastic contemplation with Dionysian exuberance, Platonic eroticism, and Renaissance magic and rituals.

3 Soul in motion, transformation, and ascent to immortality

As necessary background for Ficino, one notes that Plato's dialogues build upon a psychological motivational foundation to provide the full account of the interactive reality of all being and souls (human/cosmic/ divine). The overarching Good, the One, or Gods are manifest in the beauty, symmetry, and truth of reality. Only the divine beings of cosmic Mind (*Nous*), the Rational World Soul, and Gods possess absolute virtue and justice. Human beings can strive to be god-like in the course of their soul's embodied existence by understanding such (cosmic, divine) Gods well enough to emulate them and model their ways in their earthly life to the greatest degree possible. Thereby, their human soul may attain true immortality.

Typically, Plato underpins moral, social, and political theories with philosophic insights and scientific intuitions in which cosmic, divine entities, laws, and gods are deemed necessary to move, explain, and sustain all life and reality. In its generic meaning, soul comprises 'all soul' ('*pan psyche*' in *Phaedrus* 245c5), and, in particular, each soul, human and divine. The shared nature and resemblance of all souls thereby make soul the controlling and regulating factor of all motions, including human emotions, motivation, action, and behavior (*Laws* 904a6-10). Plato's accounts of soul are clearly taken up by Ficino, and may also be seen as precursors for Freudian and modern psychology of motivation in the human personality and character.

Specifically, one finds this human-divine kinship in the nature of their souls as self-movers: Only human beings and Gods possess such souls. Plato draws a clear metaphysical distinction between two basic types of movers and motions as the 'not self-moving' and the 'self-moving.' Primary motion is that of soul, the principle form of life, as a self-moving being. All other motion is secondary, that is, motions of non-living, unsouled forms of being or things are derivative and dependent upon ensouled living beings, whose souls move them and other soulless beings and things.

We turn now to Plato's texts that support the above-mentioned background for Ficino's Neoplatonism.

In detailed accounts of the self-moving nature and immortality of soul (*Phaedo*; *Phaedrus*; *Laws X*) Plato argued: Soul is the principle of life and motion. The essence of soul entails it is in everlasting self-motion. Hence soul is immortal. Yet his account in the *Phaedo* was subject to logical difficulties (105b-107b). There Plato presented several arguments for the immortality of the human soul, which attempt to demonstrate that soul and death are mutually exclusive. He argued that soul is the principle of life, a principle of life cannot admit of death, and thus the soul must be immortal (105c-106d).

As background, Plato could not provide a doctrine of the immortality of the human soul easily or exclusively in a convincing logical deduction (*Phaedo* 85c-d), and resorts back again to his notion of *anamnesis* or recollection in the *Meno*. Yet this rationale may only require that the soul existed before its association with a body, not necessarily after its bodily existence (*Phaedo* 77a-c). It seems easier to accept Plato's view that the soul as an *archai* or fundamental principle of motion and life entails its immortality, as a principle can be indestructible, than his view that the essence of the human soul necessitates its immortal existence. For, it is difficult to prove that the human soul is truly extricable from its existence in the human body.

In clearer common ground with Ficino's theories, Plato's maxim 'like is to like' better serves the purposes of Renaissance Neoplatonist Christianity. Here, one may postulate that Plato left the West with irresolvable ambiguities concerning the immortality of the human soul, which Ficino overcame or transcended through Christianity. The maxim illuminates a fundamental principle of Plato's religious investigation throughout his dialogues, that virtue and law represent a person's "assimilation" to personal Gods (*Laws* 716c1-d3). The "kinship" (*sungeneia*) between humans and Gods also prominently figures in *Laws* (899d4-900a9) and *Republic* (366c1-d6). One part of this assimilation process requires that an individual view oneself not only as a citizen of a State, but also as a member of the cosmos; thereby one realized more fully the pertinent cosmic affinities and duties.

However, for Plato and Ficino alike, a significantly social aspect to religion must persist (manifesting itself in frequent religious festivals and worship), because religion is tightly intertwined with the aims of the good state. Hence, the other central aspect of the assimilation process requires that one view the earthly state, like the individual, as an integral part of the cosmic community, for the state too must partake of assimilation to the divine, cosmic community. This legacy of close theological-political association is wholeheartedly taken up in Renaissance Italy with its interlocking Catholic Church and State.

Similarly, for Ficino, sharing in the life of God is sustained in an informal Christian community of friends, not from Florence alone, but also from the greater European community of believers and seekers of divine wisdom and insight

4. Purposes and outcomes of human-divine assimilation

In philosophy and religion, the use of myth and imagery convey basic moral tenets. In the case at hand, the tenet is that the moral condition of the person's soul determines the character and the nature of one's immortal soul in its afterlife. For instance, Plato often resorts to religious myth-making to explain the soul's immortality, and this move requires some explanation. Sometimes his myths portray the cycles of reincarnation of the immortal human soul. In the *Phaedo* Plato playfully portrays the souls of socially minded people as being reincarnated in ants and bees (82b), as this image makes it more transparent how the inner nature of one's soul determines the kind of life one has. The *Myth of Er* is an especially adorned, detailed account of this notion. Plato portrays human souls as freely choosing their next life, and the three Fates, working a cosmic spindle of Necessity, irrevocably spin the yarn that seals the fate each soul has chosen (*Republic* 617e1-621d3).

In his last work, *Laws*, Plato's mythologizing of the immortal soul becomes more abstract, less of a story, and more logically schematic. He states that God, acting in the role of the divine gamesman "draughts-player" shifts souls from place to place (*Laws* 903d5-10, 904e9-905a1, 728bff, 837a; *Theaetetus* 176d7-177a9). Even though Plato uses myths to portray the afterlife of the soul, the purpose of these stories is (arguably) to attempt a plausible account for the very different kinds of life that people choose to live on earth. His myths suggest that the goodness or badness of one's soul emerges from one's (voluntary) choices. Consequently, the nature of one's soul determines the quality of life, happiness, or misery on earth and beyond.

As a Christian Neoplatonist, Ficino overcomes and transcends conflicting Platonic conceptions of personal immortality of the human soul. As a Christian, Ficino readily constructs his doctrines of personal immortality quite differently, rejecting the notion of reincarnation, instead upholding the doctrine of God's unique creation of each human soul. This God-made human soul has but one earthly chance to attain its personal immortality after death, in its final separation from the human body, precluding the alternative Platonic account and possibility of reincarnation. Central to Christian doctrine, the human soul must connect and commune with God through perfecting one's love of God and other created beings in its single, earthly existence and trials.

In his Renaissance lifetime, Ficino's doctrines and practices still mirror for Christianity an underlying Platonic tenet—to be virtuous is to be like God. Only the attainment of virtue then could truly bestow immortality on the individual. This view explains why in the *Symposium* Plato argues that immortality is the ultimate aim of human eros or love:

> So when one has begotten a true virtue and has reared it up one is destined to win the friendship of heaven; ... [this one], above all humans, is immortal (212-213).

As virtues represent the excellence proper both to the human soul and to God's divine soul (*Laws* 899d4-900a9), Plato maintains human virtue originates from and depends upon divine virtue:

> Justice and temperance combined with wisdom, dwell in the animate powers of the gods, and of which some small trace may be clearly seen also residing in us (906a9-b4).

By regulating in oneself the varying revolutions of passion and reasoning, a person imitates, that is, becomes assimilated to the absolute and unchanging revolutions of God (*Timaeus* 46e9-47e3). By so doing, a human becomes virtuous and "dear" (*philein*) to God (53d10-e1), and thereby "shares in immortality" (*metexein ... athanasias*) (90c-d). Perhaps, then, Plato's recurring myths of immortality represent a sustained attempt to explain this kinship and assimilation process. In other words, in its pre-existence, the human soul and mind has originally experienced and can again revive its immortal life, clearly apart from the body. It can regain its original vision of this higher, divine reality through its mortal bodily existences or reincarnated embodiments (*Republic* 500b-d).

This belief that cosmic, divine "friendship" (*philia*) necessarily binds the cosmos together (*Timaeus* 32c1-5; *Symposium* 186a-188b), becomes mirrored in human social and spiritual bonds of friendship that bind human beings in society, and thereby human beings to God. In particular, Christian love of others, as in *agape*, manifests the proposition to 'love thy neighbor as thyself.' This love, namely, Ficino's Platonic-Christian sort is the psychic glue binding Ficino's wide reaching religious communities of diverse sorts of individuals—priests, nuns, monks, princes, and diplomats in Italy and throughout Europe, convening to pursue the theology of the Christian faith, as argued here, as a perfected form of Platonic cosmic-theology.[11]

Therefore, for Neoplatonist Christians in their ascent toward immortality and communion with God, and, for Platonists, toward perfect Goodness, Beauty, and Truth, interpersonal paths of individual human souls become necessarily intertwined in Plato's philosophy and Christian religion in these ways and means:

(1) shared desire in loving and pursuing wisdom of the following:

[11] Copenhaver and Schmitt (2002): 144; 154.

(a) Unchanging, divine, immaterial Forms and Ideas in connection with the Good and the One (respectively identified in Plato's *Republic* and *Parmenides*);

(b) Divine Mind, Psyche, World-Soul, Demiurge (*Laws* and *Timaeus*);

(c) Gods (*Laws X*).[12]

(2) Life-long assimilation process of learning these forms of immortality and divinity through philosophy and theology.

In this inquiry, the life of philosophy and religion has been presented in different varieties:

(a) dialectical learning, modeling, and mentoring;

(b) reasoning, believing, and learning with like-minded souls and friends in community;

(c) mystical spiritualism, rituals, magic, divine and prophetic revelation;

(d) philosophical and religious beliefs and practices, with a faith that transcends the bounds of reasoning.

As the foregoing analysis implies, the soul's self-motion becomes its most positive attribute: It sustains the soul's earthly striving to be immortal in striving to be god-like in its ascending virtue, wisdom, and faith.

5. Ficino: Christ; Plato: Socrates

More world-historical instances of the human-divine kinship and process of assimilation are evident in the figures of Plato's Socrates and Ficino's Christ. Socrates calls himself a "gift from the god" (*theou ... dedosthai*) (*Apology* 31b1). So too Ficino claims Socrates is a Christ-like figure, or the prefiguring of Jesus Christ, because Socrates and Christ were both founders of great theories and radically alternative ways of living, namely philosophy, and the universal religion of Christianity.[13]

Without their 'midwifery' and ultimate self-sacrifice for the Good of humanity, or for the glorification of God, humanity would be irredeemable, in profound ignorance, caught in the stain of 'original sin' that marks their fallen souls in the lower realm of their being, cast only in their discrete, individual mortal existence. Divine work, training, practice, and deeds are needed to lead souls to their immortal afterlife prepared, purified, redeemed to reap the rewards of the soul's original nature, before the Fall, and original human sin. Alternatively, for Platonists, this was the soul's condition before its descent to mortal life in bodily frame, in the course of its reincarnation(s).

[12] Lenzi (1997): 234-36.

[13] Allen and Reese (2002): 84-85.

Human beings, precisely because they possess immortal souls in mortal bodies caught up in a physical, developmental existence, need guides, inward and outward forces and beings—spirits, angels, daemons, and personal mentors. These guardians move them upward through mental reasoning, religious faith, and philosophical or ritualistic spiritual practices, walking them through the steps on the way to higher being, toward the supreme light of truth, goodness, and God. The life and teachings of such divinely inspired or simply divine intermediaries, their love and care for the souls of others, in selflessness and martyrdom transform human souls. Otherwise, humans would not know why or how to be released, nor how to become capable of lifting themselves up toward the light of the Sun, the truth and being of Forms and God to participate in the immortality of their own personal, disembodied soul.

Whether prophetic teacher, friend and (Platonic) lover, priest, and fellow-follower, their individual greatness in petitioning for the salvation of human souls, and their guidance, their prayers, teachings, and sacrifice would be in vain without abiding faith in higher divine powers of divine beings, be they Forms, Minds, World Souls or the Christian God. Even it these conditions obtain, still they would not suffice without Fortuna or the grace of God.

Fittingly this analysis ends with Ficino's mysticism and reliance on direct, inner experience and inquiry:

> [By] purifying itself from things external, the soul enters the contemplative [scholastic] life and attains a higher knowledge, discovering the … (immaterial) or intelligible … closed to the human soul while … in ordinary experience and in the troubles of the external life (of the human body). [The gradual ascent of the human soul] culminates in the immediate knowledge and vision of God.[14]

The soul accomplishes its ascent by developing its two wings—intellect and the will, desirous of immortal life experiencing complete virtue, wisdom, and happiness only in the vision of God (Ficino's *Letters, I*: 174). Ficino emphasized the superiority of will and love over mind and reason, because, as a Neoplatonist, he believed that true bliss comes from the soul's enjoyment of the beatific vision and ultimate goodness of God, and this condition of the immortal human soul transcends reasoning and intellect.

[14] Kristeller (1964): 44.

THE PLACE OF THE UNIVERSE: SCIENCE AND PLATONISM IN COPERNICUS' *DE REVOLUTIONIBUS*

Gina Zavota

Opinions concerning the extent to which Nicholas Copernicus was influenced by Platonic and Pythagorean thought are widely varied. While some authors seek to distance Copernicus' astronomical innovations as much as possible from these philosophical schools, and to downplay the references to philosophy in his texts, others have explored possible lines of influence in great detail. However, much work still needs to be done before a clear picture of Copernicus as both a Platonist and a leading figure of the Scientific Revolution can emerge. Some of the most interesting questions concern his motivation for positing a heliocentric model of the solar system in the first place, as well as the epistemological status of his claims. On the one hand, it has been suggested that Copernicus is simply trying to "save the phenomena," that is, to account for the perceived motions of the planets, sun and moon without any regard for whether his explanations correspond to empirical facts. On the other hand, writers such as Edward Grant have argued that Copernicus'

> remarkable break with the medieval tradition is not to be found in the arguments [he] gave in support of a diurnally rotating earth . . . but in the insistence by Copernicus that the earth really and truly has a physical motion and in the methodological rationale which emerged from this profound belief.[1]

What I would like to suggest is that neither of these positions truly captures the kind of claim Copernicus is making when he says, for instance, that the Earth is in motion. Copernicus' innovations sprung from his dissatisfaction with both Ptolemaic astronomy and Aristotelian metaphysics, and his masterwork *De Revolutionibus Orbium Coelestium* [*On the Revolutions of the Heavenly Spheres*] is as much a response to the latter as to the former. Philosophy cannot be separated from science in his work; the two are closely bound together, and it is only through an understanding of his metaphysical commitments that we will be able to gain insight into the genesis of his scientific innovations. In particular, his claims result not only from observation and computation, but also from a search for the harmony and beauty that he knows must be present in the world.

[1] Edward Grant, "Late Medieval Thought, Copernicus, and the Scientific Revolution," *Journal of the History of Ideas* 23, 2 (1962): 212.

Before proceeding, it is important to point out that any separation of the influences on Copernican thought into those deriving from Aristotelian science on the one hand, and those stemming from Platonic or Pythagorean cosmology and metaphysics on the other, is of necessity somewhat artificial. In Copernicus' day, no such clean division would have existed, for at least two reasons. Firstly, Aristotelianism had undergone a significant transformation in the centuries following Aristotle's death, due in large part to the work of medieval Christian and Muslim Neoplatonists who had sought to harmonize Platonic and Aristotelian thought. Thus Aristotelian models for scientific inquiry in the Renaissance were themselves quite Neoplatonic in many important ways, as we shall see over the course of this inquiry. In addition, the predominant intellectual style of the Renaissance was broadly synthetic in nature, oriented much more toward harmonizing various seemingly contradictory bodies of knowledge or belief than toward drawing dividing lines between them. Thus, while I will tend to treat Platonism and Aristotelianism as if they were easily distinguishable schools of thought, in order to clarify my analysis, this should not be taken as an accurate depiction of the way in which Copernicus himself would have experienced the ideas discussed here. Nevertheless, it will serve as a useful mechanism for exploring the philosophical commitments that I believe shaped Copernicus' groundbreaking scientific innovations.

In this essay, I will restrict my comments to the Introduction and first ten chapters of Book I of *De Revolutionibus*, as well as the prefatory letter to Pope Paul III, as they contain a more general, nontechnical treatment of the subject, along with many of the most provocative philosophical statements in the text. Before beginning this analysis, however, a few words concerning Copernicus' hypothesis itself are in order. While most people are familiar with the general characteristics of his heliocentric model of the solar system, some lesser known details bear directly on the topic at hand.[2] When *De Revolutionibus* first appeared in 1543 – the year of Copernicus' death – Western astronomy was still dominated by geocentric paradigms based on that of Ptolemy. Seen against this backdrop, Copernicus' proposal was revolutionary in many ways. In addition to displacing the Earth from its customary position at the center of the universe, he correctly ordered the first six planets (including the Earth)[3] and placed them in motion around the sun.

[2] For a comprehensive, if somewhat technical, explanation of the mechanics of Copernicus' model of the solar system, see Noel M. Swerdlow and Otto Neugebauer, *Mathematical Astronomy in Copernicus's De Revolutionibus*, 2 vols. (New York: Springer, 1984).

[3] Only Mercury, Venus, Mars, Jupiter, and Saturn were known at the time.

He also posited, against Ptolemy, that the vault of the heavens, containing the distant or so-called "fixed" stars, was stationary. He did this in part to account for the phenomenon of retrograde motion, which occurs when planets seem to stop and reverse direction during their circuit of the heavens.[4] Retrograde motion was one of the problems that had prompted Ptolemy to include a series of epicycles and deferents in his model of the solar system, and later astronomers had gradually increased the complexity of his basic system over the course of subsequent centuries in order to account for various celestial phenomena.

Although Copernicus' dissatisfaction with geocentric astronomy motivated his own inquiries, his proposal does not represent a complete break with Ptolemy. Contrary to popular conception, Copernicus was not able to completely eliminate epicycles and deferents from his system. Furthermore, he was laboring under essentially the same conditions as those under which Ptolemy had worked more than 1,300 years earlier. No significant observational technologies or mathematical techniques that might have aided him had been developed in the intervening centuries – the first telescopes, for instance, did not appear until more than fifty years after his death. Thus Copernicus operated with data that were greater in quantity, but not so different in nature, than those used by Ptolemy. Interestingly, the practical value of the two systems is roughly equivalent; in both cases, the positions of the planets, Sun and moon can be accurately predicted around 99% of the time.[5] In effect, then, the two theories are equivalent from a mathematical perspective, and neither the computational techniques nor the technology of Copernicus' day were capable of determining which of the two more accurately represented physical reality.

Given this situation, then, what could have motivated Copernicus' adoption of a heliocentric model? One view, articulated for example by Michael J. Crowe in his *Theories of the World from Antiquity to the Copernican Revolution*, holds that the new system emerged from "aesthetic considerations."[6] If we are to entertain this possibility, however, we must first clarify what those considerations might have been. To begin with, there is

[4] That is, they appear to stop their usual west-to-east motion across the sky and to move from east to west for a short period of time. We now know that this appearance results from the fact that planets closer to the sun move more quickly than those further away from it. As a result, when Mercury or Venus overtakes the Earth, it appears to reverse direction when observed from a terrestrial position.

[5] See Michael J. Crowe, *Theories of the World from Antiquity to the Copernican Revolution* (New York: Dover, 1990) for a detailed explanation of this statement.

[6] Crowe 89.

elegance, an important concern for mathematicians and physicists since Plato's time. Nearly all astronomers would agree that calculating the positions of the planets is less cumbersome using the Copernican system, and that it gives a more unified expression to the regularities of planetary motion. Copernicus himself seems to acknowledge the importance of such considerations when he states that

> heaven itself is so linked together that in no portion of it can anything be shifted without disrupting the remaining parts and the universe as a whole.[7]

Given this conviction, it would be only natural for him to seek a theory that reflects this perceived harmony. While it could certainly be argued that the quest for greater elegance and unity is, in and of itself, a sufficient reason to develop a new model of the universe,[8] in this case there is more to be said. Although there is notoriously little evidence of *how* Copernicus devised his heliocentric system, several statements he makes in the introduction and the first book of *De Revolutionibus* provide insight into the specific reasons *why* he would have felt that his model represented an advance over Ptolemy's, despite its lack of predictive superiority. It is here that we will be able to see the role played by Platonic and Pythagorean thought in one of the greatest achievements in the history of Western science.

Copernicus makes reference to philosophy and various philosophers – most prominently Plato, Aristotle, and the Pythagoreans – frequently in the early chapters of *De Revolutionibus*. In his introductory letter to Pope Paul III, he attempts to explain his motivation for proposing a heliocentric theory – an idea which he claims grew out of his frustration with the lack of consensus among the astronomers of his day with respect to some central questions. Not only was there disagreement concerning the motions of the various planets, but the optimal methods for describing and calculating those motions were also open to debate. Finding this confusion unacceptable, Copernicus

> began to be annoyed that the movements of the world machine, created for our sake by the best and most systematic Artisan of all, were not understood with greater certainty by the philosophers.[9]

[7] Nicholas Copernicus, *On the Revolutions*, ed. Jerzy Dobrzycki, trans. Edward Rosen (Baltimore: Johns Hopkins UP, 1978), Preface.

[8] One only needs to become acquainted on a superficial level with the work of present-day particle physicists to see that elegance and uniformity still play an important role in discovery in the physical sciences.

[9] *On the Revolutions*, Preface.

By proposing various conflicting theories and methods, astronomers were thus not only doing a disservice to science, but they were also failing to properly acknowledge the beauty of God's creation. In order to remedy this situation, Copernicus turns to philosophical sources for guidance. Quoting Plutarch, he states that, given that Philolaus and other Pythagoreans held that the Earth was in motion, he too feels compelled to consider this position.[10]

Whether or not this is an accurate representation of how Copernicus came upon the idea that the Earth might be in motion, the fact that he chose to give this explanation is significant. It casts the entire work as a search for a fitting expression of the world's beauty and perfection; indeed, Copernicus begins his introduction with the question

> What indeed is more beautiful than heaven, which of course contains all things of beauty? . . . On account of heaven's transcendent perfection most philosophers have called it a visible god.[11]

While "most philosophers" may be something of an overstatement, Copernicus likely has in mind Hermes Trismegistus, whose statement to this effect he quotes later in Book I,[12] as well as Plato, who calls the created world "a blessed god"[13] in the *Timaeus*. Astronomy, he declares, is the highest art, given its lofty subject matter, which allows one to be immersed in "unremitting contemplation . . . and admiration for the Maker of everything."[14] Thus a conviction, bolstered by his reading of Pythagorean and Platonic philosophers, that the universe was designed with unity and beauty in mind – and that humankind's most elevated pursuit must be the attempt to understand this design – underlies his astronomical work and finds expression within it. This Platonic conviction, in turn, leads him to propose his heliocentric model. As Morris Kline states in *Mathematics in Western Culture*,

> [h]armony in the universe demanded a heliocentric theory and he became willing to move heaven and earth in order to establish it.[15]

[10] It is important to note that Copernicus' system was not simply a revival of that of Aristarchus or any other Ancient thinker known to us who posited a heliocentric cosmos. However much he may have been inspired by them, Copernicus suggests a model that is in many ways radically different from those of Greeks.

[11] *On the Revolutions*, Introduction.

[12] Cf. *On the Revolutions* I, 10.

[13] *Timaeus* 34b.

[14] *On the Revolutions*, Introduction.

[15] Morris Kline, *Mathematics in Western Culture* (New York: Oxford UP, 1953) 110.

Thus his goal in *De Revolutionibus* is not simply to "save the phenomena" of celestial motion, but to discern, so to speak, the truth of the matter. This truth, however, is not that of later empirical science, but rather the truth of Platonic cosmology and philosophy.

Copernicus does not begin by stating that the sun is in the center of the solar system. Instead, he first affirms that the universe is spherical. He gives several reasons for this choice of shape, among which are the fact that "of all forms, the sphere is the most perfect"[16] and because

> wholes strive to be circumscribed by this boundary, as is apparent in drops of water and other fluid bodies when they seek to be self-contained.[17]

Through the same reasoning, Copernicus concludes that the Earth and the other planets must also be spherical, and furthermore that the heavenly bodies move with a uniform, eternal circular motion:

> I shall now recall to mind that the motion of the heavenly bodies is circular, since the motion appropriate to a sphere is rotation in a circle. By this very act the sphere expresses its form as the simplest body, wherein neither beginning nor end can be found.[18]

This recalls, among other things, Plato's statement that the Demiurge

> made the world in the form of a globe . . . the most perfect and the most like itself of all figures, for he considered that the like is infinitely fairer than the unlike.[19]

Moreover, Copernicus insists that

> there is no difference between the Earth's centers of gravity and magnitude. . . land and water together press upon a single center of gravity.[20]

In other words, the point to which water, earth, and all other physical objects naturally tend is the same as the physical center of the Earth's bulk.

In making this last claim, Copernicus makes an important break with Aristotelian physics and metaphysics. In Book II of *On the Heavens*, arguing against the Pythagoreans and others who held that fire, not Earth, occupies the center of the universe, Aristotle had asserted that

[16] *On the Revolutions* I, 1.

[17] *On the Revolutions* I, 1.

[18] *On the Revolutions* I, 1.

[19] *Timaeus* 33b.

[20] *On the Revolutions* I, 3.

> [t]hey hold that the most important part of the world, which is the center, should be most strictly guarded, and name it, or rather the fire which occupies that place, the 'Guard-house of Zeus,' as if the word 'center' were quite unequivocal, and the center of the mathematical figure were always the same with that of the thing or the natural center. But it is better to conceive of the case of the whole heaven as analogous to that of animals, in which the center of the animal and that of the body are different.[21]

In other words, according to Aristotle the organizational center of an entity – its animating force, such as the brain of a human being – is not necessarily the same as its center of gravity or its geometrical center. Thus in his geocentric system, while the Earth's center of gravity was identical with that of the universe as a whole, the metaphysical or "natural" center of the world was located in the sphere of the fixed stars. This outermost shell of the universe was the most ontologically elevated realm, given its proximity to the Unmoved Mover and its role as the ultimate genesis of all motion and life in the world. Copernicus' model, by contrast, represents

> the recovery of the Pythagorean conception of the center and the abandonment of the Aristotelian conception of dual centrality. The geometric center of the cosmos in Copernicus is the vital and natural center of which Aristotle spoke.[22]

One of Aristotle's problems with such models concerns their implications for the size and limitedness of the world. After reassuring readers that a geocentric world does not leave its most valuable location unguarded, Aristotle touts a further benefit of his universe, namely that

> the center will be something primary and precious; but to the mere position we should give the last place rather than the first. For the middle is what is defined, and what defines it is the limit, and that which contains or limits is more precious than that which is limited.[23]

Using this Aristotelian framework, then, we could say that, bound up with Copernicus' realignment of the metaphysical and physical centers of the

[21] *On the Heavens* 293b1-9.

[22] Miguel A. Granada, "Aristotle, Copernicus, Bruno: Centrality, the Principle of Movement and the Extension of the Universe," *Studies in the History and Philosophy of Science* 35 (2004): 91-114. This article contains an excellent exploration of the nature and importance of the notion of centrality for both Aristotle and Copernicus.

[23] *On the Heavens* 293b11-15.

universe is an implicit rethinking of the ontological weight of the principle of limit relative to that which is limited. Although the Pythagoreans had also privileged the former, Aristotle, in his critique, seems to imply that their concerns with the physical center of the world amounted to a prizing of that which is limited (matter) over that which does the limiting (the place within which the matter is contained, demarcated by the sphere of the fixed stars, or the "end" of a strictly finite universe).

In Copernicus' case, however, the situation is more complicated; in fact, as Alexandre Koyré has argued in *From the Closed World to the Infinite Universe*, Copernicus' world is not, strictly speaking, unlimited. He maintains the notion of heavenly spheres, stating that

> [t]he first and the highest of all is the sphere of the fixed stars, which contains itself and everything, and is therefore immovable. It is unquestionably the place of the universe, to which the motion and position of all the other heavenly bodies are compared.[24]

Its distance from the spheres of the planets, however, is "immense" [*immensum*]; that is,

> [f]rom Saturn, the highest of the planets, to the sphere of the fixed stars there is an additional gap of the largest size.[25]

Copernicus arrives at this conclusion after noting the lack of retrograde motion in the stars, and the fact that, unlike the planets, their distance from the Earth does not appear to change (a fact recognizable in the planets from the apparent variation in their sizes over time when observed from the Earth). However, he refuses to explicitly posit that the size of the universe is infinite, preferring to

> leave the question whether the universe is finite or infinite to be discussed by the natural philosophers.[26]

This statement is somewhat misleading, however, inasmuch as Copernicus' discussion of the heavens is couched in an analysis of Aristotle's treatment of motion in the *Physics*,[27] especially the claim that all simple motion is either

[24] *On the Revolutions* I, 10.

[25] *On the Revolutions* I, 10.

[26] *On the Revolutions* I, 8.

[27] "The motion of everything that is in process of locomotion is either rotatory or rectilinear or a compound of the two"(*Physics* 261b28-29). Much of Books V-VIII are taken up with a discussion of motion; the topic is also briefly handled in Chapters 1 and 2 of Book III.

circular, towards a center, or away from a center. He even engages Aristotle in explicitly metaphysical terms, stating that

> it would seem quite absurd to attribute motion to the framework of space or that which encloses the whole of space, and not, more appropriately, to that which is enclosed and occupies some space, namely, the earth.[28]

Thus, despite his claim that he will eschew metaphysics in *De Revolutionibus*, Copernicus overturns Aristotle using Aristotle's own language, agreeing that limit is ontologically superior to the limited, but assigning rest to it instead of motion.

Shortly before beginning his technical exposition of his system, and several chapters into the work, Copernicus introduces the notion of a heliocentric solar system. He argues for the position of the sun through a response to Aristotle, as well as to Ptolemy, using the language of gravity and the natural tendency of objects to move towards a center. When he finally states in Chapter 9 of Book I that "[l]astly, it will be realized that the sun occupies the middle of the universe," he has already developed a Platonic framework within which to place his stationary sun, and his statement is not as shocking as it otherwise might have been. He is quick to add that this fact, as well as those concerning the position and motion of the Earth,

> are disclosed to us by the principle governing the order in which the planets follow one another, and by the harmony of the entire universe, if only we look at the matter, as the saying goes, with both eyes.[29]

Copernicus' scientific innovations are thus unfolded within the context of a critique of Aristotelian metaphysics, indicating that he was concerned with more than "saving the phenomena" of celestial motion, or even with attempting to discover whether the Earth can empirically be said to revolve around the Sun. While it is impossible to know what Copernicus had in mind as he wrote the words quoted above, it is tempting to imagine that, in exhorting readers to see the universe "with both eyes," he is encouraging us not only to watch the planets as they make their way across the heavens, but also to keep our vision focused on a very different kind of heaven, a Platonic realm defined by harmony, elegance, and truth.

[28] *On the Revolutions* I, 8.

[29] *On the Revolutions* I, 9.

MAPPING KNOWLEDGE AND CONSCIOUSNESS OF BEING: CATEGORIES AS TRANSCENDENTALS IN PLOTINUS AND HEGEL

Robert M. Berchman

Introduction

F. M. Schroeder notes that A.H. Armstrong's metaphor of "intelligible architecture" has entered and informed the language of Plotinian metaphysics. [1] I would like to suggest that this metaphor fits a Hegelian language of metaphysics as well. What I shall explore in this study is an aspect of the architectural metaphor that Plotinus and Hegel share. This is their doctrines of categories understood as *transcendentalia.* [2]

It is admitted straight away that such a comparison to the medieval notion of transcendentals is at best analogical. [3] Plotinus' and Hegel's transcendentals also have nothing in common with Kant's notion of the transcendental. [4] If Plotinus' and Hegel's transcendentals have little in common with these understandings, what do they imply? First, since Plotinus' and Hegel's categories transcend all predicative classification, they transcend the categories of Aristotle and Kant. Secondly, since Plotinus' and Hegel's categories are grasped in an act of either intellect or intuition, not

[1] See Schroeder (2002) 83.

[2] The details of this theory cannot be adumbrated here but transcendentals arose out of the medieval problem of universals. This discussion began with Philip the Chanchellor's *Summa de bono*. It was continued by a variety of Scholastics including Alexander of Halles, Gregory the Great, Thomas Aquinas, Duns Scotus, Suarez, and Nicholas of Cusa. See Allan and Wippel (1969) and Aersten, (1996).

[3] Plotinus and Hegel's categories are not transcendentals in the sense developed in detail in medieval Scholasticism. This medieval doctrine presupposes an Aristotelian ontology ultimately rejected by Plotinus and Hegel. Rather what I suggest is that Plotinus' five genera and Hegel categories of Being-Becoming-Non-Being are employed in a transcendental manner akin to the way transcendentals functioned in medieval philosophy.

[4] For Kant, the term transcendental no longer signifies that which transcends our experience in the sense of providing its ground or structure. Here the pure forms of intuition [space and time] and the pure concepts of the understanding [such as substance and cause] are transcendental in the sense that they constitute the conditions for the possibility of experience.

understanding, the transcendentals are terms or concepts that refer to all things regardless of their ontological entity or kind. Thirdly, from Plotinus' and Hegel's perspective, in knowing Being by means of the transcendentals, one transcends the limits of Aristotelian and Kantian categorical language, and is able to map knowledge and consciousness of Being. Fourthly, if the above is valid Plotinus' alleged commitment to idealism requires review.

1

For Plotinus and Hegel, Being is the primary transcendental, because it is not itself one of the Aristotelian or Kantian categories, since these categories mark off kinds of being. Being, is not however, a category above other categories, an ultimate genus. This is because Being is equivocal or homonymous, i.e. there is no single generic property or nature shared by members of each category in virtue of which they are beings. Therefore, Being transcends the classificatory structure of beings in the world. Thus, the transcendentals allow for the possibility of mapping knowledge and consciousness of being - from the precipice of Plotinus' *Nous* and Hegel's *Geist*.

Plotinus' five genera - Being, Rest, Motion, Identity, and Difference, and Hegel's Being, Non-Being, and Becoming are categories, terms, or concepts that express different facets of the eternal life of *Nous* and *Geist*. It is primarily in this sense that they function as transcendentals. Basic to this theory of transcendentals are two notions: the convertibility and in-division of Being. The first notion is that the various transcendentals do not differ in reality, only in concept. Here the concept of Being is fundamental in that concepts of the other transcendentals presuppose Being. The second proposal implies that negativity yields the concept of unity in Being. We shall see that these concepts are reflected in Plotinus' interpretation of the *megista gene* of the *Sophist*; specifically in his interpretation of the relationship between Being and Non-Being as *contrariety* rather than opposites. They also surface in Hegel's reading of the dialectical relationship between Being, Non-Being, and Becoming.

Important consequences follow, if Plotinus' and Hegel's categories function as transcendentals. These categories do not merely modify, but replace those used by Aristotle and Kant. Here categories of Reason [*Nous/Vernunft*] replace categories of Understanding [*Nous/Verstand*] in mapping knowledge and consciousness of Being. If these consequences hold, then another important topic opens for inquiry. This is the subject of idealism in antiquity.

This question was originally put on the map by Myles Burnyeat who argues that not only is idealism absent from antiquity, but also that it could not have arisen. Burnyeat claims that the rise of idealism had to await Descartes' *Cogito*. [5] Later Richard Sorabji examined the possibility of idealism in Gregory of Nyssa,[6] Sara Rappe claimed the origins of Berkelean idealism in Plotinus, [7] and Robert Berchman [8] commented on the possible origins of a proto-Berkelean idealism in Origen of Alexandria.[9]

The crucial point here is that if Plotinus' categories function as *transcendentalia,* do we have the possible origins of Hegelian idealism in antiquity? There is much evidence to support such a claim. Hegel's theory of the categories is strikingly similar to Plotinus;' they are utilized by both in `transcendental' ways; and since the categories are terms or concepts that map knowledge and consciousness of Being, what we might have is a type of idealism based on Reason [*Nous*/*Vernunft*] rather than Understanding [*Nous*/*Verstand*].

I should add that an idealism based on Reason argues that physical and mental objects are ideas whose existence depends on being *known* not merely *perceived*. This last point demands some reflection. The weak point in any thesis that associates Plotinus with Berkelyean idealism is Berkeley's claim that physical objects are collections of ideas whose existence depends on being *perceived*. [10]Any type of *esse est percipi* idealism, arising from perception, would be deficient from Plotinus' perspective. A type of idealism, however, arising from the activity of thinking or reason, could be commensurate with Plotinus' position. This is Hegel's thesis and it is the fulcrum upon which any claim to Plotinian idealism could legitimately rest.

2

For Plotinus, the transcendental categories of reality are the five genera. Motion and Difference are associated with the descent into plurality

[5] Burnyeat (1982) 3-40.

[6] Sorabji (1983) 287-296.

[7] Rappe (1996) 250-274.

[8] Berchman (2003) 437-450.

[9] Here Sorabji and Rappe suggest that Gregory of Nyssa and Plotinus offer proto-examples of Berkelean idealism. They argue that Berkeley's claim that physical objects are collections of ideas whose existence depends on being *perceived* fit Gregory's, Plotinus's metaphysics rather well. According to Sorabji and Rappe that Berkeley's God produces ideas in our minds, in predictable consequences, also suggests a common ground with Gregory and Plotinus. Berchman is more reticent, but open to such a possibility given Origen's *logos*, rather than *nous, m*etaphysics.

[10] Berkeley (1970) 25-33; 60-65; 103-104.

that occurs at the phase of descent or Procession, while Being, rest, and Identity are identified with the stability acquired through ascent or Reversion [II.4.5.28-35; III.7.3.8-11]; V.1.4.30-43; VI.2.7-8]. *Nous* as a function which has determinate contents, and carries plurality within itself, is the principle through which Being proceeds forth from itself. In its descent there is the loss of knowledge; while in its ascent there is an increasing richness in the content of knowledge of Being.

Hegel proposes that Being, Non-Being, and Becoming are associated with the movement of *Geist* as a dialectical necessity. The conceptions into which *Geist* disassembles and analyzes its own content, are the categories of Being, which are the forms of the cosmic life as they unfold as the moments of a single unitary development. In this dialectical process there unfolds an increasing richness in the content of consciousness. Layer is dialectically added to layer; what went before is included in what has been realized so far. This activity is a mapping activity in that the different facets of the continuum of *Nous* and *Geist* are brought to light as members or links in the descent and ascent, and the self-unfolding of Intellect and Spirit.

Before we address these topics in more detail, it might be helpful to recall that in Hegelian idealism phenomenology deals with the nature of our knowledge or consciousness of reality, and that hermeneutics is the art of interpreting texts. These two projects are inextricably linked in this way. If phenomenologically, Plotinus and Hegel are conscious of reality in a particular way, the hermeneutical question is how do Plotinus and Hegel map knowledge of Being? It is suggested that they employ new categories to avoid confusion of an incorporeal or mental reality accessible to *Nous* or *Geist* with a corporeal reality perceived by our senses. Since the categories play a fundamental role in mapping knowledge of being, the questions addressed next are why Plotinus and Hegel introduced new categories, and how these categories function as *transcendentalia* in the mapping of being.

It is also important to recall that Plotinus and Hegel claimed that earlier attempts to map knowledge of being were incomplete and insufficient. This was so because first, not only were the instruments used, the classificatory categories lacking, but secondly, they proposed that earlier views of reality were deficient and incomplete.

Aristotle's categories fail to map knowledge of Being adequately. In their place Plotinus proposes a new set based upon his reading of the five genera of Plato's *Sophist*. In his interpretation of the five genera of the *Sophist*, in his rescue of Non-Being as a contrary, and in establishing matter as the *contrariety*, not of being as such, but of substance, Plotinus offers a novel proposition. The simple opposition which Plato had established in the *Sophist* between a part of otherness and the being of each thing [258d7-e3] has been transformed by Plotinus into an opposition between a part of otherness and the Forms [II.4.16.1-3], and that opposition has been itself transformed, through a modification of the doctrine of Aristotle's *Categories* into a *contrariety* [I.8.6.28-59], a contrariety which establishes the "form of non-being" which is contrary to all the positive characterizations of substance, as merely not beautiful, but ugly, as not merely not good, but bad [I.8.10]. Hegel's claims that both Aristotle's and Kant's categories fail. In their place he proposes a triad of categories based upon [what appears to be] his own interpretation of Plotinus' reading of the five genera of Plato's *Sophist,* and his rejection of categories of Aristotle and Kant. This is illustrated by Hegel in the dialectical relationship of the categories of Being, Non-Being, and Becoming. The dualism of [1] Being and [2] Non-Being is overcome by duality. That is to say, the duality of Being and Non-Being is dialectically "sublated" in [3] Becoming.

There are other reasons as well for thinking the classificatory categories wanting. This turns on Plotinus' and Hegel's claim that their predecessors made the fundamental mistake of treating reality as made up of discrete particulars. Aristotle and Kant misled us because their categories of thought are abstract. As abstractions these categories are discrete and do not properly represent the continuum of reality from which they are drawn. Particular things are different from each other, and the categories whose terms are abstractions from reality, highlights such differences. These categories present the identity of a particular thing – its essence – as what makes it what it is and not something else. Thus, Aristotle's and Kant's categories do not indicate that a thing's identity includes its relations to that which it is *not*. That is to say, the categories Aristotle and Kant employ to map knowledge of being mislead us because reality is a continuum in which everything in order to be itself has as part of its identity its relations to what it is *not*.

Whether Plotinus and Hegel argue for falsity or meaninglessness, their premises can be made to seem more appealing when they argue meaninglessness. In trying to represent relations, they represents them "abstractly," they treat each categorical term of a substance, quality, quantity, and relation discretely, rather than concretely. Consequently, things are related externally. What should occur is that things be related internally because relations are a part of a thing's identity. This existential claim would resonate powerfully – the concrete is internal, not external; it is something concrete not abstract.

Plotinus' and Hegel's rejections of the Aristotelian and Kantian categories ultimately rest upon their rejections of the metaphysical nature of Aristotle's and Kant's consciousness of reality, which is grounded on a principle of Understanding – *Nous* and *Verstand* not a principle of Reason – *Nous* and *Vernunft*.

The thesis that Plotinus' reading of Plato's five genera and Hegel's triad of categories function as categories of Reason [*Nous/Vernunft*], not Understanding [*Nous/Verstand*] depends on the assumption that it could only be motivated by the need to answer the question: how can we adequately map knowledge and consciousness of Being? Plotinus and Hegel propose that as products of the activity of *Nous* and *Geist,* only the `transcendentals' are legitimate, only they can be used to map knowledge of Being. There are other motives, however. This rejection of the Peripatetic and Kantian categories rests upon a prior metaphysical claim. Plotinus' *Nous* and Hegel's *Geist* are a *We* consciousness, not predominately or exclusively an *I* consciousness. Such a *We* consciousness requires new categories, otherwise Being as *We*, as a continuum, cannot be mapped and known at all.

3

Before we reach an understanding of this move, Plotinus deserves a hearing on the problem of the One and the Many. Unity is in what is intelligible rather than what is material. The supreme principle is *Nous* and the world of Forms is its thoughts. This Supreme Mind and the world of Forms which are its contents are not the highest reality. However immense the unity between *Nous* and the *Ideai*, it still involves the duality of subject and object. The absolute and unqualified unity between subject and object is reconciled in the One – which like Plato's Good is above the other Forms and is beyond being. Here Plotinus is influenced by the unity given to the Forms by the Form of the Good, and also by Plato's reading of Parmenides' notion of unity as absolute and unqualified oneness.

Multiplicity is the result of the overflow of the One "downward." This spatial term is not to be taken literally. It is an ontological term designating degrees of reality; the less unity, the less reality. The One overflows by necessity, and this overflow descends level by level to the physical universe. Plotinus often uses the metaphor of emanation for this overflow associating it with the image of the sun radiating light. Consequently, the One radiates realities. It does not become less by this radiation, so this out-pouring has no beginning or end. Although the order and structure of reality is unchanging, it is also the live of movement and change – a life of intense, self-contained, contemplative activity – of which the life of movement, change, and production of things on the physical level are faint images. Consequently, although the total order and structure of reality never change, there is a "flow" within it, which consists of a downward movement from the One and an upward movement back to the One.

How does this movement occur? For Plotinus there are three individual divine hypostases which make up the intelligible universe – One, Mind, and Soul. *Nous*, despite its immense unity, still contains the duality of subject and object. It emanates outward from the One automatically. *Nous* has the potential to know. By the activity of contemplation the world of Forms arises. This happens because Mind seeks to be united with the One from which it has radiated. However, it cannot remain itself as *Nous* and at the same time know the One. For then it is subject and the One is object. Thus the unity is not absolute. But what results from the Mind's attempts to know the One is the world of Forms and the categories. The world of Forms is the way the One or Good is known to *Nous*. The categories are the way Being is known to *Nous*. The absolute unity is known at the level of *Nous* as the multiplicity of Forms. The absolute unity of Being and Becoming is known at the level of Mind as the five genera of Plato's *Sophist*. There is a high degree of unity at both levels, for the Forms and the categories have a high degree of unity and order at the levels of *Nous* and *Ousia*. Both have a unity in that Mind in knowing its object becomes like it, and an order in that *Nous* in knowing reality becomes its own Forms or thoughts.

The activity of contemplation, Intellect's attempts to know the One, is thus productive. By its movement out from the One, Mind has the potential to know; and by its movement of return, to know the One, it generates the Forms on its own level of reality. Here the Forms represent the One at the level of contemplative Mind and the categories represent the One at the level of a contemplative mapping of Being.

The third hypostasis is Soul. It also contemplates, but is distinguished from Mind because its thought are discursive. While Intellect's thought is intuitive, Soul's thought is that in which objects are known successively. Soul is the cause of the sense-world and represents the intelligible in the sense world. Not only does it think discursively, but it also has the lower forms of sense consciousness. Nonetheless, although distinct from Intellect, Soul reaches the realm of Mind, and with Intellect it can rise in self-transcendence to union with the One.

The crucial point here is that even though One, Mind, and Soul are distinct and hierarchically arranged, they are not separate from one another. One and Intellect are always present to Soul – which is significant for the return of humans to the intelligible world – and thus the ability to map knowledge of Being. Here Soul is the *logos* of Mind and the active principles operating in the visible world through soul are *logoi* of the Forms of *Nous*. Thus, *We* who are intellects, and not *I* souls, have knowledge of the intelligible world of Being, not only because we know the Forms but also the categories of *Nous* – the five genera of the *Sophist*. Here our knowledge knows nothing of the body or the senses. It comes directly from "within" because of our contact and kinship with *Nous* which illuminates us. Indeed, Intellect provides our discursive reason with categories for mapping knowledge of being, and these categories are the five genera of Plato's *Sophist*.

4

This radical transformation of ideas taken from Plato and Aristotle is typical of the author of the *Enneads*. This is certainly the case when Plotinus turns to the problem of Non-Being in the *Sophist*. Here he associates Non-Being with matter. The origin of this connection arises out of Plotinus' association of matter with primary evil and evil *per se*, and his claim that matter is Non-Being [I.8.3.35-40; II.4.16.3; II.5.4-5; III.6.7.1-19]. It is also associated with the claim that matter is derived from the One, through the mediation of Soul [III..9.3.7-16; III.4.1].

As Denis O'Brien has shown, to comprehend what this means requires working from Plato's *megista gene* to Plotinus' interpretation of them.[11] Since it is not possible to address O'Brien's argument on matter and evil in detail, let us on focus on his analysis of Plotinus' association of Non-Being with contrariety. This insight provides an excellent way of detecting what Plotinus, metaphysically and transcendentally, is up to.

The simple opposition which Plato established in the *Sophist* between a part of Otherness and the Being of each thing [258d7-e3] is transformed by Plotinus into an opposition between a part of Otherness and the Forms [*En*., II.4.16.1-3]. Next, this opposition is then transformed, through a new interpretation of the doctrine of Aristotle's *Categories* into a *contrariety* [*En*., I.8.6.28-59]. This contrariety establishes the "Form of Non-Being" since it is contrary to all the positive characterization of substance. It is not merely not beautiful, but ugly; not merely not good, but evil [*En*., I.8.10]. In this last argument, Plato's Eleatic Stranger dismisses Parmenides' "absolute" Non-Being as an impossible and inconceivable contrary to Being [*Sophist*, 258e6-259a1]. Plotinus rescues Non-Being as a *contrary* by circumventing Aristotle's categories, and by establishing matter as the contrary, not of Being as such, but of substance. Also, following the argument of Plato's Stranger, he proposes that Non-Being implies Becoming. Consequently, by emending Aristotle's argument, Plotinus can claim that substance implies its *contrary* Non-Being.

In nuce, Plotinus' Stranger suggests that Non-Being is an essential condition of the existence of any object, since all objects, save Being-itself, participate in Otherness in relation to Being. And insofar as they are "other" than Being they must be counted as Non-Being which means that their movement and rest, their Becoming, are also Non-Beings, again not because they do not participate in Being, but because they participate in Otherness in relation to Being. Therefore, they are not identical with Being. The Stranger distinguishes Being as Form and as particular. Here Plotinus takes Plato's

[11] Following O'Brien (1996) 171-195.

second definition and identifies it with the Stranger's account of the "parts" of Otherness in his definition of Non-Being. Finally, Plotinus recasts Aristotle's definition of contraries from "things which stand furthest apart within the same genus" to "things which stand furthest apart and which are not in the same genus" which stands on the difference between qualities and elements.

The use of the contraries to designate sameness and difference, not as opposites but as relatedness allows Hegel to read Plotinus' theory as a precursor to his own notion of the dialectical unfolding of contrarieties as Being, Non-Being, Becoming. Plotinus and Hegel bring *contrariety* and dialectical *change* into metaphysics in two different, but complementary ways. Since the beginning of metaphysics, Being has shown itself as having the character of ground. This is of *Nous* for Plotinus and of *Geist* for Hegel. In the epochal clearing of Being reached by Plotinus and Hegel, Being is thought thinking itself; and thought thinking itself as Absolute Idea dialectically thinking itself.

5

The modern bridge from Plotinus to Hegel lies in Spinoza and Kant. It is with Spinoza that Hegel finds the most fully developed "standpoint of substance" [*Logic*, III.2.216ff.] - before he offered his own absolute formulation. Spinoza lets thinking begin with the absolute - substance. Here substance is not yet pure thought, *Geist*, as Hegel proposes. Nonetheless for Hegel, Spinoza understands *substantia* correctly – thinking begins with absolute substance, equally fundamentally and resolutely as thinking itself. Hegel argues next, that Kant's path is even more decisive than Spinoza's. He sees in Kant's idea of the original synthesis of apperception "one of the most profound principles for speculative development [*Logic*, III.2.216ff.]. Here Kant's notion of transcendental no longer signifies that which transcends categorical classification, but that which transcends our experience in the sense of providing its ground or structure. Thus, the pure forms of intuition, space and time, and the pure concepts of understanding, categories such as substance and cause, are transcendental in the sense that they constitute the conditions for the possibility of experience.

Kant's insistence that the categories are merely subjective concepts of the human mind precluded a use of the categories as first principles for the explanation of the world. The categories were not ontological principles of being, but epistemological principles of knowing. Nonetheless, Kant's doctrine contained the pregnant hint that the categories, as subjective universals, form a special class of universals distinct from all other universals.

Out of Spinoza and Kant, Hegel in his search for a principle of explanation, adopted like Plotinus, the belief that the first principle consists of transcendentals functioning as objective universals. This leads Plotinus and Hegel to propose that the first principle of the world, the first reason of things, is a system of pure non-sensuous universals or transcendentals. For Plotinus, these *transcendentalia* are the five genera of the *Sophist*, while for Hegel they are the triad of Being, Non-Being, and Becoming. And since Thought is concerned with Being - the primary *transcendental*, Being is absolute thought thinking itself as *Nous* and *Geist*.

In nuce, Plotinus and Hegel share the premise that Being and Thought are a continuum which must be mapped in a new way. This means that reality cannot be captured in the abstractions of the Aristotelian and Kantian categories. Thus new categories are introduced, the five genera of the *Sophist* and the categories of Being, Non-Being, and Becoming, to map this continuum. With these transcendentals the limits of classificatory language are overcome, and knowledge and consciousness of being are mapped.

How do Plotinus and map knowledge of Being? Hegel views the entire cosmos and history as the Absolute coming into greater actualization and greater articulation in multiplicity in an orderly, rationally understandable way. This view is similar to Plotinus' but with two important differences. First, in Plotinus the descent from unity to multiplicity and the ascent from multiplicity to unity are not historical movements. We do not see the past, present, and future as directed toward greater and greater realization of Being itself. For Plotinus, the One is ever complete and realized. It radiates its fullness always. Thus, there is no temporal or historical dimension to the One. Time and history are of no significance for the One itself. Second, as we move from the One, we have less and less unity and more and more multiplicity. Hence, we are further and further from true being and reality. In Hegel it is the opposite. As we get more and more concrete articulation in time and space in the course of history, we get a greater realization of *Geist* itself.

Nonetheless, whether the continuum of Being and Thought is viewed through dialectical actualization, or noetic ascent-descent-ascent, things are not, ontologically, wholly unrelated or wholly alien to each other. There is always an identity-in-difference and a unity-in-plurality among things. This means all things are not wholly alien to each other but are internally related in *Nous* and *Geist*. Thus, in the mapping of the knowledge of Being, as we descend from and ascend to the One, we see a decreasing and increasing richness in the content of *Nous* consciousness. Similarly, we encounter an increasing richness in the content of consciousness, as layer is added to layer in the dialectical development of *Geist*. Here philosophers, using transcendentals, uncover the layers of our knowledge and consciousness of Being. In this uncovering, the activities of *Nous* and *Geist* are realized.

6

Are there any further conclusions that can be drawn? We have had no time to examine Kant's position regarding the constitutive activity of the subject in relation to sensory experience [the relation being the key point]. In brief, it is a radically new theory and there is no ancient philosopher with any comparable viewpoint – including Plotinus. Thus I would suggest that what emerges in Plotinus is not any commitment to idealism - either of the Berkeleyan "Immaterial," Kantian "Transcendental," or Hegelian "Absolute" varieties. At most, what this study shows is that philosophers can arrive at strikingly similar theories by somewhat different routes. Some of the writing in [V.5] approaches the Hegelian mode, the discussion in [III.8] suggests a Berkeleyan trope, and what Plotinus says about the One in relation to Intellect's thinking parallel some things Kant says about the unity of apperception. Nonetheless, all this does not suggest a `Plotinian idealism.' [12]

Foundationally, Plotinus is a realist. By realism it is meant: 1] there are real objects that exist independently of our knowledge or experience of them; 2] that these mental and physical objects have properties and enter into relations independently of the concepts with which we understand them; or 3] the language with which we describe them. [13] Plotinus does not reject any of these three theses of realism. As Sorabji suggests, Plotinus' aversion to idealism is well illustrated by his theory of matter. [14] In [VI.3.8.12-19] he raises the question what is left over in a perceptible substance, when in imagination we strip away all its properties. He answers there must be some seat of the properties, that is, as it were, a *part* of the sensible substance, and that it is *matter*. Plotinus downgrades this part by describing matter as a mere shadow upon a shadow, a picture, an appearance [II.34-37]. Even though sensible individuals are bundles of properties conceptually known, these properties are not idealized. This passage, as A.C. Lloyd has shown, led Porphyry, Proclus, Simplicius, and Philoponus to treat the individual as a bundle of qualities, unique in that the same combination would not be found in another individual. They are referred to, in the negative language of Porphyry, Proclus, and Philoponus, as accidents [*sumbebekota*].

But even as accidents they are known not perceived which precludes the possibility of a proto-Berkeleyan idealism. [15] For Plotinus and Hegel, to exist is not merely to be *perceived*; to exist is to be *known* to *Nous* and *Geist*. Thus metaphysically, what is needed are categories of reason that allow

[12] I have argued this elsewhere. cf. Corrigan and Turner (2006) and Cleary and Gurtler (2006).

[13] Audi (1995) 488.

[14] Sorabji (1983) 292. cf. n. 21.

[15] Lloyd (1981) 67-68. cf. Porphyry, *Isagog.*, 7.21-23; *in Cat.*, 129.9-10; Proclus, *ap.* Olympiodorus, *in Alcibiadem,* 204 [Creuzer]; Philoponus, *in An. Post.*, 437; Simplicius, *in Cat.*, 229.17.

Intellect and Spirit to know the things that constitute Being. These categories do mean things thought of, and this means that things thought of are also thoughts or concepts. Plotinus identifies *Nous* with the Forms, as Hegel identifies ideas and concepts with *Geist*. Without such an association knowledge and consciousness of Being could not be mapped at all. Thus, the very same ideas, whose concurrence forms a physical or mental object, have their source in Intellect and Spirit. Consequently, our abilities to know and to be conscious of reality arise from and depend upon *Nous*, *Geist*, and the transcendentals.

Conclusion

In such activity *Nous* and *Geist* picture the intelligible architecture of Being. Plotinus and Hegel share a view of reality as a continuum; they claim that reality is known and not merely perceived; and they maintain that reality is known categorically through the *transcendentalia*. Nonetheless, none of these theories constitute a commitment by Plotinus to idealism of either the Berkeleyan, Kantian, or Hegelian varieties. If idealism enters the Neoplatonic tradition at all, it is with ps. Dionysus, Eriugena, and Cusanus. This "idealism" is a by-product of the Christianization of Platonism. The Christian God is a constitutive thinker and man who is made in his image is a constructivist thinker as well.

I would suggest that the claim that Plotinus is an idealist arises when the *Enneads* are read from the precipice of Descartes, Berkeley, Kant, and Hegel. Indeed, the claim that Plotinus is an absolute idealist is due more to Hegel's `sublation' of Plotinus, rather than a `move' by Plotinus towards idealism. If Plotinus had Berkeley, Kant, Hegel, and Husserl as predecessors, it could be argued that a Plotinian "idealism" might have occurred. But I would suggest this outcome is also unlikely. The hyper-reality of the One is too great for Plotinus to have made a move toward idealism. Thus, I concur with Burnyeat that:

> Idealism, whether we mean by that Berkeley's own
> doctrine that *esse est percipi,* or a more vaguely conceived
> thesis to the effect that everything is in some substantial sense mental or spiritual, is one of the very few philosophical positions which did not receive its first formation in antiquity. [16]

[16] Burnyeat (1982) 3.

CRITIQUE AND RESCUE: ON ADORNO'S DIAGNOSIS OF ARISTOTLE'S *METAPHYSICS*

Russell Ford

> If the immanent quality of a type of thinking, the strength manifested in it, the resistance, the imagination, the unity of critique with its opposite – if all this is not an *index veri*, it is at least an indication.[1]

Introduction

Adorno is a poor historian if we take the historian's objective to be that of providing an objective and impartial reflection of a past time. The philosophical tradition is, for him, a vast and intricate network of symptoms, each significant not in its own right but rather in the way that it indicates a more essential and generative social cause. This is not a deficiency and, indeed, the politicization of history which began with Marx, if not earlier, marks what is so deeply valuable about Adorno's thought. On the one hand, Adorno's philosophical style adroitly avoids devolving into any sort of naïve historicism that would vainly attempt to reconstruct a thinker's work according to their 'original intention.' On the other hand, by reading the philosophical tradition symptomatically, if not sympathetically, Adorno is able to accomplish two things: first he is able to indicate the structural elements that periodically form and whose repetition gives to the tradition its consistency; second, insofar as these elements are determined according to the index of a particular present, Adorno's historical diagnosis entails an immanent critique of the present by the very history it discloses.

In short, Adorno's method is dialectical – which for him means that it is comprised of two moments, critique and rescue, whose distinguishing characteristic is their temporal character. This dialectical method is often read against, or mistaken for, that of Hegel, with the presumption that Adorno's project is simply a sort of negative twist on Hegel's positive or absolute dialectic. Judging simply by the frequency with which Adorno enters into debate with Hegel, as well as the tradition of German Idealism that arises in Kant throughout his published work, this comparison seems apt. However, with the ongoing publication of Adorno's lecture courses it has become more and more clear that his dialectical method is reliant on, and responds to, a far more diverse cast of characters than that provided by German Idealism.

[1] Adorno (1983), 384-385.

Nowhere is this more clear than in his course from the summer semester of 1965, entitled *Metaphysics: Concept and Problems*. Written as he was completing his major work, *Negative Dialectics*, the *Metaphysics* course shows how Adorno's conception of dialectics is deeply influenced not only be Hegel's relation to Kant, but, perhaps more deeply, by Aristotle's relation to Plato.

It is this latter relationship that provides the starting point for an understanding of the founding moment of the tradition of thinking that Adorno recognizes as metaphysics. In Aristotle, Adorno finds the first elaboration of the dialectical structure that was merely posited by Plato in the duality between the world of appearance and the Forms. The contrast between these two thinkers, or rather between these two moments that together constitute the emergence of metaphysical thinking, is indicative of the specific concerns that will come to mark metaphysics as a distinct sort of philosophical inquiry. For Adorno, these concerns are less material than formal. In other words, although metaphysics is often marked off as a science of thinking about the ultimate, final, or foundational causes of what is, for Adorno this concern is itself marked and motivated by the Platonic doctrine of Ideas as existing in a realm that is *really* distinct from the empirical one. It is this insistence upon another distinct world, a world that is distinguished from the empirical world precisely by its constitution as the truth of this latter world, that inaugurates the trajectory of metaphysics. However, this moment is incomplete without a second moment, one in which the distance between the two worlds postulated by the first moment is sutured in an attempt to return truth to the world, but without thereby losing the distinctiveness of truth. Aristotle's metaphysical philosophy marks, for Adorno, the historical moment of critique and rescue, the inaugural moment of metaphysical thinking, insofar as he reads Aristotle as, on the one hand critically rejecting Plato's account of the distinct world of really existing Forms and, on the other hand, attempting to preserve Plato's insight into the constant character of truth.

Adorno's reading of Aristotle, then, shows that metaphysics does not attain to dialectics only with the Enlightenment – metaphysics is inherently dialectical insofar as its origin lies in Aristotle's attempt to critique the duality of Plato's Ideal and empirical worlds while at the same time drawing forth the essential and Ideal truth from out of the empirical. Adorno writes in the fourth lecture of the course:

> I believe this way of stating the matter may better define the locus of metaphysics in the history of philosophy, and thus define the essence of metaphysics as well (for I believe the essential is always historical), than would be possible in the relatively superficial lectures one might

give on the themes of metaphysics. Following from this definition one might say that metaphysics, because it attempts to regard Ideas as something linked to the empirical world but endangered by advancing secularization, was itself threatened from the first in its own development.[2]

Although the exhibition of metaphysics as a fundamentally historical (rather than, for instance, ontological) form of thinking is worthy of consideration in its own right, in this case it is also interesting for the work that this discovery performs in relation to Adorno's own philosophical project (a project that, in turn, enabled this discovery). At the end of his lecture course, Adorno turns from his explicit engagement with Aristotle's *Metaphysics* to a concern that is more familiar to his readers: how one can think after Auschwitz. Here Adorno relies upon the transformation that metaphysics undergoes in the project of the Enlightenment from a concern over the relation of the empirical and the transcendent to a concern over that of nature and culture. However, to simply repeat Aristotle's metaphysical gesture of critique and rescue upon a Kantian field runs the risk of merely reproducing the catastrophe of recent history. This recent history is the outcome of an ideology that has sought to mythically fuse nature and culture by drawing the latter from out of the former. Adorno finds the resolution of the impasse of metaphysics aptly expressed in the "unredeemed program" of the Introduction to Hegel's *Phenomenology of Spirit* which recognizes the need for what Adorno calls a "metacritique of epistemology."[3]

While Adorno is principally concerned with epistemology insofar as it provides a ground for contesting such philosophical projects as phenomenology, Heideggerian ontology, existentialism, and analytic positivism, it may also be problematized historically. Specifically, Adorno's linking of the metaphysical tradition with the problem of thinking after Auschwitz, a problem that centers on the peculiar status of epistemology, invites the question of the relation of metaphysics and epistemology in Aristotle's thought which forms the beginning of the tradition's historical trajectory. Concerning himself exclusively with the *Metaphysics*, which readily lends itself to being critiqued in a dialectical fashion, Adorno does not explore (except for a very brief rejection of Heidegger's ontological recuperation of Aristotle) Aristotle's account of individual thinking that is found in his *On The Soul*. To be sure, the *Metaphysics* exerted a much greater formative role upon the philosophical tradition through the Neoplatonists and

[2] Adorno (2000), 19.

[3] Ibid., 25.

Scholasticism, but *On The Soul*, precisely because it is by no means easily assimilated to dialectical schematization, may betray the movement of metaphysics to be more complex than Adorno describes.

Significantly, the strange and difficult account of the imagination offered in the Third Book of *On The Soul* has no ready correlate in the *Metaphysics*. This is striking insofar as the perceptive and thoughtful activity of ensouled beings recapitulates the nature of the world. It is therefore fitting to ask how and to what extent this element of Aristotle's epistemology might complicate Adorno's dialectical depiction of his metaphysics, as well as the formal account of metaphysics that is developed on the basis of this interpretation. It may be that Aristotle's account of imagination lays the groundwork for an epistemological metaphysics, a thinking about thinking, that is no longer confined to the debilitating structure of what will become dialectical metaphysics.

The Fate of Force

Adorno declares at the outset of his exposition that it will be heavily reliant upon the work of the 19th century "Hegelian" Eduard Zeller, since, in the lecture course, he is "more concerned to throw light on the problems and history of metaphysics through Aristotle than to give [you] an irreproachably punctilious account of that philosopher's work."[4] The path that Adorno follows in his exposition is one that takes as its starting point Aristotle's critique of the Platonic Ideas. Broadly speaking, Aristotle rejects the hypostatizing of concepts, derived from empirical sources, in a separate, transcendental domain. Specifically, this criticism is comprised of three components that ground and orient Adorno's account of Aristotle's *Metaphysics*. First, Aristotle rejects the substantiality of universal concepts; second, he rejects the absolute separation and autonomy of the Platonic Ideas, or of substance generally; and, finally, he rejects as inconsistent the contention that the autonomous and separate Ideas could ever function as causes in relation to empirical appearances. Together, these objections constitute and express the original problem of Aristotle's *Metaphysics*: that of the universal and the particular.

Aristotle's rejection of the Platonic solution to the problem of the universal and the particular does not take the form of a mere reversal. Following what Adorno claims is the formal mark of metaphysical thinking – a combination of a critical moment with a moment of rescue or salvage – Aristotle's *Metaphysics* is guided by a concern to simultaneously reject the

[4] Ibid., 24.

Platonic claim concerning the unreality of the empirical and the substantiality of the universal, and to salvage the Platonic notion of truthful substantiality by linking it with the empirical. Where Plato opposed the universal and the particular, going so far as to eliminate any truth value that the latter might lay claim to, Aristotle, who shares Plato's concern for the discovery of truth, and therefore also a concern for the distinction between the universal and the particular, rejects the sufficiency of this distinction for arriving at a solution.

What is at issue in the determination of the respective truth content of the universal and the particular for Aristotle, and what is forced to choose a side between them (that of the universal) by Plato, is the concept of substantiality (*ousia*). However, the universal cannot be substantial if by substance is meant something that is reliant upon nothing else for its existence. Insofar as the Platonic Ideas are hypostatized empirical qualities (and Adorno emphasizes that this is apparently one of the central lessons of the *Parmenides*, perhaps due to an influence of Aristotle upon Plato)[5], they show themselves to be insubstantial. What is substantial can then only be particular things, understood not as determinate and individuated objects of perception, but as immediate things (*tode ti*). Here by "immediate" Adorno is emphasizing that immediate things are not mediated, especially not by any sort of sensory apparatus, and therefore are uncritically and objectively real (this is Aristotle's "naïve realism"). Substance, for Aristotle, is to be seen "in terms of the immediate objectivity of the external world, and not in terms of mediation through the perceiving consciousness."[6] This is not to say, however, that there is no mediation at all, for to do so would bring an abrupt end to the inquiry. Although substances are immediate, these substances give rise to what Aristotle, in the *Categories*, calls "secondary substances." (*deuterai ousiai*)[7] With these, the account of substance and immediacy is, in Adorno's words, "turned on its head."[8]

[5] Ibid., 17.

[6] Ibid., 30.

[7] In Section 5 of the *Categories*, Aristotle writes, "A *substance* – that which is called a substance most strictly, primarily, and most of all – is that which is neither said of a subject nor in a subject, e.g. the individual man or the individual horse. The species in which the things primarily called substances are, are called *secondary substances*, as also are the genera of these species. For example, the individual man belongs in a species, man, and animal is a genus of the species; so these – both man and animal – are called secondary substances." Barnes (1984), 4.

[8] Adorno (2000), 35.

Having successfully critiqued the alleged substantiality of the Platonic Ideas by showing that these Ideas are in fact reliant upon the empirical for their existence, and thereby showing the immediately existing to be what is properly called substance, Aristotle then sets about rescuing the Platonic conception of an unchanging truth by differentiating the immediate thing (*tode ti*) from its concept. The immediate thing, substance properly called, is now to be distinguished from its conceptualizations, the "secondary substances," which are substances only to the extent that they are more or less proximate to the immediate thing. Thus Socrates is a proper substance, an immediate thing, but is only thinkable through secondary substances, concepts, such as "human," "male," and "living being," each of which warrants the appellation "substance" precisely to the degree that it specifies the individual thing and not another. The thing, substance proper, therefore always corresponds to a multiplicity of concepts while, at the same time, concepts never fully individuate a thing but remain applicable to multiple individual things. Substance thereby gives rise to a dynamic reciprocality of thing and concept that determines Aristotle's resolution of the problem of the "One in the Many."

Where Plato had sought the resolution of this problem in the rigid determination of the (untruthful apparent) thing from its (truthful ideal) conceptualization, Aristotle argues that this separation proved untenable from the standpoint of causality. Adorno's reading emphasizes that this causality is, in its problematic exposition, doubly dynamic: comprising both the immediate determination of concepts, and the conceptual determination of the immediate thing. This double dynamic is expressed in the terminological dyad "form and matter" (*morphe* and *hule*) which supersedes the Platonic distinction between "*eidos*" and "*ta onta*." What differentiates the two sets of terms is that Plato's are irreducibly different, whereas Aristotle's are necessarily interrelated (or, in Adorno's reading, mediated) insofar as they are determined by the need to resolve to problem of causality posed by the Platonic schema. However, if the generation of this dynamic duality is due to a critique of the gap (*chorismos*) in the Platonic account of the "One in the Many" then Aristotle's resolution of the problematic remains fundamentally Platonic. Here emerges Aristotle's own understanding of the central difficulty of Platonism: the problem is not accounting for the superiority of the Ideas, but rather of explaining the mechanism or the *activity* by which this superiority is exercised and preserved.

On the one hand, the Platonic *chorismos* is overcome by the interrelation of the dyad of form and matter. The conceptualization of the immediate yields these two characteristics as the two possible emphases for the individuality that this conceptualization would express. The brute thereness of the thing is most properly its matter, but, as Aristotle emphasizes, to remove all formal characteristics from the individual and immediate thing is to eliminate that thing itself. Therefore, on the other hand, another aspect of the Platonic *chorismos* is preserved in Aristotle's account insofar as determination only arises through the assumption of form by matter. Adorno summarizes this result as follows:

> On the one hand, the Platonic doctrine that Ideas or Forms have being in themselves is maintained, in the sense that reality – or at any rate, higher reality – is attributed only to them; but, on the other hand, this reality is not susceptible to thought, or only within that in which it is realized. This makes the question of the realization of form the central problem. For while form is regarded as the higher reality and that which has true being-in-itself, nevertheless, it has this being only *within* matter. Thus, the truly fundamental problem of Aristotle's philosophy becomes the realization of form. And this question is, at the same time, none other than the question about change, which relates both to the effect of form on matter and to matter itself, and finally, to the relation between the two.[9]

The consequent transformation of the dyad of matter and form into that of potentiality and actuality is the reflection of the transformation of the Platonic problematic of cause into the Aristotelian problem of change.[10] Adorno insists upon this point repeatedly throughout his lectures as a decisive difference between the two thinkers. The consequences of this transformation are decisive for metaphysics in general, but also for Aristotle's particular conclusions. Matter and form remain, for Aristotle, determinate and independent concepts (and Adorno is quick to emphasize the ease with which Aristotle converts immediacy into something conceptual[11]), but their relation is not multiple and determinate, but eternal. That is, even though matter exists in order to become form (and this is the meaning of *dunamis*) this change is never complete insofar as matter and form retain their essential distinction. This essential distinction of matter and form, whose conceptual structure

[9] Ibid., 62.

[10] Ibid., 56.

[11] Adorno writes of Aristotle's curious treatment of *hule*, "the very fact that he [Aristotle] conceives matter, as I have explained, as a pure possibility which is itself mediated categorically as that which is possible – this very fact implies a concept. What is possible is an existing thing which is determined in relation to another which it has not yet become. For this reason the concept of pure possibility already includes a kind of determinateness which, in strict accordance with Aristotle's thesis, it should not have." Adorno (2000) 75.

refigures the Platonic problem of causality as the problem of change, thus divides the famous "four causes" into two principles: the changing and the ordering form of the change (*dunamis* and *energeia*). Thus Aristotle has managed to salvage the Platonic unchanging – esteemed as more true and more valuable than the changing – precisely through a critique of the account of causality that engendered it. The eternal, as Adorno puts it, has become the pure actuality of change.[12]

> Now, the reason given by Aristotle for this eternal quality of the relationship between the two basic categories [matter and form], and thus for the eternal nature of movement itself ... is none other than that both the genesis and the disappearance of this movement, and thus of the relationship between the two, can in turn only be caused by a movement.[13]

This movement of change is not, despite Aristotle's best efforts, determined solely by the unchanging formal element. Matter has its own dynamic principle by which it is predisposed to formal determination. On the one hand this predisposition is the *fate* that befalls matter insofar as, under this term, Aristotle is able to incorporate the immediate into the conceptual.[14] This fate befalls being as its eternal past but at the same time organizes and determines that past according to the being that it becomes. The unity of this movement of change is expressed in the "unmoved mover" which, following Adorno's reading, is more properly the actuality of being than its causal agent.

Fittingly, it is with the activity of the prime mover, which, he claims, takes us from Aristotle's metaphysics to his theology that Adorno concludes his discussion of Aristotle's text.[15] Fitting, because it is this unifying conception that provides the conception adequate to the problem of change that resulted from the critique of Platonic metaphysics, and thus preserves the priority of the conceptual over the immediate. This priority is further emphasized by the character of the actuality of the unmoved mover: it is thinking about thinking (*noesis noeseos*). The activity of the unmoved mover

[12] Ibid., 81.

[13] Ibid., 87.

[14] Ibid., 74-75. The force of matter (as opposed to the movement of the concept) is a frequent theme in Adorno's work but remains almost entirely unexplored in most work on the history of philosophy and especially Aristotle and the Aristotelian tradition. A notable recent exception to this is the historical investigation of force in Lee (2004).

[15] Ibid., 88.

is a purely formal one, a purely conceptual thinking devoid of practical matter, for only in this way can its end remain immanent to its activity.

Adorno is particularly intrigued by this "apotheosis of pure thought" which seems to join together Aristotle's metaphysics, theology, and epistemology. He writes that this "is the point at which the project for an objective ontology clashes with the concept and violently absorbs it, and this in turn implies the recourse to subjectivity on which all idealist metaphysics is founded."[16] This "recourse to subjectivity" that is emphasized by Adorno's reading of the conceptual structure of Aristotle's metaphysics is at the same time troubled by the immediacy that is forsaken and forgotten in the drive to conceptualization. Having transformed the problem of cause into the problem of change, Aristotle is left to account both for the resolution of change (conceptuality; actuality) and the impulse to change (immediacy; necessity). The latter presents "a curious tension and difficulty" since the almost paradoxical conception of the immediate as matter (*hule*) is, on the one hand, "denigrated, disqualified, censured in every respect, including the moral, while on the other there is the remarkable assumption whereby this element, though heterogeneous with regard to form, is endowed with a kind of animation, a tendency, even a kind of yearning."[17] This yearning is *ananke*, the necessity that immediacy, substance, be given over to actualization, but also the necessity of this fate for actualization itself. *Dunamis* is therefore the name of the force that simultaneously engenders and eludes the conceptualization that gives it force.

Imaginary Difficulties

Adorno's insistence upon a structural reading of Aristotle's metaphysical system has the advantage of foregrounding and emphasizing the transformation of the Platonic philosophy that he inherits, and of using this relation to draw attention to a structural peculiarity of the metaphysical tradition itself: the double movement of critique and rescue. However, this interpretation fails to incorporate any other relevant portions of the Aristotelian corpus. This is no doubt due to the particular emphasis upon the situation of contemporary metaphysics that orients the overall aim of the lecture course, but such an inclusion is, to a certain extent, demanded insofar as Adorno concludes his account by explicitly linking Aristotle's metaphysics to his epistemology. This epistemology, as it is developed in *On The Soul*, clearly exhibits a number of parallels to Adorno's structural account of the

[16] Ibid., 91.

[17] Ibid., 74.

Metaphysics: the work is organized by a concern with a particular type of change (namely, that which is proper to the soul), the investigation proceeds according to the familiar conceptual duality of matter and form, and the dynamic tension of this duality is ultimately resolved in contemplation, thinking about thinking. However, what is most striking about *On The Soul* is the account of the imagination as a distinct type of change (neither perceptive nor intellectual) that properly belongs to certain kinds of ensouled beings. This account of the imagination may not only serve as something of an Aristotelian rejoinder to Adorno's claims concerning Aristotle's *Metaphysics*, but may also indicate a direction for further study of the metaphysical tradition (both before and after Aristotle) that would emphasize the difficulty in situating the imagination within purely metaphysical accounts of the human.[18]

The inquiry into the soul is a specific inquiry within the larger framework of the account of change given in the *Metaphysics*, the *Physics*, and elsewhere. Its aim is to develop a specific account of that sort of change that distinguishes the soul from other sorts of beings. The soul, in turn, is conceived as the supreme manifestation of change itself insofar as it alone is capable of attaining to the pure and self-contained activity of thinking about thinking. Aristotle develops an account of this sort of change by beginning with motion, the simplest sort of change for an ensouled being to participate in. Aristotle's definition of motion, that it is "the actuality of potency as potency,"[19] is conjoined to the distinguishing characteristic of the soul: that the source of change is that which undergoes the change. Thus the sorts of change that can be properly attributed to the soul are the nutritive, the perceptive, and the intellective. The ensouled individual thing would then be, in each case, a certain way of preserving a physical disposition amidst self-determined change.

In the commentary accompanying his translation of *On The Soul*, Joe Sachs writes that "in a certain way, the whole of the perceptible world is present in, at-work in, the animal soul, and part of its life rather than mere

[18] There is a growing body of work that deals expressly with the problem of the imagination in the history of philosophy. Notable among this body of work are Brann (1992), Kearney (1998), and Sallis (2000).

[19] Aristotle defines *kinesis* in Book III, Chapter 1 of the *Physics* as "the progress of the realizing of a potentiality, *qua* potentiality." Wicksteed & Cornford (1929) 195. At the conclusion of his discussion of the imagination in *On The Soul*, that "[i]f, then, imagination involves nothing else than we have stated, and is as we have described it, then imagination must be a movement (*kinesis*) produced by sensation actively operating." Hett (1975) 163.

material that might underlie it."[20] It is Aristotle's account of perception that the account of the soul most clearly begins to reflect Aristotle's *Metaphysics*. Perception operates in the same way for each of the senses. The thing perceived and the perceiving organ are individual bodies related by the common body of an appropriate medium. Perception then consists in the actualization of the receptive medium by the thing perceived (specifically by its being what it is) and the corresponding reception of this actualization by the sense organ, which is thereby itself actualized. Aristotle emphasizes at the conclusion of his account that it is the form and not the matter of the thing, medium, and sense organ, that determines sensation. In some ensouled beings, this is the extent of the work of the sense organs and perception and it is clear, then, how the activity of contemplative thinking agrees with the account provided in the *Metaphysics*. Aristotle writes in *On The Soul* that the mind is "the form of forms" (here using the Platonic term "*eidos*" rather than "*morphe*") meaning that it is the pure potency to be actualized as conceptualized nature according to the aspects of that nature that are reflected in perception. The unmoved mover is therefore the actualization of nature itself – which includes all ensouled beings – insofar as this actualization requires no transmission.

While this account emphasizes the parallel between the epistemology of *On The Soul* and the metaphysics (and theology) of the *Metaphysics*, it ignores an essential component of Aristotle's account of the soul: the imagination which is distinct from, but tied to, both perception and thinking. For Adorno, Aristotle's *Metaphysics* works against the very problematic that it exposes when it attempts to resolve the dual tension of change by conceptualizing the immediate thing. The difficulty encountered there is that the individual thing only becomes "thinkable," only assumes a form, insofar as it becomes conceptualized. *On The Soul* explains this transition in its account of perception and thinking, but adds the imagination as an intermediary power.

For Aristotle, imaginings "remain within" perception, but the imagination is not reducible to perception. It differs insofar as the imagination is itself a motion of the soul that is caused by the receptive actualization of the sense organs. Significantly, this motion is not actualized in thinking, although thinking relies upon this motion for its own proper activity. Moreover, this actualization is possible even in the absence of a perceived thing that would provoke the sensation. Imagination is therefore a power of sensation autonomous from the potential actualization of the sense

[20] Sachs (2001) 80.

organs, and this is confirmed by Aristotle's accounts of the accompaniment of sense perception by imagination. In terms of the metaphysical problematic sketched by Adorno, the imagination would be a power of the immediate thing to trouble its conceptuality precisely by lending this conceptuality the possibility of being fictional, which is antithetical to the actualization of the substantiality of the thing conceptualized.

Adorno concludes his discussion of *ananke*, of the fateful force of the immediate thing, by glimpsing something of this imaginative faculty when he writes:

> Because the regularity of natural causality can never equal the internal coherence of successive moments, as Aristotle seeks to describe it through his teleology, everything causal also seems to have a moment of the fortuitous. And, perhaps more important, apart from the moment of causality there are all those moments which cannot be subsumed under the principle of identity and which, in accordance with the omnipotent principle of identity in thought, must appear as extraneous and accidental. There is thus a curious correlation between causality and chance; and the more relentless the dominance of causality, of causal-mechanical thinking, becomes in the world, the more the category of chance increases, as a kind of reminder of how much meaning, how much internal coherence, has been lost through the predominance of causality. No doubt there are social reasons for this – the fact that, as rationality has increased in the means of social organization, the ends of social organization have remained irrational, fortuitous.[21]

A poor historian, Adorno is, no doubt, at best a problematic commentator on Aristotle. But his schematizing analysis of the structure of Aristotle's *Metaphysics* shows its possibilities when it indicates, even obliquely, the way that Aristotle retains the power to surprise the very tradition that his works engendered. And, it may well be the case that, following Adorno's hint concerning the fortuitous and the substantial, Aristotle's account of the imagination could come to be understood as the hidden seed of a perpetually critical power within metaphysics – one that would preserve the immediate even as it gave rise to conceptualization.

[21] Adorno (2000) 75.

WINCENTY LUTOSŁAWSKI PLATONIC STUDIES: Plato as an inspiration for Polish Messianism*

Tomasz Mróz

The purpose of this paper is a presentation of the history of 'the posthumous life of Plato' as the history of Platonism was called by František Novotný.[1] It depicts a short reconstruction of Wincenty Lutosławski's (1863-1954) research on the chronology of Plato's Dialogues, and Plato's philosophy. It is also an attempt to present the way Lutosławski positioned Plato's ideas in the history of European philosophical thought, focusing on its relationship with Polish Messianism.

Lutosławski's findings in his research on Plato's Dialogues' chronology, although a hundred years old, are considered to be a turning point in Platonic studies.[2] Lutosławski's *The Origin and Growth of Plato's Logic with an Account of Plato's Style and of the Chronology of His Writings*[3] is acknowledged to be a reliable source describing the 19th century dispute over the Dialogues' chronology and an important attempt to resolve this issue. The part of Lutosławski's philosophical views that are somewhat underestimated is the fact that his research was inspired by Plato and that the connection between Lutosławski's chronological investigation and his system of messianic philosophy does indeed exist.

The subject of the nineteenth century discourse relating to Plato's works is referred to as *Die Platonische Frage*. The initiator of the discourse was the German scholar Wilhelm Gottlieb Tennemann[4] who carried out a research on the link between the Dialogues' chronology, the evolution of Plato's ideas and an appropriate interpretation of Platonism. In 1804 Friedrich Schleiermacher[5] in the introduction to his translation of the Dialogues wrote, that Platonic philosophy in the Dialogues presented a certain unity and was consistent. In the nineteenth century German scholars rejected this 'idealized' image of Plato. These two approaches, unitarian and evolutionary, to the texts

* Translated into English by Agata Andrzejkowicz and Aleksandra Macintosh.

[1] Novotný (1977).

[2] Thesleff (1982), pp. 3-4, 68; Brandwood (1990), pp. 130, 135. Also Santayana (1957), p. 58, first published in *The International Monthly* in 1902.

[3] Lutosławski (1897).

[4] *System der platonischen Philosophie*, Leipzig 1792-1795, vol. 1-4.

[5] *Platons Werke*, translated by F. Schleiermacher, *Preface* vol. 1, Berlin 1804.

of *Corpus Platonicum* formed the basis for the discussions on Plato that continue even today.

Scholars such as Karl Friedrich Hermann[6], Friedrich Ueberweg[7] emphasized the fact that Plato's philosophy evolved, but neither of them noticed the need for research on style for the more appropriate presentation of the Dialogues' chronology with the exception of Richard Schöne[8]. However, the most important inspiration for Lutosławski, was the work of Lewis Campbell[9] who made a precise analysis of the late Dialogues' style.

Researching the vocabulary especially hiatuses, particles and other words of little semantic meaning of so-called late group of the Dialogues (these include *Sph.*, *Plt.*, *Phlb.*, *Ti.*, *Criti.*, *Lg.*), Campbell established their stylistic and chronological affinity. Many later authors, unaware of the achievements of L. Campbell and Friedrich Blass[10], who studied the frequency of use of hiatus, repeated some of their discoveries.

Accuracy of the method and new insights into it caused broader acquaintance with the work of Wilhelm Dittenberger.[11] This aroused first discussions on lexicographical-stylistic methods of establishing Plato's Dialogues' chronology. The Platonic vocabulary of the Dialogues was examined. In 1886 Martin Schanz[12] provided new material and methodological instructions for the research. Another scholar, Constantin Ritter[13], collected considerable amount of the findings from German and Austrian sources and focused on the analysis of the frequency of occurrence of various answers' formulae. Hans von Arnim[14], although without broader knowledge of literature, analysed a similar subject. Lutosławski was familiar with all these works, when he formed his own assumptions on the chronology of the Dialogues.

[6] *Geschichte und System der platonischen Philosophie*, Heidelberg 1839.

[7] *Untersuchungen über die Echtheit und Zeitfolge platonischer Schriften und über die Hauptmomente aus Platons Leben*, Wien 1861.

[8] *Ueber Platons Protagoras. Ein Beitrag zur Lösung der platonischen Frage*, Leipzig 1862.

[9] *Introduction* in: *The Sophistes and Politicus of Plato*, Oxford 1867.

[10] *Die attische Beredsamkeit in dem Zeitraum von Alexander zu Augustus* vol. 2, Leipzig 1874.

[11] „Sprachliche Kriterien für die Chronologie der platonischen Dialoge", *Hermes* vol. 16 (1881).

[12] „Zur Entwickelung des platonischen Stils", *Hermes* vol. 21 (1886).

[13] *Untersuchungen über Platon*, Stuttgart 1888.

[14] *De Platonis Dialogis Quaestiones Chronologicae*, Rostock 1896.

In his *Plato's Logic* Lutosławski included a report on the methods of linguistic-statistic research on the Dialogues, which prior to that were applied in Germany, Britain and The United States. He was identified with his research of the Dialogues' chronology, but his interpretation of the development of Plato's philosophy remained less known. He was recognized for the stylometric method and the chronological result achieved by it. His method included the biggest statistical material at that time. On the basis of the factor of statistical convergence of the Dialogues with the late group, and also the late group with *Lg.*, Lutosławski constructed a proposal of the Dialogues' chronology. He divided these into the following groups:

- the Socratic group (*Ap.*, *Eutyphr.*, *Cri.*, *Chrm.*, *La.*, *Prt.*, *Men.*, *Euthd.*, *Grg.* – we can be certain that *Grg.* is the last dialogue in this group and that it is followed by Plato's first Sicilian journey);
- the first Platonic group (*Cra.*, written before the Academy was founded and *Smp.*, *Phd.*, *R. I,* written later);
- the middle Platonic group (*R. II-X*, *Phdr.*, and *Tht.*, *Prm.* written only after Plato took twelve-year interlude from writing and the second Sicilian journey) and
- the last Platonic group (*Sph.*, *Plt.*, *Phlb.*, *Ti.*, *Criti.*, *Lg.*).

In various aspects Lutosławski's relative chronology is identical with those prepared by W. Dittenberger, M. Schanz and C. Ritter.

Lutosławski's work provoked a discussion not only on the Dialogues' chronology but also on the very sense of stylometric research in general. Thus far the attention of Lutosławski's readers was focused on the method and the selection of the linguistic material rather than on the interpretation of the development of Plato's philosophy. Even the most dissenting critics have recognized the bulk of the work undertaken by Lutoslawski on the Dialogues chronology. The first critique mainly of a philological and not philosophical nature of Lutoslawski's ideas came from Paul Natorp[15] and Eduard Zeller[16]. Many scholars researching Plato's philosophy greeted the method with enthusiasm. They published their own works concerning the Dialogues

[15] „Ueber die Methode der Chronologie platonischer Schriften nach sprachlichen Kriterien", *Archiv für Geschichte der Philosophie* 11 (1898); and three articles entitled „Untersuchungen über Platos Phaedros und Theaetet", *Archiv für Geschichte der Philosophie* 12 (1899) and 13 (1900). He also wrote some letters to Lutosławski pointing out mistakes, he found in Lutosławski's book. The letters are preserved in The Archive of Science of The Polish Academy of Sciences and The Polish Academy of Arts and Sciences in Cracow.

[16] „Die deutsche Litteratur über die sokratische, platonische und aristotelische Philosophie 1896", *Archiv für Geschichte der Philosophie* 13 (1900).

chronology[17], in which they applied different style's indicators from indicators applied by Lutosławski or different methods. In many cases they confirmed Lutosławski's findings. As Lutosławski's *Plato's Logic* was written in English, it involved the English speaking world in the debate. Prior to this, issue was taken up by the German speaking philosophers and philologists. The critique came from the unitarian stand of Paul Shorey[18], to be discussed later, similar to Schleiermacher's interpretation. Another scholar, Hans Raeder[19] summarised the discussions in his book *Platons philosophische Entwickelung*. His chronology of the Dialogues between *Cra.* and *Lg.* was in accordance with Lutosławski's chronology.

The quality of the style of the Dialogues then introduced, was a rhythmical sequence in the clauses of the sentences. The revolution in the research on the style of the Dialogues was brought about by technological advances in the use of computers towards the end of the twentieth century.[20] Recent opposition towards stylometric research and towards the importance of chronology stems mainly from the adherents of the so-called unwritten doctrines (Tűbingen School: Konrad Gaiser, Hans Krämer).

In *Plato's Logic* Lutosławski recognized the chronological order of the 'dialectical dialogues' (*Tht.*, *Prm.*, *Sph.*, *Plt.*) and settled a dispute over whether they fall in the early or late period of Plato's work. By opposing himself to E. Zeller, Lutosławski put the dialectical dialogues in the later period of Plato's work (after *Smp.*, *Phd.*, and *R.*). By placing the dialogues in the later period, Lutosławski expressed the essence of Plato's philosophical evolution and his abandonment of the first version of the theory of ideas. According to him the dialectical dialogues depict turning point in Plato's philosophical development, similar to the critical period of I. Kant's philosophy. These were not just a juvenile exercise in dialectics.

Four groups of stylistic similarity of the Dialogues (the Socratic group, the first Platonic group, the middle Platonic group and the last Platonic group) translate into six stages of Plato's philosophical development:

- Socratic – the Socratic group;
- beginnings of the theory of ideas – *Cra.*, *Smp.*, *Phd.*;

[17] E.g.: A.W. Benn, „The later ontology of Plato", Mind 11, 1902; P. Bovet, *Le dieu de Platon d'apres l'ordre chronologique des dialogues*, Paris 1902.

[18] Shorey (1903).

[19] Leipzig 1905.

[20] D. Wishart & S. V. Leach, "A Multivariate Analysis of Platonic Prose Rhythm", *Computer Studies in the Humanities and Verbal Behaviour* 3 (1970); G. R. Ledger, *Re-counting Plato: A Computer Analysis of Plato's Style*, Oxford 1989.

- Middle Platonism – *R.*, *Phdr.*;
- the reform of logic – *Tht.*, *Prm.*;
- the new theory of science – *Sph.*, *Plt.*, *Phlb.*, and
- the last works – *Ti.*, *Criti.*, *Lg.*).

According to Lutosławski the most important points of Plato's philosophical evolution are as follows: Plato in his early philosophical development considered ethical issues, applying Socratic induction, and did not attach much significance to logic as such. Any logical issues that had already occurred, were not a reflection upon logic as such, but rather the use of the laws of logic in ethical deliberations. Later in *Men.* the distinction between the right belief and knowledge, which would be connected with pre-existence of the soul can be found. Hypothetical reasoning, examining the consequences of using some theorems before judging their truthfulness, also appears in *Men.* The first serious logical issue which was examined by Plato in another dialogue, *Cra.*, is the relationship between thought and language. The next issue appeared in *Smp.* and it concerned independently existing, unchanging ideas of almost mystical vision.

The language of poetry, in which the theory of ideas was presented, was to Lutosławski a sign, that Plato did indeed realize the difficulties of his own concept. *Phd.*, *R.* and *Phdr.* confirm the existence of ideas beyond the material world. Ideas are its complete opposition; the reality of ideas is a perfect, true Being, shaping the material reality of appearances.

At the same time Plato's interest in logic was increasing. He recommended the classification of notions and the quest for the most general, highest principles. The subject of the truth are the eternal ideas and the world of *phaenomena* is the subject of beliefs. Coherence became the basic criterion of the truth and the Good became the most important of ideas.

In this very moment the highest kinds, categories come to the fore in Platonic philosophy, in *Tht.* and *Prm.* These categories do not exist beyond the human mind and soul. The soul itself, as the principle of motion, becomes a more and more important element of the system. After the criticism of the theory of ideas in *Prm.*, Plato proposes a new theory of knowledge. According to this new theory man's intuition should not take part in the recognition of truth. Truth should be recognized by the individual when he discovers the notional order, through a synthesis and an analysis. As a result the system of ideas is superseded by a hierarchy of souls, which is predominated with divine providence. Ideas form the model of sensory reality, but their existence consists of being discovered by human souls and being reproduced in the matter by the Demiurge. Plato at the last stage of his work had already formed his methods of dividing and combining the notions, classifications and generalizations. He recommends the use of dichotomy only on condition that it does not break the natural division of the reality into the kinds. This was a modification of the simple dialectic present in Plato's earlier works. He also formulated recommendations concerning the definitions that are very similar to those known from *Corpus Aristotelicum*. In the whole consistent system of notions every single class of beings, small or large, was supposed to be given its own nature by God. This allowed one to distinguish several other classes within the same kind. This proves that Plato's awareness of logic was increasing since the time he wrote his first dialogues. However, it is not the only evidence of that. Plato's earlier dialogues contain errors and sophistries which are largely absent from his later dialogues.

Lutosławki insisted that Plato's greatest philosophical achievement was the recognition of the spiritual reality as the driving force of the changes and the reason for existence of the world in general.

The last period of Plato's philosophical development, which was expressed in *Ti.* and *Lg.*, was the most disputed by scholars. Lutosławski's aim was to prove that Plato in the late period of his work was more of a spiritualist than an idealist. On the basis of the fragment of *Ti.* 28a (no®sei metà lógou perilhptón) he claimed that Plato 'repeatedly represents ideas as included in thought.'[21] Lutosławski had his own interpretative method. The aim of it was to draw attention to souls reviving all bodies and world. On one hand the ideas were losing objective existence, on the other – the spiritual sphere was gaining fundamental meaning. Another fragment of the dialogue, 69c-d, enabled Lutosławski to draw conclusions concerning the human soul. These were that Plato separated the mortal element connected to corporeality from the immortal soul. The soul's task was to discover the eternal (90d).

After the analysis of *Ti.* and noticing the absence of the theory of ideas in *Lg.*, Lutosławski drew the following conclusion:

> Plato's philosophy is not a mere theory of knowledge, and his theory of knowledge is not limited to the conception of ideas. The soul is not an idea, and acts a more important part in later Platonism than all ideas of Middle Platonism. It is the soul, and not the ideas, which is the central point of Plato's later theory of knowledge.[22]

Therefore Plato became the first representative of spiritualistic pluralism which is based on the assumption that the reality is constituted by spiritual beings of different levels of perfection:

[21] Lutosławski (1897), p. 477.

[22] Lutosławski (1897), p. 494.

> the ideas which were at first credited with a substantial existence out of the mind have been later enclosed in souls, and the hierarchy of souls became the highest reality, the last explanation of the problem of existence.[23]

Ideas are the subject of objective knowledge, but the substantial existence does not always follow the objective character. Plato did not reach this conclusion until the late period of his work. Thus the existence of ideas is possible only in connection with souls recognizing them:

> Ideas exist only in souls – they are eternal and unchangeable because their first model is created by God in his own thought. Thus ideas are the patterns of reality, and their existence in souls is named true Being. [...] They must be created and elaborated by each soul in its own turn, and sought for by the logical exercises of classification, generalization, and division.[24]

According to Lutosławski Plato anticipated some trends of future philosophy. Lutosławski wrote:

> he anticipated that new course of philosophy which led Descartes two thousand years later to seek the origin of all knowledge in individual consciousness[25]

According to Lutosławski, spiritualism, i.e. the recognition of the substantial existence of the spiritual sphere, connected Plato to French philosophy.

This interpretation was met with harsh criticism from P. Shorey, a famous Platonic scholar from Chicago, who was an opponent of stylometric research. He pointed out fundamental defects in Lutosławski's interpretation of Plato's philosophy. Shorey argued that Plato formed the whole of the system in his early years and was fragmentarily announcing it piecemeal in his successive dialogues. Shorey was therefore sceptical towards the importance of research on chronology. He represented the unitarian interpretation of Plato, whereas Lutosławski was in favour of Plato's philosophical evolution. This was made possible to follow due to the Dialogues' chronology, which was set by the examination of the Dialogues' style. As can be seen they are standing on polar opposites of the methodology of research on Platonic legacy.

Lutosławski was given to over-elaboration in some fragments of the late group of the dialogues, of which Shorey points out several examples.

[23] Lutosławski (1897), p. 516.

[24] Lutosławski (1897), pp. 523-524.

[25] Lutosławski (1897), p. 525.

Shorey drew attention to these 'errors' but he did not present any arguments opposing the spiritualistic interpretation as such. With philological meticulousness he disputed every single translative and interpretative deviation of *Plato's Logic*. Shorey also criticized some commentaries by L. Campbell, E. Zeller and P. Natorp.

We will adduce two of Lutosławski's errors, which undermine the legitimacy of his arguments. At this point the only argument in Lutosławski's favour would be invoking the whole interpretative context. On the basis of the following fragments of *Ti.*: 27e and 29a, Lutosławski explained the relationship between ideas-models and the intellect as an ontological relation. The text of the Dialogues, however, explicitly points not to the existence of ideas in the mind, but to the need of intellectual learning of what is unchangeable – ideas. Shorey described that commentary as a 'mistranslation'.[26] The second example, described by Shorey as a 'misinterpretation'[27], concerns *Cra.* The last line of Socrates (440a-d) contains a complete terminology of the Platonic theory of ideas (eĭdoV, aütò äò Ésti, Ésti då tò Âgajðón). In spite of this, Lutosławski did not ascribe the awareness of their transcendental existence to Plato at this stage.

An important point of Shorey's criticism was to draw attention to the futility of stylistic research, *platonische Forschung* after Lutosławski's book appeared, turned into an enumeration of the possible Dialogues' chronologies. It appeared that Plato's philosophy itself was declining in importance. Philosophers were arguing over its history instead. Lutosławski, however, did not study the Dialogues' chronology in isolation from their content. Stylometry was just a basis for the genetic presentation of the development of Plato's philosophy. Although some doubts are raised as to Lutosławski's interpretation. He was not one of the „enumerators of kajðáper and t™ m®n"[28] – as Shorey refers to the statisticians. In 1948, at the age of 85, Lutosławski wrote:

> My book on Plato's logic published in 1897 and showing the development of Plato's thought did not sufficiently insist on the novelty and originality of Plato's last views.[29]

[26] Shorey (1903), p. 38.

[27] Shorey (1903), p. 33.

[28] Shorey (1903), p. 3.

[29] Lutosławski (1948), p. 71. Lutosławski's name was printed there as „Lutostawski". He was complaining about this insouciance concerning the spelling of his name particularly in the USA, when he was traveling there with lectures.

Indeed, language statistics itself was not the final aim of the Lutosławski's stylometric experiments. He treated stylometry only as a means to an end. He continuously described the mystical experience, which he had while reading *Smp.*, during the preparations for the exams at the University of Dorpat in 1888. Plato's philosophy became also an element of messianistic and personalistic philosophy of Lutosławski.

Thirty years after publishing his *Plato's Logic,* Lutosławski wrote a history of metaphysics, a peculiar history of philosophical standpoints, showing the importance of Plato's role in the history of thought. Lutosławski in his book *The Knowledge of Reality*[30] made a classification of philosophical (i.e. metaphysical or ontological) views, which he named *theasies*, after the Greek word jðeasíV. In Lutosławski's concept of the development of metaphysics, Plato was regarded as the author of the idealistic and spiritualistic philosophy.

According to Lutosławski, the metaphysical cognition is synthetic and it encompasses the whole of being. Also at the same time, metaphysical cognition is not based on the authority of religion. Moreover, metaphysics has its additional justification – the acceptance of a particular metaphysical standpoint shapes human life and is a foundation of ethics. Metaphysics is the only science closely bound up with morality, and the latter one is a test of the former one.

> Every theasy depends on two factors: first, the subject who looks at the world; and secondly, the subject or world which he complies.[31]

Hence the subject of the cognition remains fixed, despite changes that might occur in it. There are only as many metaphysical stages of a subject's development as there are layers of reality. All of these are subsequent and necessary stages of evolution and express certain truths.

According to Lutosławski, the development of the six possible world views is outlined as follows: materialism, idealism, pantheism, spiritualism, mysticism, and messianism.

Materialism, with all its aspects of the relationship between spirit and matter, is the most naive and primitive view. Idealism is antithetical to materialism. Conflict is not merely a theoretical contradiction, but it translates into divergent interests of people who represent these two opposite

[30] Lutosławski (1930).

[31] Lutosławski (1930), p. 4. The final Polish version of that book supplemented with Lutosławski's theory of personality and the ways of discovering the God was remaining ready to publish in typescript since the death of the philosopher in 1954. It appeared recently entitled *Metafizyka* [*Metaphysics*], ed. T. Mróz, Drozdowo 2004.

viewpoints. Pantheism is synthetic, in comparison with materialism and idealism, since it solves that first conflict of views. Pluralistic spiritualism is antithetical to pantheistic monism. However, dialectical inconsistency between these two views forms the contradiction on the higher level of metaphysical reflection. An appropriate understanding of these views must be preceded by the understanding of the earlier ones. The synthesis of pantheism and spiritualism is mysticism:

> Twice has the struggle between two opposed points of view led to a reconciliation at a higher stage.[32]

The last, third conflict of the world views occurs between spiritualist and mystic, e.g. Plato and Plotinus. Both do not doubt the existence of the spiritual sphere, but to the first one the most important indicator of the ontological hierarchy is diversity and freedom of spiritual individuals, whereas to the second one the true reality is being formed in a mystical experience of a bond between the spirit and the highest being in the spiritual hierarchy.

Mysticism together with spiritualism forms a foundation of the final view – national messianism. The fundamental notion in the spiritualistic outlook is the existence of the free soul, in mysticism – a mystical experience – enlightenment. Then the last possible view should use these two notions and raise them to the higher level.

Messianism is the crowning achievement of the philosophy's history. It is also the final possibility of the outlook's evolution of the individual. Similarly to mysticism, messianism places the emphasis on the relationship between spiritual beings, yet not only between God and an individual, but also between separate individuals. According to Lutosławski, messianism, let us stress the importance of the proper understanding of what messianism is, is a view encompassing the spiritual sphere – after all it derives from spiritualism, discovered by Plato, and mysticism. An exemplification of the messianistic outlook happens rarely, because the higher and more advanced the view is, the smaller circle of people share it. Therefore messianism is an exclusive view, but its aim is to overcome this exclusiveness.

> Mystic union, such as is experienced between creature and Creator, is also possible between creatures of like nature, who establish mystic links between themselves and with their Creator simultaneously [...] Such a group would live on inspiration, drawn from infinite wisdom.[33]

[32] Lutosławski (1930), p. 139.

[33] Lutosławski (1930), pp. 141-142.

The freedom of the will of the spiritualist and the mystical submitting to God's will are being gathered in national mission, which was closely related to the history of Poland. National mission is the nation's humanity-oriented activity; it is similar to the individual's nation-oriented activity. Its aim was to transform the relationship between different nations and to bring them to coexistence and cooperation in near future. An individual without losing his freedom in acting gains the possibility of acting for other individuals and together with them in fulfilling the God's plan for the human race in the practice of love,

> the active love of the Messianist becomes national consciousness. We may distinguish it from all kinds of emotions or feelings, as being eminently active and creative.[34]

The discovery of national consciousness and appearance of messianism would not be possible without Plato's discovery of the role of spiritual reality – according to Lutosławski.

> The above sketch of the essential alternatives of metaphysical conception is, like every other philosophical work, an outcome of the moral, intellectual and spiritual experience of the author, who has in very fact lived through all the stages he indicates, and has devoted more than forty years to the study of his predecessors in philosophy. He is humbly grateful for the privilege of having enjoyed both the leisure and vitality necessary to the pursuit of these arduous studies, and further for a certain quality of character which has enabled him to be, in a sense, independent of the limiting influences of period, environment, or, in short, of any motive other than the passionate love of truth.[35]

– in these words Lutosławski completed his survey of outlooks, the crown of which is messianism.

Fifty years after publishing *Plato's Logic* Lutosławski reminded international audiences of his own interpretation of the development of Plato's philosophy. What inspired him to do so was on one hand a minimal reception of that interpretation from pages of *Plato's Logic*, and on the other a new, extremely dramatic situation of Europe and Poland after World War II. In the 1950's, in his eighties, Lutosławski prepared a new edition of his book. The new version excluded the philological methodology and included the elements indicating the link between Plato and personalism and messianism.

[34] Lutosławski (1930), p. 142.

[35] Lutosławski (1930), pp. 138-139.

Lutosławski perceived Plato's philosophy as one of the ideological antidotes to communism, which was spreading across the world at that time. He wrote:

> But while the reviewers of my book on Plato's logic were eloquent about the merits of stylometry, they cared much less about the logical development, and Plato was still considered an idealist for whom true being consisted in ideas only without recognizing the true existence of the souls.[36]

The political situation of Poland created favourable conditions for reminding the world of Lutosławski's own interpretation of Platonism.

> This change of mind of Plato has now acquired a singular actuality in view of the conflict usually termed as between communism and Christianity, Christianity being the popular exposition of the modern spiritualism, called now by some American philosophers personalism.[37]

Although Lutosławski recognized the basis for communist ideology which was 'more radical than any contemporary communism'[38] in *R.* written by Plato after the third Sicilian journey, when idealism gave way to spiritualism, he also insisted that,

> Plato reached in his latest works a view of the world very much akin to Christianity.[39]

The message of the new book aimed to reach a wide range of readers, especially under the ideology, which was negating the primacy of the individuals' freedom over the totalitarian state. Its purpose was to indicate the appropriate outlook during the political conflict, which was to Lutosławski another exemplification of the old philosophical dispute over the ontological priority of ideas over free spirits. Only the recognition of spiritualism in ontology could unify individuals in a messianistic act for the good of mankind –

> and on this way no greater teacher has ever lived than Plato. If all men could become similar to the greatest thinker of all ages, they would agree in action and despise the idle strife of words.[40]

Bernhard Mollenhauer, one of the Lutosławski's correspondents mentioned Lutosławski's hitherto unpublished book in one of the American

[36] Lutosławski (1948), p. 70.

[37] Lutosławski (1948), p. 70.

[38] Lutosławski (1948), p. 70.

[39] Lutosławski (1948), p. 71.

[40] Lutosławski (1948), p. 72.

periodicals. In his article he also quoted one of Lutosławski's letters from October 30, 1954, in which Lutosławski stated:

> The connection of the latest Platonism with Polish Messianism is almost unknown, so in my work on Plato's logic I made it evident. There is no causal connection between the Platonism of 350 BC and the Polish Messianism of 1848, but I made it evident in my (later) work and therefore my Platonic studies are an introduction to the study of Polish Messianism.[41]

However, *Plato's Change of Mind* was not published. In 1947 the book was turned down by the Longman's publishers, and up to now its typescript is kept in The Archive of Science of The Polish Academy of Sciences and The Polish Academy of Arts and Sciences. The book is now gaining in importance especially in comparison with K.R. Popper's *The Open Society and its Enemies*[42], where Popper attacks Plato's political philosophy. While Popper blamed Plato for totalitarian ideology, Lutosławski defended Platonism, as a cure for political situation, especially communism.

Only a few books by Polish philosophers were as widely known and discussed in the West as *Plato's Logic*. Lutosławski's work, erudite, well-crafted, though not without a personal involvement, certainly is the best known all over the world work of Polish authorship from the field of the history of philosophy. Nevertheless his work was unknown to Polish reader. Even the philosophical circle perceived Lutosławski mainly from his messianistic philosophy. Most critics agreed that he was an expert on Plato, but hardly anyone read *Plato's Logic*. Abroad Lutosławski was perceived as the author of contentious work about Plato, and a supporter of the spiritualistic view of the world. Lutosławski had contributed an extensive statistical research on style to the researches on Plato. Even if the rightness of the method or the chronological conclusions would be questioned, undoubted remains the fact, that thanks to *Plato's Logic* the scientific world considered the Platonic problem again. However, it was not the method, but the interpretation which was in the centre of Lutosławski's attention. The majority of scholars, who accept genetic-evolutionary approach to the Dialogues, agree with the outline of chronology, which is determined by Lutosławski and two equally important scholars: H. Raeder and C. Ritter.[43]

[41] Mollenhauer (1954), p. 247. The letter was written only two months before philosopher's death.

[42] Vol. I, *The Spell of Plato*, London 1945.

[43] Thesleff (1982), p. 4.

Lutosławski named materialism as the first philosophical outlook in the history of European philosophy. Idealism, pantheism, spiritualism, mysticism and national messianism were further stages of the worldviews' evolution. The most significant truths of messianism were the existence of a free and immortal soul and the acknowledgment of a relationship between the human being and God as well as a bond between similar individuals.
According to Lutosławski the first of these truths, the fundament of spiritualistic philosophy was discovered in the philosophical sphere by Plato, which makes his spiritualism one of the inspirations of messianism. Messianistic philosophy became a philosophical system, which was not just a nineteenth century's creation of Polish Romanticism, but had one of its real roots in ancient philosophy. This was meant by Lutosławski to increase its value in the history of philosophy.

* * *

The readers interested in Lutosławski's studies on Plato, in his linguistic method, or in his Platonism, might like to consult the papers listed below, which were published in English and French, apart from numerous Polish works on the subject.

Mróz T., *Philebus Interpreted by Paul Natorp and Wincenty Lutosławski*, in: *Plato's Philebus. Selected Papers from the Eighth Symposium Platonicum*, edds. John Dillon and Luc Brisson, "International Plato Studies" 26, Sankt Augustin 2010, pp. 382-389.

Pawłowski A., *Les Aspects Linguistiques dans l'Œuvre Scientifique de Wincenty Lutosławski*, "Organon" 37 (40): 2008, pp. 149-176.

Pawłowski A., *Wincenty Lutosławski (1863-1954). A Forgotten Father of Stylometry*, "Glottometrics" 8 2004, pp. 83-89.

Pawłowski A., Pacewicz A., *Wincenty Lutosławski (1863-1954). Philosophe, helléniste ou fondateur sous-estimé de la stylométrie*, "Historiographia Linguistica" XXXI 2/3 (2004), pp. 423-447.

NEOPLATONISM IN SCIENCE PAST AND FUTURE

Bruce MacLennan

I. Introduction

In this article I argue that modern Neoplatonism can contribute to a revitalization of science and an improved human relationship to nature. I begin by considering the role of Neoplatonism in the history of science, considering both ideas that have contributed to the constitution of contemporary science, and those that have been abandoned by it. Then I mention two especially Pythagorean developments in contemporary science. Finally, I turn to the future, to the contributions that I believe Neoplatonic ideas can make toward the future of science.

II. The Past

Recall the alternative views of nature and science that competed in Europe in the 16th and 17th centuries.[1] We may take as our starting point the Aristotelian-Thomistic cosmology, which resulted from Aquinas' rehabilitation and Christianization of Aristotelian cosmology and Ptolemaic astronomy, and which dominated European thinking from the thirteenth century. A value system was implicit in this cosmology, which placed a stationary Earth at the center of the universe, in the center of which was Hell and the Devil (Easlea 1980, pp. 43, 57–8). In polar opposition was God in His heaven, the active force outside the circumference of the Primum Mobile. Correlated with this polarity of good and evil were other oppositions, many of which can be found in the Pythagorean Table of Opposites: form / matter, mind / body, active / passive, male / female, heaven / earth, and so forth (Easlea 1980, pp. 46–50). The causes of these associations and correspondences are complex and not entirely cultural, for they also have psychological and biological roots, but that is beyond the scope of this article (Hillman 1978, Pt. III; Stevens 1998, pp. 116–23).

As the weaknesses of the Thomistic-Aristotelian philosophy became apparent, two philosophical orientations presented themselves as the chief

[1] In this brief overview I am indebted to the work of Brian Easlea (1980) and especially to the classic works by D. P. Walker (1958) and Frances Yates (1964, 1966). The primary sources are very numerous, but the citations may be found in these works.

contenders for a new philosophy of nature (Easlea 1980, pp. 89–90). On one hand was the *mechanical philosophy*, as developed especially by Gassendi and Descartes, and on the other was the (so-called) *magical philosophy*, which was advocated in one form or another by Neoplatonists, alchemists, Hermeticists, adherents of the supposed *prisca theologia*, and so forth. A principal difference between the two was their view of nature. In accord with Cartesian dualism, the mechanical philosophers viewed non-human nature as inanimate and sought to understand natural processes in terms of mechanical principles, such as shape, position, and motion, rather than in terms of sensory qualities, which were considered fundamentally illusory. On the other hand, in general accord with Neoplatonic cosmology (stemming ultimately from the *Timaeus*), the magical philosophers understood nature in terms of an *anima mundi*, which vitalizes and governs the material world (Merchant 1980, ch. 4). One consequence of these differences was that mechanical philosophers were stronger advocates of using mechanistic principles to appropriate and exploit non-human nature for human benefit, a foundation of the industrial revolution (Easlea 1980, ch. 5). The magical philosophy, however, entailed a degree of reverence for Nature and implied circumspection in possessing and exploiting "her" (Easlea 1980, pp. 102–4, 111–12, 139). Against this background I will mention some Neoplatonic ideas that were either adopted or abandoned by modern science as it emerged at this time.

As is well known, discussion of the *Corpus Hermeticum* by Lactantius (*Div. Inst.*, I.vi, *De ira Dei*, XI) led to the impression that these texts were of enormous antiquity, that Hermes Trismegistus was a contemporary of Moses, and that the Hermetic tracts represented the *prisca theologia*, the primordial theology revealed by God. This misperception persisted until corrected in 1614 by the textual analysis of Isaac Casaubon. In the interim, the texts' apparent antiquity and the respect accorded them by Lactantius lent them considerable credibility. In particular, acceptance of the *philosophically* oriented *Hermetica* encouraged acceptance of the more overtly *magical* tracts. Thus we have the roots of Renaissance Hermeticism.

Although the *Hermetica* are not homogeneous, they are broadly in agreement with Neoplatonic theory and practice (e.g., Fowden 1986, pp. 188–95), and so Marsilio Ficino and his followers found little difficulty in crafting a Hermetic philosophy, which they considered to be consistent with Christianity (Yates 1964, ch. VI). It is the theoretical and practical core of the magical philosophy, but let us consider its relation to modern science.

Aside from its scientific impact, the eventual shift to a heliocentric cosmology was a development of enormous symbolic significance. The astronomical reasons for this change are familiar, but it is important not to forget the philosophical background. The Central Fire—often misinterpreted as the Central Sun—was an idea inherited from ancient Pythagoreanism, and Copernicus called his heliocentric model "the Pythagorean theory" and quoted the *Hermetica* in its defense (*De revol. orb. cael.*, Thorn ed., 1873, p. 30; Yates 1964, p. 154). Heliocentrism was motivated as much by religious and philosophical considerations as by astronomical ones, for Neoplatonism, Hermeticism, and related philosophies considered the Sun to be "the visible god," associated with the Demiurge, and a potent symbol for the One and its power, irradiating the material world and bringing it life (Yates 1964, pp. 153–4). From this perspective, the Sun *belonged* in the center of the universe, which thereby became the fountainhead of the Good rather than the central abyss. Giordano Bruno, in his defense of Copernicanism, referred back to the solar magic of Ficino's book *De vita coelitus comparanda*, his most overtly magical work.[2] Consistently with the heliocentric view, Bruno (*Ash Wed. Supper*, Dial. I, p. 61) argued that the Earth, "our perpetual nurse and mother," as he called her, *must* move because she is alive and eternal by virtue of her continual self-renewal. It was a tenet of the magical philosophy, which we find for example in Cornelius Agrippa (1651/1993, II.56), that the stars and planets are sources of vitality and motion, and therefore that they have souls and are alive themselves (Yates 1964, p. 243). Similarly Kepler, who was influenced by Agrippa, the Paracelsans, Proclus, and other Neoplatonists, said the earth is a living being with an *anima terrae* structured like the *anima hominis* (Pauli 1955, pp. 156–77).

Qabalah, in the form in which it emerged in the Middle Ages, incorporated many Neopythagorean ideas, especially in its decad of *Sephiroth* or divine emanations (Yates 1964, pp. 92–3).[3] Indeed, Scholem (1965, p. 167) has argued that the *Sefer Yezirah*, a principal Qabalistic text, was written by a Jewish Neopythagorean, perhaps in the first centuries CE. The other principal text, the *Zohar*, was written in Spain in the thirteenth century, where Ramon Lull was active (Yates 1966, p. 178). Significantly influenced by the Neoplatonic systems of pseudo-Dionysius and John Scotus Erigena (Yates 1966, pp. 177–8), as well as by the Qabalah, Lull is best known for his system of rotating wheels labeled with letters corresponding to the dignities of God, which are, in effect, simultaneously the divine names of pseudo-Dionysius and the Sephiroth of the Qabalah (Yates 1966, pp. 178–9). To put it in other terms, we have in the Lullian art a system of archetypal ideas, whose

[2] Yates (1964, pp. 155, 208–9). See Ficino (1998, Bk. III) for *De vit. coel. comp.*

[3] A good example of Neopythagorean treatment of the decad is pseudo-Iamblichus' *Theologumena arithmeticae* (ed. de Falco, 1922; tr. Waterfield as *The Theology of Arithmetic*, Phanes, 1988).

interrelationships can be explored combinatorially by rotating the wheels (Yates 1966, p. 178).

It is significant, as Yates has stressed, that in Lull's art these archetypal ideas were represented by letters, not by the symbolically rich images used in prior systems for organizing ideas, such as the magical memory systems of Bruno and Campanella (Yates 1966, pp. 176–7). In this, Lull is connecting with Qabalistic interpretation of the letters of the Hebrew alphabet as the atomic constituents, as it were, of the Name of God, and with the Qabalistic practice of *gematria*, by which hidden correspondences and connections between ideas were found by means of the numerical values of the Hebrew letters, and with Neopythagorean use of the numerical values of the Greek letters for numerological speculation (Yates 1964, p. 92; 1966, pp. 178–9). Although these practices are found primarily in Gnosticism, they were commonly attributed to the ancient Pythagoreans (e.g., Hippolytus, *Refutatio*, 6.25, 6.47, 7.14, 8.5-8).

Another important aspect of Lull's art, as Yates (1966, p. 178) emphasizes, is that it was intended as a *method* for discovering and demonstrating truths, specifically the truths of Christianity. The symbolical and mystical meanings of Lull's characters were closely tied to his medieval world-view, but in the seventeenth century, several philosophers were inspired to improve on his idea and to apply it to the discovery, codification, and demonstration of scientific knowledge.[4] Chief among these was Leibniz, who was deeply influenced by Lull, Bruno, Qabalah, alchemy, and Hermetic philosophy with a Rosicrucian accent.[5] According to Yates (1966, p. 370), he defined his project as:

> a general science, a new logic, a new method, an *Ars reminiscendi* or Mnemonica, an *Ars Characteristica* or Symbolica, an *Ars Combinatoria* or Lulliana, a Cabala of the Wise, a Magia Naturalis, in short all sciences will be here contained as in an Ocean.

There is a direct line of descent from the ideas of Leibniz and his contemporaries for formal knowledge-representation languages and mechanized reasoning, through the development of symbolic logic and formalized mathematics, to the computational models of knowledge and cognition used in artificial intelligence and cognitive science, but that is outside the scope of this paper. It suffices here to observe that the Lullian vision affected the pursuit of *method*, which occupied many seventeenth-

[4] Yates (1966, ch. 17, esp. pp. 356–7, 361–2, 364–5); see also Ong (1958) and Rossi (2000).

[5] Yates (1966, pp. 367, 372–3). For more, see Coudert (1995) and Rossi (2000).

century philosophers, including Descartes, Bacon, and Leibniz, for this pursuit was redirected toward a methodology of abstract relationships among monadic ideas (Ong 1958; Yates 1966, ch. 17; Rossi 2000, ch. 5). Although this drive reached its apex in the logical positivist philosophy of the early twentieth century, it still survives in the preference for mathematical abstraction in all scientific theories.

It is interesting to recall that contemporary with the Lullian art, there were other systems for organizing ideas, dating to classical antiquity, used for memory, spiritual contemplation, or magic, which (in contrast to Lull's art) made use of symbolically rich images rather than abstract characters (Bolzoni 2001; Carruthers & Ziolkowski 2002; Yates 1966; Rossi 2000). These systems also had roots in Neoplatonism, and had applications in religion, alchemy, and other spiritual disciplines. They arose from a confluence between the ancient art of memory, attributed to Simonides of Ceos, and the Platonic explanation of knowledge as recollection. The art of memory, as known primarily through the *Ad Herennium*, recommended placing vivid, active symbolic images for ideas (*imagines agentes*) in distinct spatially-organized visualizable places (*loci*), so that their relationships could be recalled (Yates 1966, ch. 1). Platonic epistemology, in comparison, understood the Forms or Ideas to have an eternal structure and fixed relationships.

Already in the Pythagorean revival of late antiquity memory was connected with spiritual practices, and biographers attributed a prodigious memory to such figures as Pythagoras and Apollonius of Tyana (Yates 1966, p. 56). Also beginning in antiquity was the use of cosmologically significant structures, such as the zodiac, decans, and planetary spheres, to organize ideas and their images (Yates 1966, p. 54). In this way the art of memory allowed the macrocosm to be reflected in the microcosm of the individual mind.

In the Middle Ages there was increasing use of the art of memory to internalize religiously significant ideas, such as the articles of faith, the virtues and vices, and the paths to salvation and damnation (Yates 1966, pp.67–9). (Recall also the *Tablet of Cebes*, named for a famous Pythagorean and described as a dedication of a follower of the Pythagorean and Parmenidean way of life.) Albertus Magnus said that the images of the virtues, for example, contained their own *intentiones*, which were efficacious for imparting the virtues (Yates 1966, p. 76). Further, Aquinas introduced a devotional focus into the art of memory by suggesting that the images should be contemplated with solicitude and affection (Yates 1966, pp. 83–7). (Contributing to this development was the medieval practice of *Ars Notaria*, a magical art of memory, attributed to Pythagoras, in which one sought illumination by contemplating esoteric figures while reciting magical prayers; Yates 1966, pp. 56–7.)

In the Renaissance these developments reached their culmination in the spiritual magic of Ficino and Pico, who took practices from the *Asclepius* and other *Hermetica* for the "ensouling" (ἐμψύχωσις, *animatio*) of images, and synthesized them with the art of memory, the astral magic of the *Picatrix*, and the Neoplatonic theurgy of Iamblichus and Proclus. In this art properly structured memory images were regarded as "inner talismans," which through their theurgic power could draw down celestial influences and unite the divine part of the human mind with the divine powers of the cosmos (Yates 1966, pp. 149–62).

However, these symbolically rich images did not lend themselves so well to the newborn mechanical philosophy, with its emphasis on quantifiable size, shape, and motion in preference to phenomenological qualities (Yates 1966, pp. 360–5). Indeed, the imagistic systems were more suited to expressing psychological structures than physical relationships, and so they have been used, especially by Jungian psychologists (von Franz 1974, chs. 10, 11; Jung 1969a, chs. XIII, XIV). In summary we may say that the new science took up the more formal, logical, and abstract aspects of Neoplatonism, but left the more concrete, imaginative, and symbolic aspects to the magi and their successors.

Another aspect of Neoplatonic philosophy that influenced the new science was the idea that there are hidden causes behind the phenomena of the sensible world. That is, all change in the phenomenal world is an effect of an eternal structure of abstract ideas. Thus the reality we ordinarily experience is not the true, or most fundamental reality; it is rather an image, shadow, or reflection, in fact, an illusion. True reality is an immaterial abstract structure, imperceptible to our senses, accessible only through reason and indirect experimentation.

This reductionist perspective is already apparent in Newton's explanation of color as wavelength. His division, on the basis of wavelength, of the continuous spectrum into seven colors, explicitly analogized with the seven tones of the diatonic scale, is just one example of Newton's intentionally Pythagorean approach, in which the hidden *quantities* are real, and the manifest *qualities*, illusions (Bortoft 1996, pp. 38–40, 192–212; Gage 1993, ch. 13, esp. p. 232). Indeed, the reduction of experiential qualities to imperceptible quantities has been typical in physics ever since the development of atomic theory. However, modern science understands the hidden causes to be abstract and mathematical, whereas Neoplatonism and the magical philosophy understood them to be living, psychical, and divine actions of the World Soul (a contrast already apparent in the Kepler-Fludd controversy; see Yates 1964, pp. 440–4; Pauli 1955).

The Renaissance magi understood that different material objects might be irradiated by the same archetypal idea, and that this hidden connection was the cause of sympathies and antipathies between material objects (Easlea 1980, pp. 92–4). The doctrine of cosmic sympathy originated with the Stoics (Wallis 1972, pp. 70–1, 110), but the Neoplatonists adopted it, and Agrippa, for example, cites Iamblichus, Proclus, and "the Platonists" as authorities on "occult virtues" (e.g., Agrippa 1651/1993, I.22, 38, III.59; 1694, ch. 44).

Although the notion that there might be occult affinities between objects was anathema to the mechanical philosophers, it was essential to the theory of gravity. Newton protested *hypotheses non fingo*, but his acceptance of occult forces no doubt facilitated his mathematical description of gravitational force in the absence of mechanical interactions (Easlea 1980, pp. 90, 111, 164–83); in fact, he thought Pythagoras had already discovered the inverse-square law by means of his harmonic theory (White 1997, pp. 348–9). As a closet alchemist and Hermetic philosopher, Newton believed that universal gravity demonstrated the active presence of God in the world, whereas the mechanical philosophers generally believed that God had left the physical world alone since the end of the Age of Miracles (Easlea 1980, pp. 22, 182).

However, due to the hidden nature of the causes, these sympathetic relations were difficult to determine by reason alone (Easlea 1980, p. 93). Therefore, practicing magi, such as Paracelsus, that is, those who, among other things, were actually trying to cure the physical and mental ills of humankind, were forced to resort to experiment to discover the occult sympathies in the material world (Easlea 1980, pp. 100–3; see also Webster, 1982). As the limitations of a purely rationalistic approach to the mechanical philosophy became apparent, some philosophers, such as Francis Bacon and Robert Boyle, began to adopt these empirical methods (Easlea 1980, pp. 90, 126–9, 194–5, 202). Boyle, of course, had been an alchemist and Hermetic philosopher with Rosicrucian sympathies (Easlea 1980, pp. 136–9). However, he abandoned, along with his Hermetic ideas, the notion that the natural world is divine, saying (*Inq. Vulg. Rec. Notion Nature*), "the veneration, wherewith men are imbued for what they call Nature, has been a discouraging impediment to the empire of man over the inferior creatures of God" (Easlea 1980, p. 139). Thus he enunciated an attitude that has contributed to our environmental crisis.

Similarly Bacon, with metaphors that would have warmed the cockles of Freud's heart, enthused that the experimental method would allow men to "penetrate further," through "the outer courts of nature," to "find a way at length into her inner chamber," in order to find the "secrets still locked in Nature's bosom" (Easlea 1980, p. 129). By the "trials and vexations" of experiment, Nature would be put on the rack and compelled to answer (Easlea 1980, p. 128). Nature and all her children would be men's slaves, Bacon promised (Easlea 1980, p. 129). Nor was he alone. Many of the adherents of the new "Masculine Philosophy" (as they called it) saw Dame Nature as a subject of torture, domination, and exploitation (Easlea 1980, pp. 128–9, 213–14, 236, 241–52). Surely it is not coincidental that these remarks were made during the culmination of the witchcraze (see also Merchant 1980).

Of course, like the mechanical philosophers, the magical philosophers were also interested in practical results, but their understanding of nature as having a soul and being divine led them to take a more cooperative and less dominating stance toward her (Easlea 1980, pp. 94, 103, 112). Also, the magical philosophers understood themselves to be a part of this same nature, a unified emanation of the One, whereas Descartes had taught the mechanical philosophers that human souls were essentially separate from a soulless nonhuman world. So also, the magical philosophers understood themselves as *participants* in nature (Yates 1964, pp. 31–2), whereas the mechanical philosophers took the stance of *observers* separate from the object of their observation, a view that has interfered with scientific understanding in areas as disparate as quantum mechanics, ecology, psychology, and sociology.

Against the development of modern science, I must mention a notable dissenting voice.[6] Goethe's well-known campaign against Newtonian science (Sepper 1988) was rooted in a different conception of the proper role of science in human life (Heisenberg 1974b). His view has much in common with Neoplatonic and Hermetic philosophy, which is not unexpected since he was influenced by Neoplatonic ideas, by alchemy, by Boehmist mysticism, and so forth (Gray 1952, Pt. I; Raphael 1965, Pt. I).[7] Whereas modern science can be characterized as *analytic*, *observational*, and *reductive*, Goethe's approach is *empathetic*, *participatory*, and *holistic* (Barnes 2000; Bortoft

[6] Goethe (1988) includes some of Goethe's most important writings on the philosophy of science, whereas Goethe (1996) has shorter, often aphoristic, extracts; the commentary in both collections is useful. Bortoft (1996) analyzes Goethe's philosophy of science from a phenomenological perspective. Seamon & Zajonc (1998) collect recent articles on Goethean science.

[7] Goethe was more directly influenced by alchemy and Hermeticism than by Neoplatonism, but he claimed the latter was the foundation of his religious beliefs and that he had read the *Enneads* by the time he was fifteen; later he studied Iamblichus and Bruno (Gray 1952, pp. 49–50, 105).

1996, pp. 3–26, 49–76, 321–30; Goethe 1995, pp. 12, 22, 28, 41, 48; Pauli 1955, pp. 205–6). In essence it recognizes our kinship with the rest of the natural world, and accesses the universal archetypes within our minds to facilitate our assimilation to, and our empathetic understanding of, nature (Bortoft 1996; Goethe 1995, pp. 22–4, 103–109). In more Platonic terms, "like knows like" and intuitive understanding comes with participation in the *energeia* of the archetypal forms. Let me explain.

Goethe's scientific methodology is essentially phenomenological (Barnes 2000; Bortoft 1996; Goethe 1995, p. 11; Seamon 1978; Seamon & Zajonc 1998). First, it focuses on the qualities of things as experienced by the whole person, that is, by the senses, emotions, reason, intuition, and all the other faculties of the observer, rather than on abstract quantities hypothesized to lie behind an effectively illusory sensory world (Bortoft 1996, II.4, III.3–4; Goethe 1995, pp. 9–11, 17–20, 28–30, 36, 64; Heisenberg 1974b). Thus we may contrast Newton's theory of color, which reduces it to a single quantity, wavelength, with Goethe's, which embraces the full range of color phenomena, such as experienced by a painter, poet, or sensitive naturalist (Bortoft 1996, II.2, III.4; Goethe 1995, p. 18; Pauli 1955, p. 206). But Goethe is emphatic that his approach is not subjective (Bortoft 1996, p. 34–5; Goethe 1995, pp. 34, 37–8). Rather, by sensitive observation of, experimentation with, and participation in nature, the mind of the naturalist achieves a kind of harmony, or empathetic attunment, with natural phenomena (Goethe 1995, pp. 11–12, 24, 33, 48).[8] Understanding arises from a coincidence of inner form and outer fact. That is, the mind of the Goethean scientist participates in the same archetypal idea—which Goethe called the *Urphänomen*—as does the natural process (Bortoft 1996, pp. 22–3, Pt. III, ch. 5; Goethe 1995, ch. 7; Heisenberg 1974b). Like knows like.

Goethean science has been described as both Platonic and anti-Platonic (Bortoft 1996, III.5; Dieckmann 1972, p. 8; Goethe 1996, pp. 11–12; Heisenberg 1974b), a paradox that can be explained as follows. On the one hand, Goethean science stays focused on direct experience of nature, and seeks to understand natural phenomena in themselves, eschewing theories

[8] Pauli (1955, pp. 205–6) compares Goethe's criticism of Newton to Fludd's criticism of Kepler. In both cases the former has an intuitive-feeling personality with a holistic (synthetic) orientation, whereas the latter has a sensation-thinking personality with an analytic orientation. The types are complementary and both are necessary for a comprehensive understanding. (Pauli notes the relation to ancient theories of beauty: the holistic theory of Plotinus (focusing on the whole) vs. the analytic theory of the Stoics and Aristotle (focusing on the parts). Heisenberg (1974c) explores the role of these complementary notions of beauty in the history of science.)

couched in terms of hidden realities supposed to be the ultimate causes of the visible world. Understanding is rooted in sensory experience, and in this sense it can be described as anti-Platonic. On the other hand, by seeking the *Urphänomene*, Goethean science is directed toward discovering the objective archetypal ideas that simultaneously structure nature and our possible experience and understanding of it. Therefore, these objectively existing archetypal ideas organize existence and are the foundation of any understanding of being, and so in this sense Goethean science is Platonic, for the archetypal ideas define the sensory world. Indeed Nisbet (2002) argues that Goethe's archetypal ideas are specifically Neoplatonic, in particular Plotinian, because they are "not transcendental entities, but immanent principles active within the natural world."

III. The Present

Modern science, especially physics, has continued on the trajectory established by Newton and is becoming more Pythagorean. For example, the most promising current scientific account of reality reduces everything to multidimensional *strings* vibrating harmonically in various patterns (e.g., Greene 1999). Truly, a Pythagorean vision! Since long before the arrival of string theory, however, the scientific perspective has been that the true structure of reality is very different from our sensory experience of it. Famously, the eminent physicist John Archibald Wheeler (1994) proposed the ontological maxim "it from bit" to express the idea that all the fundamental laws of physics are formal information relationships; there is no "stuff" that they are about, or to put it differently, the apparent stuff (such as strings, wavefunctions, fields, and particles) is constituted entirely by formal mathematical relationships. "Everything is number," indeed.

Another example of Pythagoreanism in contemporary science is *complex systems theory*, which attempts to find mathematical laws of emergence and self-organization throughout nature (e.g., Solé & Goodwin 2000).[9] The same laws are found to operate at many different levels, from atoms, to neurons, to embryological development, to social behavior and communication, to evolution, both cosmic and terrestrial. To put it differently, we find the same archetypal forms actualized in many different natural

[9] I do not claim that developments in complex systems theory were motivated in any direct way by Pythagorean or Neoplatonic philosophy. My point is that complex systems theory is Pythagorean in spirit, in that processes throughout nature are governed by a few fundamental mathematical archetypes, such as we find in Pythagorean philosophy.

systems, and these archetypes govern the formation and transformation of these systems in space and time. These are laws dealing with the dynamics of opposites: expansion and contraction, cooperation and competition, uniformity and diversity, randomness and order, definiteness and indefiniteness, discreteness and continuity, and so forth. That is, Pythagorean ideas of unity, duality, conjunction and mediation, balance and equilibrium, and so forth, are found to be the fundamental principles at all levels of the cosmos, and so the structure of these Pythagorean archetypes is the structure of the universe, at least insofar as we can understand it.

IV. The Future

Next I will discuss several areas in which Neoplatonism can contribute to the future development of science by righting some of its imbalances and opening new paths for its progress.

One is in our orientation toward the natural world. For example, Preus (2002) argues that Plotinus (and later Neoplatonists) made "some very important contributions to the development of later biological thought, and in particular to the development of biological concepts which broke away from the dominance of Aristotelianism." They are among the sources of evolutionary theory, "the modern synthetic theory of living nature," and "the turn toward biological science, and away from the radical reductionism of modern physics, during the last hundred years or so." Indeed, it has been said that if the twentieth century was the century of physics, then the twenty-first will be the century of biology.

In MacLennan (2005) I argued that Neoplatonism, Jungian psychology, and evolutionary psychology are mutually consistent and mutually informative, so I will not repeat that discussion here (see also MacLennan 2003, 2006, in press). However, I will mention the following. On the one hand, Jungian psychology uses psychoanalytic techniques to investigate the archetypal structures common to the experience of all people, so its perspective is interior and phenomenological. On the other hand, evolutionary psychology (e.g., Buss 2004) seeks to explain various perceptual and behavioral structures common to all humans in terms of the evolution of *Homo sapiens* adapting to its historical environment; thus it explains these archetypal structures from an external perspective, that is, in behavioral or neuropsychological terms (Stevens 2003, chs. 1, 4). Both arrive at archetypal structures similar to those discovered by Neoplatonists and described in terms of gods, *daimones*, and archetypal numerical structures.

The mutual consistency of these perspectives is a consequence of the fact that the human genome defines the neural structures common to all people, and that these structures shape perception, experience, and behavior in ways that have proved providential for our species. These archetypal structures are not innate images, but "active living dispositions, ideas in the Platonic sense" (Jung 1969b, ¶154); indeed, many of them behave as autonomous personalities (gods, *daimones*), others as numinous structures and processes, such as triads, mandalas, and spiritual transformations (e.g., Jung 1969b, 1970, 1972). The deepest archetypes are the psychical correlates of neurophysiological and physical processes ultimately coextensive with nature itself (Jung 1968, ¶291, 1969b, ¶420; von Franz 1974, chs. 1–3; Jung & Pauli 1955; Stevens 2003, pp. 80–5). Thus they are the ultimate and unchanging ground of existence and of transpersonal meaning in our souls and in the universe. Neoplatonists know the various forms of them as the Ideas, "intellectuals," "intelligibles," henads, etc. (MacLennan 2005).

Furthermore, various psychoanalytic practices, such as "active imagination," which have proved valuable in the process of psychocognitive integration, have significant similarities to theurgy and other Neoplatonic spiritual practices (MacLennan 2005, in press). They are also consistent with shamanic and initiatory practices, which evolutionary psychologists explain in terms of their selective advantage for our species (Ryan 2002; Stevens 2003, ch. 10; Winkelman 2000).

The evolutionary Jungian perspective allows the insights and discoveries of Neoplatonists to make a positive contribution to the modern world-view, and to benefit from it in turn. On the one hand, evolutionary psychology can contribute to both Jungian psychology and Neoplatonism. It expands our understanding of the archetypal ideas and the process of psychological integration by placing them in their evolutionary context and by providing an approach to investigating their neurological correlates; in this way Jungian psychology may be coordinated with contemporary biology and neuroscience without abandoning its valuable and essential phenomenological orientation (Stevens 2003). Similarly, understanding the neurological correlates of Neoplatonic archetypal structures supplements the dialectical and phenomenological investigations of historical Neoplatonism with new, empirical techniques and insights from other scientific disciplines, which will revitalize Neoplatonism by resolving long standing problems and by suggesting new directions for its development (MacLennan 2005).

Conversely, Jungian psychology and Neoplatonism complement the primarily behavioral orientation of contemporary evolutionary psychology by contributing a phenomenological perspective, which takes seriously peoples' subjective experiences; thus it does not negate spiritual experiences in its attempt to explain them. The one-sided, primarily mechanistic and materialistic, orientation of evolutionary psychology will be completed by the psychospiritual dimension necessary for a humane understanding of the human psyche that is both intellectually and emotionally satisfying (MacLennan 2006).

Thus, combining Neoplatonism with evolutionary Jungian psychology promises to unite our understanding of mind and matter in a theory transcending Cartesian dualism, which has perpetuated the intellectual and cultural hostility between science and spirituality. Perhaps it is not too optimistic to hope that this could help heal the widening rift between scientific and spiritual values in our culture.[10]

Balaguer (1998) analyzes the arguments for and against Platonic and anti-Platonic philosophies of mathematics, that is, of approaches to the ontological problem of the existence of mathematical objects. Of course, there are many variants of each of these philosophies, but Balaguer concludes that only one version of each is viable. On the Platonic side is *plenitudinous* or *full-bodied Platonism*, which is—roughly!—the idea that "all logically possible mathematical objects exist" (Balaguer 1998, p. 5). Balaguer concludes that both full-bodied Platonism and so-called anti-Platonic *fictionalism* are defensible, in that there are no sound arguments against either of them. He draws the further conclusion that there is no "fact of the matter" as to which view is correct, and indeed that there is no such fact of the matter for any abstract objects. Certainly, the latter conclusion can be considered a weakness of Platonism—and of anti-Platonism too—but I believe that additional sources of evidence can be found in support of Platonism.

Jungian psychology provides a different perspective on mathematical objects from that which is typical in the philosophy of mathematics, for Jungian psychologists have established that certain numbers and shapes are psychologically potent independently of any cultural or personal associations (Card 1996; von Franz 1974; Robertson 1989, 1995, ch. 19). For example, the number two has, in addition to its familiar quantitative properties, a qualitative aspect encompassing psychological experiences of duality, opposition, complementarity, and so forth (Jung 1970).

What is the foundation of the universal qualities of numbers, shapes, and other mathematical objects? Many of these are universal because they are rooted in the neuropsychology common to all humans. In particular, I think it is likely that the qualitative character of the numbers, especially in their more dynamical aspects, can be found in the neurodynamics of the nervous system (von Franz 1974, p. 7; Jung 1969b, ¶420; MacLennan 2006). For example, neurodynamical processes underlie our experiences of clear differentiation,

[10] So also Card (1996) argues for a Jungian *archetypal* philosophy of nature, in the tradition of nineteenth-century *Naturphilosophie*, which was inspired by Goethean science and further developed the Neoplatonic concept of the *anima mundi*.

cognitive dissonance, and so forth, which are part of the qualitative experience of the dyad. So also experiences associated with unity, such as mental coherence and settling on a conclusion, are rooted in neurological processes. Indeed, Lakoff and Núñez (2000) have shown that many mathematical concepts, even in such abstract systems as set theory, are rooted in our embodied interactions with the physical world, for which our nervous systems have been adapted by evolution.

Therefore, a Neoplatonic or, more precisely, a Neopythagorean approach to the foundations of mathematics that is understood in the context of evolutionary Jungian psychology offers potential advantages over the usual philosophies of mathematics, for it will expose the neurophenomenological foundations of mathematical concepts in their psychological fullness, that is, their qualitative aspects as well as the quantitative (von Franz 1974). From this perspective, mathematical objects, like the other archetypes, are both psychical and objective, for they reside in what Jung called the objective psyche, the network of psychological structures common to all humans (Stevens 2003, p. 65).[11]

Since contemporary science is essentially mathematical, such an enriched understanding of mathematics can help us to understand the unconscious cognitive-emotional structures that condition all of our scientific enterprises (Pauli 1955, pp. 208–9). It may help us to understand criteria of symmetry, beauty, and elegance by which mathematical and scientific theories are judged, which contribute to their acceptance, and which motivate the search for confirming evidence (Curtin 1982; Heisenberg 1974c). It may help explain the, essentially non-scientific, sources of scientific hypotheses and models, especially when they are mathematical in form. Thus, in a previously unpublished paper, Pauli argues for "a future description of nature that uniformly comprises physis and psyche," and that to achieve such "it appears to be essential to have *recourse* to the archetypal *background of scientific terms and concepts*" (Meier 2001, p. 180). At a more fundamental level, this unified description may deepen our understanding of the psychological components of scientists' preference for quantification, clear and distinct mathematical structures, definite standards of proof, abstraction and formalism, and other features of contemporary scientific practice that are familiar but not inevitable. Therefore Pauli (1955, p. 208) argues that henceforth the only acceptable scientific view will be "the one that recognizes *both* sides of reality—the quantitative and the qualitative, the physical and the

[11] Interestingly, Kepler attributes to Proclus ("his favorite author") the idea that innate archetypes, especially of mathematics, are instincts (*instinctus*) (Pauli 1955, pp. 162, 165).

psychical—as compatible with each other, and can embrace them simultaneously."[12]

V. Conclusions

As modern science emerged in the seventeenth century and displaced the magical philosophy, it incorporated a number of ideas from the Neoplatonic and Neopythagorean tradition, including the notion that there is a hidden structure of abstract, and especially mathematical, ideas underlying reality and giving rise to visible phenomena. However, these notions were imported into a dualist framework in which an inanimate, or soulless, mechanical world is opposed to *man*—and I use the gendered term intentionally—as observer and exploiter. Over the past four hundred years, the self-reinforcing processes of science and society have widened this gap, and an increasingly remote and abstract relation to physical reality has led scientists, technologists, and consumers to withdraw from empathetic participation in living nature. Further, with the advance of materialist, quantitative science the human soul has, of course, been pushed further and further into the margins, alienating many people from science.

I think that some of these disharmonies among ourselves, and between humans and the rest of nature, may be eliminated by returning to the Neoplatonic well, which has already nourished science, and by drinking deeply from it again. For Neoplatonism can unite with evolutionary Jungian psychology to reveal the objective archetypal Ideas, which inform our relations to each other, to the natural world, and to the spiritual realm, but which also underlie our scientific concepts and our most abstract theories. In particular, by acknowledging the psychological and phenomenological reality of our experience of these archetypal Ideas, we transcend the Cartesian gap, not by reducing all phenomena to inert matter, but by recognizing the equally objective psychical and physical aspects of a unitary reality.

For these archetypal Ideas are not abstract, inert quantities, but qualities full of the richness of human experience, living and dynamic, brimming with symbolic meaning, emotional and spiritual as well as intellectual. From this perspective, even the most materialist of issues are understood to have an equally valid and objective spiritual aspect, accessible to empirical investigation, in the broad sense. Materialist values are not complete in themselves, but must be complemented by non-materialist, but nevertheless objective, values.

[12] See Card (1996) for the prospects for a future archetypal philosophy of nature and its application in several scientific disciplines.

Certainly, the goal of such a Neoplatonic renewal of science and technology is not to replace current approaches to science, but to expand the human relation to nature in ways that will enrich our understanding, and to lay a foundation for an environmentally sensitive technology. As a consequence we may also anticipate the continued evolution of Neoplatonism as a *living* philosophy.

THE PRIMORDIAL TRADITION OF THE WORLD'S RELIGIONS AND THE RECONSTRUCTION OF NEOPLATONIC METAPHYSICS

Atsushi Sumi

It is unnecessary to dwell on the historical fact that the affinity between Neoplatonism and a variety of religious traditions, both in the East and the West, has testified to what I call the "potential openness" of Plotinus' philosophy to diverse cultural and religious traditions.[1] This paper does not address any individual religion but "the common vision of the world's religions" as entertained by Huston Smith who authors *The World's Religions*, a college textbook widely read in North America. In his *Forgotten Truth*, subtitled *The Common Vision of the World's Religions,* Smith maintains that, when the individual outlooks of the enduring religions are gathered together, one finds a remarkable unity underlying the surface differences, where an invisible geometry has ubiquitously been working to form them to a single truth.[2] This single truth, rooted in the unchanging depths of the universe, is forgotten by the science-dominated, contemporary mind whose gauge of reality is quantity.[3] The traditional view of reality that preceded modern science was hierarchical, centering on the human plane and open to the heavens and hells of traditional cosmologies. Its yardstick was quality, which meant euphoria to the popular mind, but importance, significance, and meaning as derived from being, to reflective minds.[4] Civilizations refined the hierarchical perspective whose minimum had consisted in a precivilized dichotomy between the sacred and the profane. For philosophy, Plato forged its paradigm, placing the Form of the Good on the top of the hierarchy.[5] Lovejoy holds that most educated men had accepted, without question, the conception of the universe as a "Great Chain of Being" up to the late eighteenth century,[6] with Smith arguing that the hierarchical outlook constituted "man's primordial tradition and what might almost be called the

[1] Sumi (2002a), 60. Evangeliou (2002), 397, otherwise expresses this openness as the "perennial and ecumenical values" of the Platonic and Neoplatonic tradition.

[2] Smith (1992), v.

[3] Smith (1992), 1-2.

[4] Smith (1992), 2-4.

[5] Smith (1992), 3-5.

[6] Lovejoy (1936), 59.

human unanimity."[7] Now this common, hierarchical vision of reality in the world's religions consists of the terrestrial, the intermediate or psychic, and the celestial or divine planes, with the Infinite which is the uncreated source beyond them. And insofar as the isomorphism of man and the cosmos holds as a basic premise of the traditional outlook, the common view of selfhood is fourfold, consisting of body, mind, soul, and spirit. We will see the former in detail later, with only a glimpse at the latter. Incidentally, in his article in *Neoplatonism and Contemporary Thought*, Smith uses the Great Chain of Being and Neoplatonism's hierarchical metaphysics interchangeably.[8] One recognizes that the levels of reality in Smith's delineation roughly apply to Plotinus' scheme of the One, Intellect, Soul, and the sensible world. A comparison between them reconfirms that the primordial tradition can justifiably be called "Neoplatonic."

That Platonism embodies the perennial tradition is not original to Smith, having already been put forth by Ficino and Augustinus Steuchus. Smith confesses, however, that it took him two decades to see how the enduring religions, including those in the East, converge.[9] But there remain the methodological problem of how we know the common vision of the world's religions as such and the epistemological problem of how we know that Smith's view is really common to the world's religions. In this paper I do not consider these problems, leaving his conviction concerning the primordial tradition unquestioned.[10]

The contemporary relevance of Neoplatonism is not exhausted by its traditional aspects. My paper in *Neoplatonism and Contemporary Thought* explores the possibility of reconstructing Neoplatonic metaphysics in the intellectual climate of today, by conceiving a coherent system interwoven from seven Platonic notions which Whitehead highlights as "important for us now" in *Adventures of Ideas*.[11] I inaugurated this reconstructive project with the consideration of how Psyche, Eros, Form and Receptacle, from among the

[7] Smith (1992), 5.

[8] Smith (2002), 1.

[9] Smith (1992), 5.

[10] O'Meara (1996), 78, maintains that the notions of hierarchy and chain of being "are too vague and too open to anachronism to be useful in coming nearer to Plotinus' views." But this remark does not apply to the primordial tradition. In order to provide comprehensive coverage of the world's religions, the underlying unity is doomed to be vague and open to some extent.

[11] Sumi (2002b), 221-69. For the significance of the seven Platonic notions, see Whitehead (1967), 146-7, 158, 275-6.

seven notions, can serve, both separately and together, to avoid pitfalls disclosed by two basic assumptions underlying scientific materialism, namely the doctrine of simple location and substance-quality metaphysics.[12] Regarding the interweaving of the two key notions of Psyche and Forms, the latter are conceptually realized in the basic Psyche, which is hardly indifferent to the actual conditioning of the process of becoming.[13] The dependence of the togetherness among Forms on the basic Psyche's organizing activity secures the inexhaustible domain of possibility in terms of which the creative advance of the universe toward novelty is interpreted.[14] At this point I introduce "the creative One," named after the Plotinian One, but made analogous to creativity, the ultimate notion of boundless, abstract possibility in Whitehead, for two reasons. First, the creative One, as the self-creative and unifying activity instantiated by all actualities, incessantly underlies both the basic Psyche and finite souls of varying grades, so that the unending physical realization of the inexhaustible domain of possibility is carried on by them. Second, it is always instantiated by the basic Psyche, so that the latter perpetually realizes the infinitude of Forms in itself.[15] Thus this creative One appears as a "more pluralistic and immanentistic counterpart" to the Plotinian One.[16]

It is easy to see some conformity of my philosophical project and the primordial tradition of religions because both are adventurous hypotheses of Platonic or Neoplatonic origin.[17] The aim of this paper is to discuss the

[12] Sumi (2002b), 224-33.

[13] Ford (2002), 215, maintains that the basic Psyche combines "both primordial Mind with the temporal dynamism of Soul." But the basic Psyche is defined as the non-temporal actuality. This combination holds when the cooperation of the basic Psyche with other souls of varying grades for the ordering of the universe is considered. Ford seems to believe that my notion of the basic Psyche combines Intellect with the world soul in Plotinus as the dipolar nature of God in Whitehead does. Since the world soul, as well as the individual soul, is "one of the partial souls" (IV 3 [27],2,57-59), however, it is not "basic," and may belong to finite souls of varying grades. The basic Psyche, as developed in Sumi (2002b), would be something combining Intellect with the Soul Hypostasis.

[14] Sumi (2002b), 242-5.

[15] Sumi (2002b), 245-52.

[16] Ford (2002), 215.

[17] Being adventurous is not foreign to Neoplatonism. Plotinus is aware that the ontological status of the One as the first activity without being is a bold challenge to the Aristotelian tradition (VI 8 [39],20,9-11). See also Sumi (2002b), 269, n 115.

problems which may arise when we try to see the modes of this conformity with regard to the levels of reality.

According to Smith, returning to our inner eye might reveal "ontological spaces" which the modern mind has forgotten, or "landscapes crowded with presences the knowing of which can turn men into saints."[18] The common ranking of such primordial worlds is threefold: terrestrial, intermediary, and celestial. Beyond them lies the Infinite, their uncreated source. The intermediate plane houses the various species of departed souls that are provisionally in limbo and is called alternatively the subtle, animate, or psychic plane. We encounter the archetypes here as reflections of originals whose actual abode is on the celestial plane. Since the intermediate plane does not elude space and time entirely, it and the terrestrial together constitute the manifest world in its inclusive sense.[19] "Ontological logic," aided by the eyes of what might be called "ontic sensibility,"[20] points invariably toward a higher celestial plane of greater being and less division. Here we encounter the archetypes unalloyed, the Platonic Forms that Plotinus converts unequivocally into living beings.[21] The celestial plane is the realm of theism in its classic Western sense and the sphere of the personal God.[22] But theism's vision of God is modeled after capacities that are distinctly human, and so God's personal mode is not his final mode. Smith keenly points out a truism that "a God we could comprehend would not command our worship."[23] Therefore the Infinite, God in his ultimate and transpersonal nature, lies beyond the celestial plane. It is literally characterized only by negative terms, such as *nir-guna* (without qualities) in Hinduism, *nir-vana* (non-drawing) and *sunyata* (emptiness) in Buddhism, the ineffable *Tao* in Taoism, and *'en-sof,*

[18] Smith (1992), 36.

[19] Smith (1992), 38-48. Smith's opposition to the modern restriction of the word "nature" to the terrestrial plane ([1992], 47, n 14) follows in the tracks of Plotinus whose *physis* is the soul-principle immanent in the sensible world.

[20] Smith (1992), 50, n 17, defines "ontic sensibility" as the "intuitive discernment that (a) nothing can arise without a cause, (b) causes are greater than their effects, (c) the greater is more integrated, and (d) the sequences of greaters cannot stop short of the Greatest, the Infinite."

[21] For more details about Plotinus' notion of Forms as living, see Sumi (1997), 410-12.

[22] Smith (1992), 48-51.

[23] Smith (1992), 52-3.

the non-finite in Judaism.[24] Of these negative predicates, the most important two are "unbounded" and "undifferentiated." On the other hand, positive terms apply to the Infinite only analogically.[25] The vertical causation is such that the "terrestrial plane proceeds from and is explained by the intermediate, the intermediate by the celestial, and the celestial by the Infinite," and so "everything derives, ultimately, from the Infinite" and "abides in the Infinite's luster."[26]

My reconstructive project of Neoplatonic metaphysics conforms schematically to this common vision of the world's religions as delineated above; the basic Psyche and other souls of varying grades hierarchically express agents on the celestial and intermediate planes, the creative One is my contemporary Neoplatonic version of the Infinite, and the Platonic theory of Forms is validated. There arise three problems related to this conformity, the consideration of which will contribute to the deepening of not only my own position but the primordial tradition. In other words, my philosophical project will have an orientation toward ecumenism and the primordial tradition an appeal to the modern mind.

The first problem concerns the objects we encounter on the intermediate plane. I have no objection to Smith's view of them as reflections of Forms, because that view keeps paradigmatism[27] and hardly compromises the Form's singularity. Philosophers, however, do not often talk about immaterial instantiation of Forms on the psychic plane. This fact seems to be partly due to the lessened significance of this plane to philosophy. Whereas religion must help ordinary people achieve peace of mind by showing the afterlife, philosophy is intrinsically endowed with an urge to attain higher

[24] As regards negative theology of the Infinite, Smith also refers to the namelessness of the Godhead in Dionysius the Areopagite, the inhibition from pronouncing the tetragrammaton YHVH in Judaism, and the hundredth name of Allah which is silent in Islam. Relying on Mircea Eliade's work, he includes an Akka pygmy chief's declaration that "God is He whose Name must not even be pronounced," as in keeping with them. This point is important because it leads to "the conviction that the primordial tradition covers not only the great historical traditions but archaic ones as well" (Smith [1992], 54, n 23). Incidentally, the supreme Deity called *Su-no-Kami* in the Shinto tradition inaugurated by Onisaburo Deguchi (1871-1948), also, is not an exception to this negative theology.

[25] Smith (1992), 52-9.

[26] Smith (1992), 42. Wilber (2000), ch. 4, correlates the common vision of reality and selfhood to his theory of four quadrants. For the relevance of this theory to Neoplatonism, see Kealey (2002), 77-80.

[27] For more details about my position on paradigmatism, see Sumi (2002b), 231-2.

realities. But Hades as portrayed in the *Phaedo* and *Republic* X unmistakably constitutes a distinct realm.[28] According to Plotinus, spiritualism is suitable for "those who require confidence supported by the evidence of the senses" (IV 7 [2],15,2-4). Moreover, various virtues possessed by human souls are surely non-physical instances of ethical Forms. Are there then two *immaterial* realms of Forms? We are thus faced with the problem of what insures the distinctness of the incorporeal instantiation of Forms on the intermediate plane from the conceptual realization of them on the celestial and, at the same time, from the material instantiation of them on the terrestrial. A solution is suggested by Plotinus' introduction of "intelligible matter," in III 5 (50),6,44-45, to distinguish daemons from Hellenic gods. This intelligible matter is distinct from the substrate in the noetic world which is developed in II 4 (12) and, as Wolters notes, is the indeterminacy of soul.[29]

The Receptacle, one of the seven Platonic notions serving as the matrix of interconnectedness, was introduced to avoid the isolation fallacy involved in substance-quality metaphysics, that the disjunction of substances made any explanation of change impossible.[30] Therefore the introduction of some substrate, distinct from the Receptacle, to the psychic plane is necessary. But this further calls for another substrate on the celestial plane for the coherence of the distinction of images of Forms from the Forms themselves. After all, the crux is how to justify the universality of hylomorphism, in terms of which separate substrates are introduced to all the three planes. This universality would be justified, if at all, by such an intuitive discernment that eidetic determinacy and hylic indeterminacy are complementary, a

[28] Hades is called "a certain demonic place" in *Rep.* 614c1, which can be compared with "marvelous regions" in *Phd.* 108c6. Hackforth (1955), 175, points out that in the *Phaedo* Plato attempts to combine the two-world metaphysical antithesis between the intelligible and the sensible realms with the four-world scheme of eschatology consisting of earthly existence, Elysium, Tartarus, and celestial existence. This four-world scheme is congruous with the primordial tradition because Smith (1992), 46, proposes to split the intermediate plane in two, "its beatific components in heavens above the earth and its hellish ones in realms below." Plotinus mentions Tartarus in III 2 (47),17,66, but does not explicitly refer to Elysium or the Isles of the Blessed.

[29] Wolters (1972), 66. Bréhier (1924-8), 3:82, n 1, wrongly takes "intelligible matter" as soul. Dillon (1969), 36, does not explain his view that the indeterminacy of soul must be the same as "matter in the intelligible world" in II 4 (12). Fielder (1976), 114, maintains that the material principle for soul is absent from Plotinus' metaphysics. The nature of matter for soul is highly disputed in this way, but Plotinus adumbrates it in II 4 (12),3,4-5.

[30] Sumi (2002b), 230-31.

discernment of unambiguously Pythagorean and Platonic origin. Secondary to such a question is whether the recollection argument in the *Phaedo* may be invalidated because the soul's prenatal knowledge is based on the images of Forms on the intermediate plane rather than the Forms themselves.

Second, my reconstructive project proposes to populate more densely the celestial and the intermediate planes. Before explicating this proposal, we may briefly touch on the subtle difference between Smith and me with respect to the basic Psyche. The basic Psyche is to the creative One in my project as God in his personal mode is to God in his infinite mode in the primordial tradition. In Plotinian terms, the basic Psyche combines Intellect and the All Soul, while the world soul belongs to finite souls of varying grades. In my project the abode of the Hypostasis Soul is the celestial plane.[31] On the contrary, Smith does not fully distinguish the "universal or total soul" from the "world mind," the All Soul from the cosmic soul, considering them to belong to the intermediate plane.[32] Now my position rejects the notion of the world as a *plenum formarum* and the principle of plenitude, the linking principle of the fullness of the realization of conceptual possibilities in actuality, because they make the creative advance of the universe toward novelty unintelligible.[33] The following Plotinian portrayal of the hierarchical structure of reality is, nevertheless, embodied in the totality of the basic Psyche and finite souls by virtue of the conceptual linkage between soul and life:

> All things coming from the One are then like a long life stretched out at length; each part is different from that which comes next in order, but the whole is continuous with itself, but with one part differentiated from another, and the

[31] See n 13.

[32] Smith (1992), 48.

[33] Lovejoy (1936), 333, supposes that Whitehead's identification of God as the principle of limitation would have horrified those thinkers who supported the infinite fecundity of emanationism which was linked with the principle of plenitude. But this supposition is not convincing. The fact that the physical realization of possibility will sometime attain the plenitude may imply the finiteness of the Infinite's fecundity, since the plenitude is something circumscribed. The infinite fecundity of the Infinite will be more fully explained by the interdependence of the inexhaustible domain of possibility and the creative One, and therefore I claim that this unending sustenance of actualities by the creative One is the same as the Neoplatonic doctrine of undiminished giving. See Sumi (2002b), 246-7.

> earlier does not perish in the later (V 2 [11],2,26-29, translated by A. H. Armstrong, adapted).[34]

This chain of being is not made sufficiently intelligible by paradigmatism in eidetic causation. When we try to conform to the enduring religions, Psyche is roughly graded into five subspecies. On the celestial plane reside (1) the basic Psyche conceptually realizing the totality of Forms and (2) diverse divine or angelic souls. On the intermediate plane cohabit (3) the world soul responsible for the actual ordering of the world[35] and (4) individual souls of human and other creatures. There are possibly (5) souls of blessed humans or others who can commute between the psychic and the celestial planes, with those of great spiritual leaders incarnated as avatars of the Infinite. The basic Psyche and the world soul in their cooperation are a counterpart of the dipolar God of Whitehead consisting of his primordial and consequent natures.

Unfortunately various grades of souls do not intrinsically account for the demarcation between the celestial and the psychic planes.[36] For this demarcation we have to appeal to the above distinction between substrates for those planes. This "population increase" has the advantage of reconciling the monotheism of the basic Psyche and the creative One with the polytheism of diverse divine or angelic souls, an advantage which Smith had never contemplated, so that Shinto, Taoism and Hinduism become more amenable to the primordial tradition. In other words, it intensifies the generality of the common vision. A Neoplatonic reconciliation between monotheism and polytheism has actually been entertained by Armstrong whose Christian Platonism presents an inclusive monotheism that might coincide with the henotheistic polytheism of the ancient Greeks.[37] But I would like to make my position clear by saying that my project is oriented to pluralism rather than inclusivism insofar as it is allied with what is claimed to be the common

[34] O'Meara (1996), 75-6, does not subscribe to the validity of the notion of chain of being in Plotinus and regards this passage as expressing "the structure of reality in general." Compare this with Lovejoy's reference to the present passage for the definite fusion of the principle of plenitude with the principle of continuity and gradation ([1936], 63).

[35]. I accept Smith's view of the world mind as "the supreme expression of the divine in the manifest world" ([1992], 48). See also Plotinus, II 2 (40),5,3-4; 7,20; VI 7 (38),1,1.

[36] Plotinus is confronted with a similar problem concerning the demarcation of the undescending soul from Intellect. See Sumi (2002a), 69, n 54. It is possible to consider my position on the celestial abode of the All Soul to turn this difficulty shrewdly to my own advantage.

[37] Bregman (2002), 337-8.

vision of the Infinite rather than some particular dogma of it. My position becomes more coherent by my reference to the "avatars of the Infinite."

Although it is certain that the hierarchical vision of reality is essential to the primordial tradition, it is not certain whether Smith accepts the principle of plenitude, either in its original, Platonic expression or its temporalized version.[38] The reasons why we refuse the principle of plenitude are that it implies "a sort of absolute cosmical determinism" in which "there is no room for any contingency anywhere in the universe"[39] and that the world as the *plenum formarum* is "an absolutely rigid and static scheme of things" in which no emergence of novelty is possible.[40] But Lovejoy believes that the rejection of the principle in its original conception may result in the unintelligibility of the connection between the intelligible and the sensible realms, because it transforms the constitution of the two realms into "a haphazard and arbitrary thing."[41] This belief is not, however, well founded. The finite realization of the inexhaustible domain of possibility is hardly haphazard, since the relative relevance of Forms for the process of becoming is determined by the actuality of the basic Psyche's primordial valuation.[42] The finiteness in question is not the result of imperfection, but of the fact, which Whitehead could see, that "there are possibilities of harmony which either produce evil in joint realization, or are incapable of such conjunction."[43]

Finally, my project, in which the creative One serves as an immanentistic counterpart to the Plotinian One, provocatively points out that an immanentistic aspect of the Infinite is even "forgotten" by the primordial tradition. By "immanentistic" I do not mean that the Infinite is really "immanent" in the world.[44] The creative One is immanentistic in the sense

[38] For the temporalizing of the principle, see Lovejoy (1936), 244.

[39] Lovejoy (1936), 54.

[40] Lovejoy (1936), 242-3.

[41] Lovejoy (1936), 52.

[42] Sumi (2002b), 239.

[43] Whitehead (1967), 276, cited in Sumi (2002b), 241. For more details of the application of the principle of intrinsic incompatibility to Whitehead's philosophy of religion, see Sumi (2001), 364-7.

[44] Perl (1997), 308-11, attempts to explain the One's immanence in terms of its being "the differential structuring of being in virtue of which all things are themselves" or "the constructive distribution of all things." But I am reluctant to follow this strategy, because Perl seems to confuse immanence and omnipresence in referring to V 5 (32),9,13-23. Plotinus here explicitly denies the One's immanence by saying that "it may not be in something else (*hina mê en allôi*)" (9,22). This *hina*-clause is not counterfactual because no verb appears in the indicative mode of the secondary tense.

that it is instantiated by finite souls responsible for the actual ordering of the universe as well as by the basic Psyche. Since the creative One is the unity underlying all psyches,[45] the scheme of instantiation harmonizes the continuity of one long life with the fragmentation of soul in the Plotinian terms above,[46] satisfying the necessary condition of conformity to the chain of being and so to the primordial tradition.

At the same time, my project satisfies the minimum requirement for the creative One's transcendence, by appealing to the distinctness of the categories of the ultimate from those of existence in Whitehead and claiming that it is distinct from Psyche and Form.[47] From creativity of Whitehead the creative One inherits the nature of boundlessness,[48] one of the most important predicates applying literally to the Infinite in the manner of negative theology.[49] Bussanich argues that "the infinity . . . of the One is ultimately compromised if we maintain that there is something the One is not" and "Plotinus speaks of the One's omnipresence in part to eliminate this tendency."[50] My project entertains a notion of infinity which Plotinus does not conceive, that the creative One is the boundless, abstract possibility instantiated by *all* the actualities. This implication of infinity as being "protean" and an infinite and unordered multiplicity of Forms require each other.[51] In this way my project proposes the immanentistic conception of the creative One. It does not force its own view on the traditional outlook but suggests that the primordial tradition can internally retrieve the immanentistic aspect of the Infinite.

In the chapter on the three dimensional cross, the most adequate model of reality, Smith contrasts two kinds of resolution, a principle decisive for spiritual existence. The first is the "union of complements." It is, as it were, a Western yin-yang in which the male or active principle and the female or receptive one are complementary. The second is the "resolution of opposites," the principle that the tension between two exclusive opposites

[45] Sumi (2002b), 246.

[46] For the problem about the tension between the continuity of the three hypostases and the discontinuity of soul at the lowest level, with which Plotinus is confronted in V 2 (11), see Armstrong (1966-88), 5:56.

[47] Sumi (2002b), 251-2.

[48] Sumi (2002b), 249-51.

[49] Smith (1992), 57

[50] Bussanich (1987), 183.

[51] See n 33.

disappear in a centered life.[52] The crucial point is that the union of complements applies to the vertical duality of the paternal Heaven and the maternal Earth. Notice that the intermediate plane presupposes this duality because it is exactly intermediary between the celestial and the terrestrial planes, and that it is split in two, "its beatific components in heavens above the earth and its hellish ones in realms below."[53] Of course, the above complementary relation between determinacy and indeterminacy is categorized into this notion. But it is hard to think that the union is caused intrinsically by the two complements. Instead this duality must be shaped to union by a hidden unity, namely the Infinite. It must be the Infinite that gives the ultimate reason for the discernment that the Earth exists insofar as the Heaven exists and the one that the Infinite is responsible for the very unity of the levels of reality as a whole.

According to Lovejoy, Plato's expression of the principle of plenitude implies that the intelligible world is declared to be deficient without the sensible.[54] Insofar as we refuse that principle, we call for something else to sustain the Heaven-Earth duality. This appeal to the union of complements marks a significant shift from the notion of *coincidentia oppositorum* in Nicholas of Cusa which is applied to the Infinite as a kind of resolution of opposites.[55] Moreover, the Infinite is of course omnipresent because it is free from boundaries. Yet the proposition that the Infinite unifies Heaven and Earth leads us to a more invigorating image of it as a roaring cataract with innumerable falls, while the proposition that it is simply omnipresent may entail such quiescent and monolithic images like a cloudless sky and a field of

[52] Smith (1992), 26-7. With the principle of intrinsic incompatibility which my project applies to the physical realization of Forms, the mutually exclusive opposites are not resolved. See Sumi (2002b), 241.

[53] Smith (1992), 46. It is not recommended to reduce complements and opposites to contradictories and contraries, the distinction which Plato appreciated at *Prot.* 346d1-3 (Taylor [1976], 147). A pure limbo which is neither celestial nor terrestrial may lead us to regard Heaven and Earth as contraries, but even so it cannot infringe on their duality and complementary relation.

[54] Lovejoy (1936), 52-4.

[55] Notice that the union of complements and the resolution of opposites do not exclude each other. The latter goes well with negative theology of the Infinite. After comparing Intellect to a circle and the One to its center, Plotinus writes as if he anticipated the Cusanian notion of "coincidence of opposites": "Just as in our example also the radii and the circle were not the center, but it is the father of circle and radii giving traces of itself and with an abiding power generating radii and circle . . ." (VI 8 [39],18,22-25, translated by A. H. Armstrong).

unbroken light, which Smith regards as misleading.[56] The most difficult problem we have to work out would be how to avoid conceiving and imaging the Infinite as monolithic without compromising its simplicity. This is the very lesson that we must learn from Plotinus' theory of the One's knowledge or inner life. To the question why the Infinite *must* be immanentistic, or at least not wholly transcendent, we can reply by revising Smith's remark above. It is a deeper truism that our worship would be commanded by a God whom we could not comprehend and, at the same time, who would impartially reign over Heaven and Earth.[57]

Due to the limited length of this paper, I regret that I cannot discuss problems related to the levels of selfhood. Incidentally, Smith closes his chapter on the levels of selfhood with the following tale of Sufi, "The Tale of Sands": A stream whose destiny was to cross the desert was afraid that it might disappear and lose his individuality by getting absorbed into the sands. But the stream accepted advice from a hidden voice coming from the desert itself and raised his vapor into the welcoming arms of the wind, which let it fall as soon as they reached the roof of a mountain, many, many miles away. Through this journey the stream could remember in his mind the details of the experience that he had once been held in the arms of a wind, and learned his true identity.[58]

If today's students of Neoplatonism go on clinging to the *ancien régime* and hesitate to launch into the reconstruction of its metaphysics, we will be incapable of dismissing the wide-spread opinion that all present appearances point in the direction of the burial of metaphysics.[59] In this paper we have further tried to intensify the ecumenical value of our reconstructive project of Neoplatonic metaphysics by confronting it with the common vision of the world's religions. Also in this confrontation we have not been content with the conformity between the two, but dealt with several difficult problems

[56] Smith (1992), 57-8, n 26. Compare this proposed image of the Infinite with Plotinus' metaphor of the One as a spring which has no other origin and remains itself at rest in III 8 (30),10,5-10. For more details about the static aspect of the One, see Bussanich (1987), 164-7. An advantage, if any, of the notion of the creative One and the dynamic image of the Infinite lies in its appeal to spirituality of post-modernity. Gregorios (2002b), 309, regards "a conception of the universe as permeated by Divine energy," rather than "belief in a personal God," as a mark of post-modern spirituality.

[57] There still remains a problem concerning the possibility of non-temporal subjectivity. Ford (2002), 212, believes that this problem is not applicable to the One but to Intellect, therefore to the basic Psyche in my project.

[58] Smith (1992), 94-5.

[59] For this opinion, see Wallis (1972), 177, mentioned in Sumi (2002b), 221.

in prospect of a higher integration of them. The Sufi tale tells us how to realize the true identity of Neoplatonism in our age. It is the continuation of a philosophical adventure that alone can protect it against getting swallowed up by the torrential flow of material civilization. This is the reason why I keep my quixotic, if not bombastic, adventure going. I feel responsible for revitalizing our perennial philosophy in this new century and integrating it with the primordial tradition of the world's religions, with the serious and not frivolous conscience of a proponent of the reconstruction of Neoplatonic metaphysics.[60]

[60] The revision of this paper has benefited greatly from the helpful comments made by Father Gary M. Gurtler, *S.J.* of Boston College.

Bibliography

Primary Sources

Aristotelis (1957, 1973), *Metaphysica*, ed. W. Jaeger, Oxford.

Aristotelis , (1950, 1973), *Physica*, ed. W.D. Ross, Oxford.

Augustine, *The Literal Meaning of Genesis*. http://www.augustinus.it/latino/genesi_lettera/index2.htm

Cicero (1975) *De Divinatione*, ed. R.Giomini , Leipzig.

Dorotheus of Sidon (1976), *Fragmenta Graeca*, ed. D. Pingree, Leipzig.

Eriugena, Johannes Scottus (1978), *Iohannis Scotti Eriugenae Periphyseon (De Diuisione Naturae). Liber Primus, edited by I.P. Sheldon-Williams*, Dublin.

Eriugena, Johannes Scottus (1996-2003), *Periphyseon I-V, edited by E. Jeauneau*, Turnhout. CCCM 161-165.

Ficino, M. (2001-3), *Platonic Theology*, 3 vols, M.J.B. Allen, with J. Warden (English translation), and J. Hankins, with W. Bowen (Latin text), *The I Tatti Renaissance Library*, Cambridge, MA.

Ficino, M. (1998), *Three Books on Life: A Critical Edition and Translation with Introduction and Notes*, ed. & tr., C.V. Kaske & J.R. Clark, Temple.

Ficino, M. (1996), *Meditations on the Soul: Selected Letters of Marsilio Ficino*, translated by the Language Dept. of the School of Economic Science, London, Rochester, Vt.

Iamblichus, (2003), *On the Mysteries*, trs. and eds. E.C. Clarke, J.M. Dillon and J.P. Hershbell, Atlanta.

Keats, J. Letter of December 21, 1817, http://www.mrbauld.com/negcap.html.

Lutosławski Wincenty: manuscript of the book *The Origin and Growth of Plato's Logic* (popular edition) – Plato's Change of Mind. (Archival sources preserved in The Archive of Science of The Polish Academy of Sciences and The Polish Academy of Arts and Sciences)

Natorp Paul, the letters to W. Lutosławski (esp. the one dated: February 18th 1898). (Archival sources preserved in The Archive of Science of The Polish Academy of Sciences and The Polish Academy of Arts and Sciences)

Ocellus Lucanus (1926), *De universi natura*, in *Neue philologische Untersuchungen*, Vol. 1, ed. R. Harder, Berlin.

Plato (1907-50), *Platonis: Opera*, 5 vols, ed., Burnet, J., Oxford.

Proclus, *The Elements of Theology*, (1933), tr. and ed. E.R. Dodds, Oxford.

Vettius Valens (1908, 1973), *Anthologiarum libri ix*, ed. W. Kroll, Berlin.

Secondary Sources

Adorno, T. (1983), *Negative Dialectics*, New York.

Adorno, T. (2000), *Metaphysics: Concept and Problems*, Stanford.

Aersten, J. (1996), *Medieval Philosophy and the Transcendentals*, New York.

Aertsen, J.A. and M. Pickavé (eds.) (2002), *Ende und Vollendung. Eschatologische Perspektiven im Mittelalter*, Berlin. Miscellanea Mediaevalia Band 29.

Agrippa, H.C. (1694), *The Vanity of Arts and Sciences*, London.

Agrippa, H.C. (1651, 1993) *Three Books of Occult Philosophy*, tr. by J. Freake, ed. & ann. by D. Tyson, St. Paul.

Alexandrakis, A. (ed.) (2002), *Neoplatonism and Western Aesthetics*, Albany.

Alexandrakis, A. and Moutafakis, N. Eds. (2002), *Neoplatonism and Western Aesthetics,* Albany

Alfino, M. (1989), "Plotinus and the Possibility of Non-Propositional Thought", *Ancient Philosophy*, 8, 273-284.

Allan, A.B. and J.F. Wippel, J.F (1969), *Medieval Philosophy from St. Augustine to Nicholas of Cusa*, London.

Allard, G.H. (1982), "The Primacy of Existence in the Thought of Eriugena," in O'Meara (ed.) (1982), 89-96

Allen, M.J.B. and V. Reese, with M. Davies (eds.) (2002), *Marsilio Ficino: His Theology, His Philosophy, His Legacy*, Leiden.

Armstrong, A.H. (ed.) (1967), *The Cambridge History of Later Greek and Early Medieval Philosophy*, Cambridge.

Amand, D. (1945), *Fatalisme et Liberté dans L'Antiquité Grecqué*, Lovain.

Armitage, A. (1947), *Sun, Stand Thou Still*, New York.

Armstrong, A.H. (1966-88), *Plotinus*, 7 vols, London and Cambridge (Mass.).

Armstrong, A.H. (ed.) (1980), *Classical Mediterranean Spirituality*, London.

Armstrong, A.H. (1987), "Iamblichus and Egypt," *Les Etudes Philosophiques* 2-3, 179-188.

Arzt, T. (in press), *Wegmarken der Individuation*, Würtzburg.

Athanassiadi, P. (1993), "Dreams, Theurgy and Freelance Divination: The Testimony of Iamblichus," *Journal of Roman Studies* 83, 115-130.

Babbitt, F.C., tr (1957), *Plutarch, Moralia, v 5 LCL,* Cambridge MA repr.

Balaguer, M. (1998), *Platonism and Anti-Platonism in Mathematics*, Oxford.

Balthasar, H.U. von (2003), *Cosmic Liturgy: The Universe According to St. Maximus the Confessor*, tr. B.E. Daley, San Francisco, CA.

Balthasar, H.U. von (1995), *Presence and Thought: An Essay on the Religious Philosophy of Gregory of Nyssa*, tr. M. Sebanc, San Francisco, CA.

Barnes, J. (1984), *The Complete Works of Aristotle*, 2 vols., Princeton.

Barnes, J. (1990), "Heidegger speleologue", *Revue de Metaphysique et de Morale*, 95.

Barnes, J. (2000), "Participatory Science as the Basis for a Healing Culture," in Steiner (2000), 219–301.

Barton, T.S. (1994a), *Ancient Astrology*, London.

Barton, T.S. (1994b), *Power and Knowledge: Astrology, Physiognomics, and Medicine under the Roman Empire*, Ann Arbor, MI.

Beach, E. A. (1994), *The Potencies of the God(s): Schelling's Philosophy of Mythology*, Albany

Bechtle, G. (1999), *The Anonymous Commentary on Plato's* Parmenides, Bern.

Beck, R. (1976), 'Interpreting the Ponza Zodiac, I', *Journal of Mithraic Studies* 1, 1-19.

Beierwaltes, W. (1980), "The Love of Beauty and the Love of God", in Armstrong (ed.) (1980), 293-313.

Beierwaltes, W. (1985), *Denken des Einen. Studien zur neuplatonischen Philosophie und ihrer Wirkungsgeschichte*, Frankfurt a.M.

Berchman, R.M. (1984), *From Philo to Origen: Middle Platonism in Transition*, Brown Judaic Studies 69, Chico, CA

Beierwaltes, W. (1994a), *Eriugena. Grundzüge seines Denkens*, Frankfurt am Main.

Beierwaltes, W. (1994b), "Zur Wirkungsgeschichte Eriugenas im Deutschen Idealismus (I) und Danach (II). Eine kurze, unsystematische Nachlese," in Beierwaltes (1994a), 313-330.

Berchman, R. (ed.) (1998), *Mediators of the Divine: Horizons of Prophecy, Divination, Dreams and Theurgy in Mediterranean Antiquity*, Atlanta.

Berchman, R.M. (2003), "Self-Knowledge and Subjectivity in Origen of Alexandria," in *Origeniana Octava*, Vol. I Leuven, 437-450.

Berkeley, G. (1970), *Principles of Human Knowledge*, Indianapolis.

Berthold, G. (tr.) (1985), *Maximus Confessor: Selected Writings*, Mahwah, NJ.

Blumenthal, H.J. and E.G. Clark (eds.) (1993), *The Divine Iamblichus: Philosopher and Man of Gods*, Bristol.

Bobzien, S. (1998), *Determinism and Freedom in Stoic Philosophy,* Oxford.

Boer, C. (1980), *Marsilio Ficino: The Book of Life*, Dallas.

Bolzoni, L. (2001), *The Gallery of Memory: Literary and Iconographic Models in the Age of the Printing Press*, tr. by J. Parzen, Toronto.

Bortoft, H. (1996), *The Wholeness of Nature: Goethe's Way toward a Science of Conscious Participation in Nature*, Hudson.

Bouché-Leclercq, A. (1899), *L'Astrologie grecque*, Paris.

Bradshaw, D. (1999), "Neoplatonic Origins of the Act of Being", *Review of Metaphysics* 53, 383-401.

Bradshaw, D. (2004), *Aristotle East and West: Metaphysics and the Division of Christendom*, Cambridge.

Brandwood L. (1990), *The Chronology of Plato's Dialogues*, Cambridge.

Brann, Eva. (1992), *The World of the Imagination*, Lanham.

Bregman, J., (1982) *Synesius of Cyrene: Philosopher-Bishop,* Berkeley, LA.

Bregman, J., (1995) "Judaism as Theurgy in the Religious Thought of the Emperor Julian, *The Ancient World: Mystery Cults in Late Antiquity, vol. XXVI, no. 2,* 133-149.

Bregman, J., (1999) "Elements of the Emperor Julian's Theology", *Traditions of Platonism: Essays in Honour of John Dillon,* ed. J .J. Cleary, Aldershot, Hampshire

Bregman, J. (2002), "The Contemporary Christian Platonism of A. H. Armstrong," in Harris (ed.) (2002a), 335-45.

Bréhier, É. (1924-8), *Plotin: Ennéades,* texte etabli et traduit, 6 vols, in 7, Paris.

Bruno, G. (1975), *The Ash Wednesday Supper: La Cena de le Ceneri*, tr. & intro., S.L. Jaki, The Hague.

Buell, L. (2003), *Emerson*, Cambridge MA.

Burnyeat, M. (1982), "Idealism in Greek Philosophy: what Descartes saw and Berkeley missed," *PR* 91, 3-40.

Burtt, A.E. (1932), *The Metaphysical Foundations of Modern Physical Science*, 2nd ed., London.

Bury, R.G. (tr.) (1949) Sextus Empiricus. *Against the Professors*, Vol. IV, Cambridge, MA.

Buss, D.M. (2004), *Evolutionary Psychology: The New Science of the Mind*, Boston.

Bussanich, J. (1987), "Plotinus on the Inner Life of the One," *Ancient Philosophy* 7, 163-89.

Bussanich, J. (1988), *The One and its Relation to Intellect in Plotinus: A Commentary on Selected Texts*, Philosophia Antiqua Vol. 49, Leiden.

Bussanich, J. (1994), "Mystical Elements in the Thought of Plotinus", in Temporini and Haase (ed.) (1994), 5300-330.

Bussanich, J. (1997a), "Plotinian Mysticism in Theoretical and Comparative Perspective", *American Catholic Philosophical Quarterly* 71, 339-65.

Bussanich, J. (1997b), "Non-discursive Thought in Plotinus and Proclus", *Documenti e Studi sulla Tradizione Filosofica Medievale* 8, 191-210.

Butterworth, G.W. (tr.) (1966), Origen, *On First Principles*, New York, NY.

Cappuyns, M., O.S.B. (1969), *Jean Scot Érigène: sa vie, son oeuvre, sa pensée*, Brussels. Originally published in 1933.

Card, C.R. (1996), "The Emergence of Archetypes in Present-Day Science And Its Significance for a Contemporary Philosophy of Nature," *Dynamical Psychology* 1996, from http: //www.goertzel.org/dynapsyc/1996/natphil.html; reprinted in Combs, Goertzel & Germine (2002), 259–94.

Carruthers, M. and Ziolkowski, J.M. (eds.) (2002), *The Medieval Craft of Memory: An Anthology of Texts and Pictures*, Philadelphia.

Cavell, S. (1994), *A Pitch of Philosophy*, Cambridge Mass.

Cavell, S. (2003), *Emerson's Transcendental Etudes*, Stanford.

Chrétien, J.-L. (1989), "L'analogie selon Plotin", *Les Études philosophiques*, 1989-3/4, 305-18.

Cilento, V. (1971), Introduction and Commentary to Plotino, *Paideia antignostica. Ricostruzione di un unico trattato da Enneadi III.8, V.8, V.5, II.9*, Firenze: Le Monnier.

Clarke, E.C. (2003), "Introduction," in Clarke, Dillon and Hershbell (eds. and trs.) (2003), xiii-lii.

Clark, E. C., Dillon, J. M. and Hershbell, J. P., (2003), *Iamblichus*, *On the Mysteries,* translated with introduction and notes, Atlanta.

Collins, A.B. (1974), *The Secular is Sacred: Platonism and Thomism in Marsilio Ficino's Platonic Theology*, The Hague.

Combs, A., B. Goertzel, and M. Germine (eds.) (2002), *Mind in Time: The Dynamics of Thought, Reality, and Consciousness*, Cresskill.

Copenhaver, B.P. and C.B. Schmitt (2002), *Renaissance Philosophy*, Oxford.

Cornelius, G. (1991), "Psychoanalysis, Divination, Astrology," http://coa.hubcom.net/wzpatalk.htm

Cornelius, G. (1999), "Is Astrology Divination and Does it Matter?" http://cura.free.fr/quinq/01gfcor.html

Cornelius, G. (2003), *The Moment of Astrology: Origins of Divination*, Bournemouth, UK.

Cornford, F. M. (1937), *Plato's Cosmology: The* Timaeus *of Plato*, London 1937 rpt. Indianapolis 1997.

Coudert, A.P. (1995), *Leibniz and the Kabbalah*, Boston.

Cramer, F.H. (1959), *Astrology in Roman Law and Politics*, Philadelphia, PA.

Creuzer, F. and Moser, G.H. (1835), *Plotini opera omnia*, Oxford.

Crosby, D.A. and D.H. Hardwick (eds) (2001), *Religion in a Pluralistic Age*, New York.

Crowe, M.J. (1990), *Theories of the World from Antiquity to the Copernican Revolution*, New York.

Crystal, I. (1998), "Plotinus on the Structure of Self-Intellection", *Phronesis*, 43.

Curtin, D.W. (ed.) (1982), *The Aesthetic Dimension of Science, The Sixteenth Nobel Conference, 1980*, New York.

Davis, L.D. (1983), *The First Seven Ecumenical Councils (325-787): Their History and Theology*, Collegeville, MN.

De Lacy, P.H. & B. Einarson (tr.) (1959) Plutarch. *Moralia*, Vol. VII, Cambridge, MA

De Lacy, P. (1972), "Galen's Platonism," *AJPh* 93, 27-39.

De Lacy, P. (1978-1984), *Galen: On the Doctrines of Hippocrates and Plato* Vols. 1-3, Berlin.

)es Places, E. (1973), *Numénius Fragments*, Paris.

)ieckmann, L. (1972), *Goethe's* Faust*: A Critical Reading*, Englewood Cliffs.

)illon, J. (1969), "*Enn.* III 5: Plotinus' Exegesis of the *Symposium* Myth," *Agon* 3, 24-44.

)illon, J. M. (1973), *Iamblichi Chalcidensis In Platonis Dialogos Commentarium Fragmenta,* Leiden.

)illon, J. M. (1977), *The Middle Platonists*, New York.

)illon, J.M. (1987), "Iamblichus of Chalcis (c.240 – 325 A.D.)," *ANRW* II.36.2 , 862-909.

)illon, J.M. (1982), 'Origen's Doctrine of the Trinity and Some Later Neoplatonic Theories', in *Neoplatonism and Christian Thought*, Norfolk, VA.

)illon, J.M. (1992), "Porphyry's Doctrine of the One", in Goulet-Cazé, Madec, and D. O'Brien (1992) (ed.), 356-66.

)illon, J. M. (1993), *Alcinous: The Handbook of Platonism*, Oxford.

)illon, J.M. and Morrow, G.R. (eds. and trs.) (1987), *Proclus: Commentary on Plato's Parmenides*, Princeton.

)obrzycki, J. (ed.) (1978), *On the Revolutions*, trans. E. Rosen, Baltimore.

)odds, E. R. (1951, rpt. 1964) *The Greeks and the Irrational, Berkeley.*

)odds, E. R. (1960) *Euripides, Bacchae,* Oxford

)odds, E.R. (1963), *Proclus: The Elements of Theology*, Oxford.

)ods, M. (1950), *Augustine*, *The City of God*, New York.

)upré, L. (1991), *Passage to Modernity. An Essay in the Hermeneutics of Nature and Culture*, New Haven.

;aslea, B. (1980), *Witch Hunting, Magic and the New Philosophy: An Introduction to Debates of the Scientific Revolution 1450–1750*, Sussex.

;dinger, E. F. (1994) *The Eternal Drama: The Inner Meaning of Greek Mythology,* Atlanta.

.dwards, M.J. (1990), "Porphyry and the Intelligible Triad", *JHS* 110, 14-25.

.merson, R.W. (1903-04), *The Complete Works of Ralph Waldo Emerson, edited by E.W. Emerson. 12 vols.*, Boston. Concord Edition.

.merson, R.W. (1958), *The Heart of Emerson's Journals, edited by B. Perry*, New York. Originally published in 1929.

milsson, E.K. (1996), "Cognition and its object", in L.P. Gerson, *The Cambridge Companion to Plotinus*, Cambridge: CUP.

vangeliou, Ch. (2002), "The Place of Neoplatonism in the Post-Modern World," in Harris (ed.) (2002a), 387-403.

aggin, P. (1992), ed., Plotino, *Enneadi*, Milano: Rusconi libri.

alconer, W.A. (tr.) (1923), *Cicero: De Divinatione*, London and New York.

ideler, D. (1987), *The Pythagorean Sourcebook and Library*, trans. K.S. Guthrie, Grand Rapids, MI.

Fielder, J. (1976), "Chorismos and Emanation in the Philosophy of Plotinus," in Harris (ed.) (1976), 101-20.

Finamore, J. (1985), *Iamblichus and the Theory of the Vehicle of the Soul*, Chico, CA.

Finamore, J. (1993), "Iamblichus on Light and the Transparent," in Blumenthal and Clark (eds.) (1993), 55-64.

Finamore, J. and Berchman, R. (2005), *History of Platonism: Plato Redivivus*, New Orleans.

Finamore, J. and Dillon, J. M. (2002), *Iamblichus: De Anima,* text, translation, and commentary, Leiden.

Findlay, J.N. (1967), *The Transcendence of the Cave*, London.

Ford, L.S. (2002), "Process and Eternity: Whitehead Contemplates Plotinus," in Harris (ed.) (2002a), 205-20.

Fowden, G. (1986), *The Egyptian Hermes: A Historical Approach to the Late Pagan Mind*, Princeton.

Fowler, H.N. (tr.) (1914), *Plato: Phaedrus*, London and Cambridge, MA.

Franz, M.-L. von (1974), *Number and Time: Reflections Leading toward a Unification of Depth Psychology and Physics*, tr. A. Dykes, Evanston.

Gadamer, H.G. (1976), "Plato und Heidegger", in *Der Idealismus und seine Gegenwart*, Hamburg: Meiner.

Gage, J. (1993), *Color and Culture: Practice and Meaning from Antiquity to Abstraction*, Boston.

Gerson, L. (1990), *God and Greek Philosophy*, London.

Gerson, L. (1991), "Causality, Univocity, and First Philosophy in *Metaphysics* ii" *Ancient Philosophy* 11, 331-49.

Gerson, L. (1994), *Plotinus*, London.

Gerson, L.P. (ed.) (1996), *The Cambridge Companion to Plotinus*, Cambridge.

Gilson, E. (1952), *Being and Some Philosophers*, Toronto.

Goethe, J.W. von (1996), *Goethe on Science: A Selection of Goethe's Writings*, ed. & intro., J. Naydler. Edinburgh.

Goethe, J.W. von (1988), *Scientifiic Studies: Goethe's Collected Works, Vol. 12* ed. & tr., D. Miller, New York.

Goold, G.P. (tr.) (1977), Manilius. *Astronomica*, Cambridge, MA.

Goulet-Cazé, M.-O., Madec, G., and O'Brien, D. (ed.) (1992), *Sophies Maietores* Paris.

Granada, M.A. (2004), "Aristotle, Copernicus, Bruno: Centrality, the Principle of Movement and the Extension of the Universe." *Studies in the History and Philosophy of Science* 35, 91-114.

Grant, E. (1962), "Late Medieval Thought, Copernicus, and the Scientific Revolution," *Journal of the History of Ideas* 23.2, 197-220.

Gray, R.D. (1952), *Goethe the Alchemist: A Study of Alchemical Symbolism in Goethe's Literary and Scientific Works*, Cambridge.

Green, R.P.H. (1995), *Augustine* De Doctrina Christiana, (ed. and trans.), Oxford.

Greene, B. (1999), *The Elegant Universe: Superstrings, Hidden Dimensions, and the Quest for the Ultimate Theory*, New York.

Gregg, R.C. and D. Groh (1981), *Early Arianism: A View of Salvation*, Philadelphia, PA.

Gregorios, P. M. (1988), *Cosmic Man: The Theology of St. Gregory of Nyssa,* New York, NY.

Gregorios, P.M. (ed.) (2002a), *Neoplatonism and Indian Philosophy*, Albany.

Gregorios, P.M. (2002b), "Does Neoplatonism Have Anything to Say to Post-Modern Spirituality?," in Harris (ed.) (2002b), 303-20.

Guidelli, C. (1991), "Verità ed arte nel trattato «Sul bello intellegibile» di Plotino, *Rivista di estetica*, XXXI.

Guthrie, K.S. (1917, 1987), *The Neoplatonic Writings of Numenius*, Lawrence, KS.

Guthrie, K.S. (tr.) (1987), Ocellus Lucanus, *On the Nature of the Universe*, in *The Pythagorean Sourcebook and Library*, Grand Rapids, MI, 203-214.

Haase, W. (1987), *Aufstieg und Niedergang der Römischen Welt* II.36.2, Tübingen.

Hackforth, R. (1955), *Plato's Phaedo*, translated with an Introduction and Commentary, Cambridge.

Hadot, P. (1968), *Porphyre et Victorinus*, Paris.

Hadot, P. (1988), *Plotin: Traité 38 [VI, 7]*, Paris.

Hamilton, E. and H. Cairns (eds.) (1961), *The Collected Dialogues of Plato*, Princeton.

Hankinson, R. J. (1991), "Galen's Anatomy of the Soul," *Phronesis* 36.2, 197-233.

Harder, R. (1936), "Eine neue Schrift Plotins", *Hermes*, 71.

Hardy, E.R. (ed.) (1954), *Christology of the Later Fathers*, Philadelphia, PA.

Harkins, P. W. and Riese, W. (1963), *Galen on the Passions and Errors of the Soul*, Columbus.

Harnack, A. (1898), *History of Dogma*, vol. 4, tr. Williams, London.

Harris, R.B. (ed.) (1976), *The Significance of Neoplatonism*, Albany.

Harris, R.B. (ed.) (2002a), *Neoplatonism and Contemporary Thought*, Part I, Albany.

Harris, R.B. (ed.) (2002b), *Neoplatonism and Contemporary Thought*, Part II, Albany

Hatab, L. J., (2001) *"Apollo and Dionysus: Nietzschean Expressions of the Sacred", in Nietzsche and the Gods,* ed. Santaniello, W., Albany

Heidegger, M. (1976), *Platons Lehre von der Wahreit*, in Id., *Wegmarken*, Frankfurt am Main: Vittorio Klosterman.

Heisenberg, W. (1974a), *Across the Frontiers*, tr. by P. Heath, New York.

Heisenberg, W. (1974b), "Goethe's View of Nature and the World of Science anc Technology," in Heisenberg (1974a), 122–53.

Heisenberg, W. (1974c), "The Meaning of Beauty in the Exact Sciences," in Heisenberg (1974a), 166–83.

Hendrix, J. (2004), *Platonic Architectonics*, New York.

Henry, P. and Schwyzer, H.-R. (1964-82), *Plotini Opera*, 3 vols, Oxford (*editic minor*).

Hett, W.S. (1975), *Aristotle: On the Soul, Parva Naturalia, On Breath*, Cambridge.

Hill, E. (2002), *Augustine On Genesis,* introduction, translation and notes, Hyde Park, NY.

Hillman, J. (1978), *The Myth of Analysis: Three Essays in Archetypal Psychology* New York.

Hubler, J.N. (2002), "The Role of Aesthetics in Plotinus' Ascent of the Soul", in Alexandrakis (ed.) (2002), 193-205.

Inge, W.R. (1968[3]), *The Philosophy of Plotinus*, vol. 2, New York.

Jones. A. (1997), 'Studies in the Astronomy of the Roman Period', *Centaurus,* 39 1-36.

Jones, J.D. (tr.) (1980), *Pseudo-Dionysius the Areopagite: The Divine Names anc Mystical Theology,* Milwaukee, WI.

Joseph, R. (ed.) (2003), *NeuroTheology: Brain, Science, Spirituality, Religiou. Experience*, 2nd ed., San Jose.

Jung, C.G. (1968), *The Archetypes and the Collective Unconscious*, *CW* 9, Pt. I, 2nd ed., tr. R. F.C. Hull, Princeton.

Jung, C.G. (1969a), *Aion: Researches into the Phenomenology of the Self*, *CW* 9 Pt. II, 2nd ed., tr. R.F.C. Hull, Princeton.

Jung, C.G. (1969b), *The Structure and Dynamics of the Psyche*, *CW* 8, transl R.F.C. Hull, Princeton.

Jung, C.G. (1970), *Mysterium Coniunctionis: An Inquiry into the Separation anc Synthesis of Psychic Opposites in Alchemy*, *CW* 14, 2nd ed., tr. R.F.C. Hull Princeton.

Jung, C.G. (1972), *Mandala Symbolism*, tr. by R.F.C. Hull, Princeton.

Jung, C.G. and W. Pauli (1955), *The Interpretation of Nature and the Psyche*, New York.

Kaufmann, W., ed., (1967) *The Portable Nietzsche,* New York

Kealey, D. (2002), "Neoplatonism in Transpersonal Psychology: The Thought of Ken Wilber," in Harris (ed.) (2002b), 71-80.

Kearney, Richard. (1998), *The Wake of Imagination: Toward a Postmodern Culture*, New York.

Kelly, J.N.D. (1978), *Early Christian Doctrines, revised edition,* San Francisco CA.

Kerenyi, C., (1976) *Dionysus: Archetypal Image of Indestructible Life,* tr. Mannheim, Princeton

Kline, M. (1953), *Mathematics in Western Culture*, New York.

Knoll, P. (1896), *Sancti Aurelii Augustini* Confessiones, CSEL 33, Vienna.

Koyré, A. (1957), *From the Closed World to the Infinite Universe*, Baltimore.

Koyré, A (1973), *The Astronomical Revolution: Copernicus-Kepler-Borelli*, trans. R. E. W. Maddison, Paris.

Kremer, K. (1966), *Die Neuplatonische Seinsphilosophie und ihre Wirkung auf Thomas von Aquin*, Leiden.

Kristeller, P.O. (1972), *Renaissance Concepts of Man and Other Essays*, New York.

Kristeller, P.O. (1964), *Eight Philosophers of the Italian Renaissance*, Stanford, CA.

Kristeller, P.O. (1961), *Renaissance Thought: The Classic, Scholastic, and Humanist Strains,* New York.

Kuhn, T.S. (1957), *The Copernican Revolution*, Cambridge.

Lakoff, G. and R.E. Núñez (2000), *Where Mathematics Comes From: How the Embodied Mind Brings Mathematics Into Being*, New York.

Lamb, W.R.M. (tr.) (1925), *Plato: Ion*, London and Cambridge, MA.

Lawrence. M. (2005), 'Hellenistic Astrology', in *Internet Encyclopedia of Philosophy*, http://www.iep.utm.edu/a/astr-hel.htm.

Lee, Richard. (2004), *The Force of Reason and the Logic of Force*, New York.

Lenzi, M. (1997), ‘Platonic Polypsychic Pantheism’, *The Monist*, 80.2, 232-50.

Ley, D. and M.S. Samuels (eds.) (1978), *Humanistic Geography: Prospects and Problems*, Chicago.

Lloyd, A.C. (1970), “Non-discursive thought. An enigma of Greek Philosophy”, *Proceedings of the Aristotelian Society*, 70.

Lloyd, A.C. (1981) *Form and Universal in Aristotle*, Liverpool.

Lloyd, A.C. (1986), “Non-Discursive Thought in Plotinus”, *Phronesis* 31, 258-65.

Lloyd, A.C. (1990), *The Anatomy of Neoplatonism*, Oxford.

Lossky, V. (1995), 'Apophasis and Trinitarian Theology', in *Eastern Orthodox Theology: A Contemporary Reader*, Grand Rapids, MI.

Lovejoy, A.O. (1936), *The Great Chain of Being*, Cambridge, MA.

Luibheid, C. (tr.) (1987), *Pseudo-Dionysius: The Complete Works*, New York, NY.

Lutosławski W. (1897), *The Origin and Growth of Plato's Logic with an Account of Plato's Style and of the Chronology of His Writings*, London.

Lutosławski W. (1930), *The Knowledge of Reality*, Cambridge.

Lutosławski W. (1948), “Plato's Change of Mind”, *Proceedings of the Xth International Congress of Philosophy*, Amsterdam, vol. I.

Maas, M, (2000) *Readings in Late Antiquity: A Sourcebook,* New York

MacLennan, B.J. (2003), "Evolutionary Neurotheology and the Varieties of Religious Experience," in Joseph (ed.) (2003), 305–5.

MacLennan, B.J. (2005), "Evolution, Jung, and Theurgy: Their Role in Modern Neoplatonism," in Finamore & Berchman (eds.) (2005), 305–22.

MacLennan, B.J. (2006), "Evolutionary Jungian Psychology," *Psychological Perspectives* 49, in press.

MacLennan, B.J. (in press), "Individual Soul and World Soul: The Process of Individuation in Neoplatonism and Jung," in Arzt (ed.) (in press).

Majercik, Ruth, (1989), *The Chaldean Oracles*, text, translation and commentary, Leiden.

Marshall. P., (2005) *Mystical Encounters with the Natural World: experiences and explanations* Oxford

Massagli, M. (1981), "L'Uno al di sopra del bello e della bellezza nelle *Enneadi* di Plotino", *Rivista di filosofia neo-scolastica* 73, 111-31.

McGinn, B. and W. Otten (eds.) (1994), *Eriugena. East and West. Papers of the Eighth International Colloquium of the Society for the Promotion of Eriugenian Studies. Chicago and Notre Dame, 18-20 October 1991*, Notre Dame.

McGuckin, J.A. (ed.) (2004), *The Westminster Handbook to Patristic Theology,* Louisville, KY.

McKenna, S. (1991), ed., Plotinus, *The Enneads*, Penguin: London.

Meier, C.A. (ed.) (2001), *Atom and Archetype: The Pauli/Jung Letters, 1928–1958*, Princeton.

Merchant, C. (1980), *The Death of Nature: Women, Ecology, and the Scientific Revolution*, San Francisco.

Michel, P.H. (1973), *The Cosmology of Giordano Bruno*, trans. R. E. W. Maddison, Ithaca, NY.

Miles, M.R. (1999), *Plotinus on Body and Beauty*, Oxford.

Mollenhauer B. (1954), "Lutosławski and the Knight among Nations", *The American Slavic and East European Review*, vol. XIII, no 2.

Moore, E. (2005), *Origen of Alexandria and St. Maximus the Confessor: An Analysis and Critical Evaluation of Their Eschatological Doctrines*, Boca Raton, FL.

Moore, E. (2003), 'Origen of Alexandria and *apokatastasis*: Some Notes on the Development of a Noble Notion', in *Quodlibet: Online Journal of Christian Theology and Philosophy*, vol. 5, no. 1.

Moran, D. (1989), *The Philosophy of Johannes Scottus Eriugena. A Study of Idealism in the Middle Ages*, Cambridge.

Moran, D. (1999), "Idealism in Medieval Philosophy: The Case of Johannes Scottus Eriugena," *Medieval Philosophy and Theology* 8, 53-82.

ʼlueller-Jourdain, P. (2005), *Typologie Spatio-temporelle De L'Ecclesia Byzantine: La Mystagogie De Maxime Le Confesseur Dans La Culture Philosophique de l'Antiquite Tardive,* Leiden.

ʼlurray, G., *(1960) Five Stages of Greek Religion,* New York PB reprint 3rd edition.

ʼNarbonne, J.-M. and Reckermann, A. (éd.) (2004), *Pensées de l'"Un" dans l'histoire de la philosophie*, Québec and Paris.

ʼleugebauer, O. and H.B. van Hoesen (1959), *Greek Horoscopes*, Philadelphia, PA.

ʼlietzsche, F. (1967a), *Werke in zwei Bänden*, München.

ʼlietzsche, F. (1967b) "Vom Nutzen und Nachteil der Geschichte," in Nietzsche (1967a) I, 113-175.

ʼlisbet, H.B. (2002), "Religion and Philosophy," in Sharpe (ed.) (2002), 219–31.

ʼock, A.D. (1969) *Conversion: The Old and the New in Religion, From Alexander the Great to Augustine o f Hippo,* Oxford PB repr.

ʼlovotný F. (1977), *The Posthumous Life of Plato*, Prague.

ʼlussbaum, Martha and Rorty, Amélie. (1992), *Essays on Aristotle's De Anima*, Oxford.

ʼ'Brien, D. (1996) "Plotinus on matter and evil," in *The Cambridge Companion to Plotinus*, Cambridge, 171-195.

ʼ'Donnell, J. J., (1979) *"The Demise of Paganism", Traditio 35,* 45-84

ʼlivieri, D. et. al. (ed.) (1898-1953), *Catalogus Codicum Astrologorum Graecorum*, 12 vols., Brussels.

ʼ'Meara, D.J. (ed.) (1982). *Neoplatonism and Christian Thought*, Albany.

ʼ'Meara, D.J. (1996), "The Hierarchical Ordering of Reality in Plotinus," in Gerson (ed.) (1996), 66-81.

ʼ'Meara, D.J. (1993), *Plotinus. An Introduction to the Enneads*, Oxford and New York.

ʼ'Meara, D.J., (2003) *Platonopolis: Platonic Political Philosophy in Late Antiquity,* Oxford

ʼng, W.J. (1958), *Ramus, Method, and the Decay of Dialogue: From the Art of Discourse to the Art of Reason,* Cambridge.

ʼtten, W. (1991), *The Anthropology of Johannes Scottus Eriugena*, Leiden.

ʼtten, W. (1994), "Eriugena's *Periphyseon*: A Carolingian Contribution to the Theological Tradition," in McGinn and Otten (1994), 69-93.

ʼtten, W. (2002), "Realized Eschatology or Philosophical Idealism: The Case of Eriugena's "Periphyseon"," in Aertsen and Pickavé (eds.) (2002), 373-387

ʼtten, W. (2006), "Anthropology between *Imago Mundi* and *Imago Dei*: The Place of Johannes Scottus Eriugena in the Tradition of Christian Thought," in Wiles and Yarnold (2006), 325-338.

ʼalmer, R.B. and R.G. Hamerton-Kelly (eds.) (1971), *Philomathes: Studies and Essays in the Humanities in Memory of Philip Merlan*, The Hague.

Perl, E.D. (1997), "The Power of All Things: The One as Pure Giving in Plotinus," *American Catholic Philosophical Quarterly* 71, 301-13.

Rappe, S. (1996) "Self-knowledge and subjectivity in the Enneads" in *The Cambridge Companion to Plotinus*, Cambridge, 250-274.

Pauli, W. (1955), "The Influence of Archetypal Ideas on the Scientific Theories of Kepler," in Jung & Pauli (1955), 147–240.

Pelikan, J. (1993), *Christianity and Classical Culture: The Metamorphosis of Natural Theology in the Christian Encounter with Hellenism*, New Haven CT.

Perl, E. (2002), "Signifying Nothing: Being as Sign in Neoplatonism and Derrida" in *Neoplatonism and Contemporary Thought Part Two*, in Harris (ed.) 125 52.

Pingree, D. (1977), 'Antiochus and Rhetorius', in *Classical Philology*, 72, 203-223

Pingree. D. (1997), *From Astral Omens to Astrology from Babylon to Bikaner* Rome.

Pingree. D. (1978), *Yavanajataka of Sphujidhavaja*, 2 Vols., Cambridge, MA.

Placher, W.C. (1983), *A History of Christian Theology,* Philadelphia, PA.

Pollmann, Karla (1996) *Doctrina Christiana. Untersuchungen zu den Anfängen der christlichen Hermeneutik unter besonderer Berücksichtigung von Augustinus'* De doctrina christiana, Freiburg.

Pranger, M.B. (1995), "Augustine and the Return of the Senses", in Giselle de Nie Karl.F. Morrison and Marco Mosterd (eds.), *Seeing the Invisible in Late Antiquity and the Early Middle Ages*, Turnhout, 53-69.

Pranger, M.B. (2001), "Time and Narrative in Augustine's *Confessiones*", *The Journal of Religion* 81, 3, 2001, 399-94.

Pranger, M.B. (2002), "The Unfathomability of Sincerity. On the Seriousness of Augustine's *Confession*", *Actas do Congresso International As* Confissões *de santo Agostinho 1600 Anos Depois: Presença e Actualidade,* Lisbon 193-242.

Prestige, G.L. (1952), *God in Patristic Thought*, London.

Preus, A. (2002), "Plotinus and Biology," in Wagner (ed.) (2002), 43–55.

Proust, M. (1971), *Within a Budding Grove*, Part Two, C.K. Scott Moncrief (trans.). London.

Raphael, A. (1965), *Goethe and the Philosophers' Stone: Symbolic Patterns in 'The Parable' and the Second Part of 'Faust'*, London.

Rice, E.F. (1958), *The Renaissance Idea of Wisdom*, Westport, CT.

Rist, J.M. (1964a), *Amor and Psyche*, Toronto.

Rist, J.M. (1964b), "Mysticism and Transcendence in Later Neoplatonism" *Hermes* 92, 213-25.

Rist, J.M. (1967), *Plotinus: The Road to Reality*, Cambridge.

Robertson, R. (1989), "The Evolution of Number: Self-Reflection and the Archetype of Order," *Psychological Perspectives* 20, 128–41.

Robertson, R. (1995), *Jungian Archetypes: Jung, Gödel, and the History of Archetypes*, York Beach.

Robbins, F.E. (tr.) (1956), Claudius Ptolemy. *Tetrabiblos*, Cambridge, MA.

Rochberg, F. (1998), *Babylonian Horoscopes*, Philadelphia, PA.

Rosen, E. (1984), *Copernicus and the Scientific Revolution*, Malabar, FL.

Rossi, P. (2000), *Logic and the Art of Memory: The Quest for a Universal Language*, tr. & intro., S. Clucas, Chicago.

Ryan, R.E. (2002), *Shamanism and the Psychology of C. G. Jung: The Great Circle*, London.

Sachs, Joe. (2001), *Aristotle: On the Soul and On Memory and Recollection*, Santa Fe.

Saffrey, H.D. (1971), "Abammon, Pseudonyme de Jamblique," in Palmer and Hamerton-Kelly (eds.) (1971), 227-239.

Sallis, John. (2000), *The Force of Imagination: The Sense of the Elemental*, Bloomington.

Sambursky, S. and Pines, S. (1971), *The Concept of Time in Later Platonism,* text and translation, Jerusalem.

Santayana G. (1957), "Search for the True Plato", *The Idler and His Works and Other Essays*, ed. D. Cory, New York.

Scholem, G. (1965), *On the Kabbalah and Its Symbolism*, New York.

Schroeder, F. (2002) "Plotinus and Interior Space" in *Neoplatonism and Indian Thought*, Albany 83-96.

Schroeder, F.M. (2004), "The Hermeneutics of Unity in Plotinus", in Narbonne and Reckermann (éd.) (2004), 108-22.

Scott, A. (1991), *Origen and the Life of the Stars*, Oxford.

Scott, W. (tr.) (1924, rpt. 2001), *Hermetica*, Boston, MA.

Seamon, D. (1978), "Goethe's Approach to the Natural World: Implications for Environmental Theory and Education," in Ley & Samuels (ed.) (1978), 238–50.

Seamon, D. and A. Zajonc (eds.) (1998), *Goethe's Way of Science: A Phenomenology of Nature*, Albany.

Sepper, D.L. (1988), *Goethe Contra Newton: Polemics and the Project for a New Science of Color*, Cambridge.

Sharpe, L. (ed.) (2002), *The Cambridge Companion to Goethe*, Cambridge.

Shaw, G. (1985), "Theurgy: Rituals of Unification in the Neoplatonism of Iamblichus," *Traditio* 41, 1-28.

Shaw, G. (1995), *Theurgy and the Soul: The Neoplatonism of Iamblichus*, Pennsylvania.

Shaw, G. (1998), "Divination in the Neoplatonism of Iamblichus," in Berchman (ed.) (1998), 225-267.

Sheppard, A. (1993), "Iamblichus on Inspiration: *De Mysteriis* 3.4-8," in Blumenthal and Clark (eds.) (1993), 138-143.

Shorey P. (1903), *The Unity of Plato's Thought*, Chicago.

Shorey, P. (tr.) (1937), *Plato: Republic*, London and Cambridge, MA.

Shumaker, W. (1972), *The Occult Sciences in the Renaissance: A Study in Intellectual Patterns*, Berkeley.

Smith, H. (1992), *Forgotten Truth: The Common Vision of the World's Religions*, 1st paperback edition, San Francisco.

Smith, H. (2002), "Science and the Great Chain of Being," in Harris (ed.) (2002a), 1-11.

Solé, R. and B. Goodwin (2000), *Signs of Life: How Complexity Pervades Biology*, New York.

Sorabji, R. (1982), "Myths about non-propositional thought", in M.Nussbaum and M.Schofield, eds., *Language and Logos. Studies presented to G.E.L. Owen*, Cambridge: Cambridge University Press.

Sorabji, R. (1983) *Time, Creation, and the Continuum*, Ithaca.

Stavropoulos, C. (1995), 'Partakers of Divine Nature', in *Eastern Orthodox Theology: A Contemporary Reader,* Grand Rapids, MI.

Steel, Carlos. (2001), "The Moral Purpose of the Human Body: A Reading of *Timaeus* 69-72," *Phronesis* 46, 105-128.

Steiner, R. (2000), *Nature's Open Secret: Introductions to Goethe's Scientific Writings*, tr. by J. Barnes & M. Spiegler, Spring Valley.

Stern, S.M. and A. Hourani, V. Brown (ed.) (1972), *Islamic Philosophy and the Classical Tradition*, Columbia.

Stern-Gillet, S. (2000), "Le Principe du Beau chez Plotin: Réflexions sur *Ennéades* VI.7.32 et 33", *Phronesis* 45, 38-63.

Stevens, A. (1998), *Ariadne's Clue: A Guide to the Symbols of Humankind*, Princeton.

Stevens, A. (2003), *Archetype Revisited: An Updated Natural History of the Self*, Toronto.

Stevenson, J., (ed.) (1957), *A New Eusebius: Documents Illustrative of the History of the Church to A.D. 337,* London.

Stock, B. (1990), *Listening for the Text. On the Uses of the Past*, Baltimore.

Strange, S. (1987), "Plotinus, Porphyry, and the Categories", in Haase (ed.) (1987), 955-74.

Struck, P.T. (2000), "Iamblichus, *De Mysteriis*, Book 1," in Valantasis (ed.) (2000), 489-505.

Struck, P.T. (2004), *Birth of the Symbol: Ancient Readers at the limits of their Texts*, Princeton.

Sumi, A. (1997), “Plotinus on *Phaedrus* 247D7-E1: The Platonic *Locus Classicus* of the Identity of Intellect with the Intelligible Objects,” *American Catholic Philosophical Quarterly* 71, 404-20.

Sumi, A. (2001), “Whitehead on Religion, Civilization and Adventure,” in Crosby and Hardwick (eds) (2001), 357-73.

Sumi, A. (2002a), “The Omnipresence of Being, the Intellect-Intelligible Identity and the Undescending Part of the Soul: An Essay on the Dispute about Indian Influences on Plotinus,” in Gregorios (ed.) (2002a), 45-69.

Sumi, A. (2002b), “The Psyche, the Forms and the Creative One: Toward Reconstruction of Neoplatonic Metaphysics,” in Harris (ed.) (2002a), 221-69.

Susanetti, D. (1995), *Plotino: Sul Bello, Enneade, I, 6*, Padova.

Sweeney, L. (1992), “Another Interpretation of Plotinus’ *Enneads*, VI, 7, 32”, in *Divine Infinity in Greek and Medieval Thought*, New York, 223-41.

Swerdlow, N.M. and O. Neugebauer (1984), *Mathematical Astronomy in Copernicus's* De Revolutionibus, 2 vols, New York.

Swift, P.A., (2005) *Becoming Nietzsche: Early Reflections on Democritus, Schopenhauer and Kant.* Lanham, MD

Szlez·k, T.A. (1979), *Platon und Aristoteles in der Nusleher Plotins*, Basel Stuttgart: Schwabe Verlag.

Tanner, M ed., (1993) *Nietzsche, F., the Birth of Tragedy Out of the Spirit of Music,* tr., Whiteside, S., London

Tatakis, B. (2003), *Byzantine Philosophy*, tr. N.J. Moutafakis, Indianapolis, IN.

Taylor, C.C.W. (1976), *Plato: Protagoras*, Translation with Notes, Oxford.

Temporini, H. and Haase, W. (ed.) (1994), *Aufstieg und Niedergang der Römischen Welt* II.36.7, Tübingen.

Theiler, W. (1972), “Von der begrenzten Form zur unbegrenzten Liebe bei Plotin”, in Stern (ed.) (1972), 467-72.

Thesleff H. (1982), *Studies in Platonic chronology*, Commentationes Humanarum Litterarum nr 70, Helsinki.

Thunberg, L. (1985), *Man and the Cosmos: The Vision of St. Maximus the Confessor*, Crestwood, NY.

Tieleman, Teun. (1996), *Galen and Chrysippus on the Soul*, Leiden.

Tieleman, Teun. (1998), "Plotinus on the seat of the soul," *Phronesis* 43, 306-325.

Toomer, G.J. (tr.) (1998), *Ptolemy's Almagest*, Princeton, NJ.

Tracy, T. J. (1976), "Plato, Galen, and the Center of Consciousness," *Illinois Classical Studies*, I, 43-52.

Tredennick, H. (tr.) (1933), *Aristotle: Metaphysics*, London and Cambridge, MA.

Trouillard, J. (1955), La *purification plotinienne*, Paris.

Uzdavinys, A. ed., (2004) *The Golden Chain: An Anthology of Pythagorean and Platonic Philosophy,* Bloomington, IN

Valantasis, R. (ed.) (2000), *Religions of Late Antiquity in Practice*, Princeton.

Voss, A. (1992), *Magic, Astrology & Music: The Background to Marsilio Ficino's Music Therapy and his Role as a Renaissance Magus*, unpublished Ph.D. thesis, City University, London.

Voss, A. (2001), *The Astrology of Marsilio Ficino: Divination or Science?*, http://cura.free.fr/decem/10voss.html

Wagner, M.F. (ed.) (2002), *Neoplatonism and Nature: Studies in Plotinus'* Enneads, Albany.

Walker, D.P. (1958), *Spiritual & Demonic Magic from Ficino to Campanella*, London.

Wallis, R.T. (1972), *Neo-Platonism*, London.

Wallis, R.T. (1976), "NOUS as Experience", in Harris (ed.) (1976), 121-54.

Webster, C. (1982), *From Paracelsus to Newton: Magic and the Making of Modern Science*, Cambridge.

Westerink, L. G., (1977), *The Greek Commentaries on Plato's Phaedo*, Vol. II, *Damascius*, text and translation, Amsterdam.

Wheeler, J.A. (1994), *At Home in the Universe*, Woodbury.

White, M. (1997), *Isaac Newton: The Last Sorcerer*, Reading.

Whitehead, A.N. (1967), *Adventures of Ideas*, New York.

Wicksteed, Philip and Cornford, Francis. (1929-1934), *Aristotle: Physics, Books I-IV*, Cambridge.

Wilber, K. (2000), *A Theory of Everything: An Integral Vision for Business, Politics, Science, and Spirituality*, Boston.

Wilcox, D.J. (1987), *In Search of God and Self: Renaissance and Reformation Thought*, Prospect Heights, IL.

Wiles, M.F. and E. Yarnold (eds.) (2006), *Studia Patristica*, Louvain.

Winkelman, M. (2000), *Shamanism: The Neural Ecology of Consciousness and Healing*, Westport & London.

Wolters, A.M. (1972), *Plotinus 'On Eros,'* a Detailed Exegetical Study of *Enn*. III 5, Diss. Amsterdam.

Woodhouse, C.M. (1986), *George Gemistos Plethon: The Last of the Hellenes*, Oxford.

Wright, W. C. (1922) *Eunapius, Lives of the Philosophers and Sophists (VS)* Cambridge, MA

Wright, W. C. (1913-23) *The Emperor Julian, Works, 3 volumes,* Cambridge, MA

Yates, F.A. (1964), *Giordano Bruno and the Hermetic Tradition*, Chicago.

Yates, F.A. (1966), *The Art of Memory*, London.

Young, Julian, (1993) *Nietzsche's Philosophy of Art,* Cambridge; New York

Zajonc, A. (1998), "Goethe and the Science of His Time: An Historical Introduction," in Seamon & Zajonc (1998), 15–30.

The Prometheus Trust Catalogue

Platonic Texts and Translations Series

I Iamblichi Chalcidensis in Platonis Dialogos Commentariorum Fragmenta

John M Dillon 978-1-898910-45-9

II The Greek Commentaries on Plato's Phaedo (I – Olympiodorus)

L G Westerink 978-1-898910-46-6

III The Greek Commentaries on Plato's Phaedo (II – Damascius)

L G Westerink 978-1-898910-47-3

IV Damascius, Lectures on the Philebus

L G Westerink 978-1-898910-48-0

V The Anonymous Prolegomena to Platonic Philosophy

L G Westerink 978-1-898910-51-0

VI Proclus Commentary on the First Alcibiades

Text L G Westerink Trans. W O'Neill 978-1-898910-49-7

VII The Fragments of Numenius

R Petty 978-1-898910-52-7

VIII The Chaldean Oracles

R Majercik 978-1-898910-53-4

The Music of Philosophy Series

A Casting of Light by the Platonic Tradition 978-1-898910-57-2

The Song of Proclus 978-1-898910-62-6

The Chant of Plotinus 978-1-898910-65-7

The Music of Plato 978-1-898910-67-1

The Hymn of Thomas Taylor 978-1-898910-68-1

The Thomas Taylor Series

1 Proclus' Elements of Theology

Proclus' Elements of Theology - 211 propositions which frame the metaphysics of the Late Athenian Academy. 978-1-898910-00-8

2 Select Works of Porphyry

Abstinence from Animal Food; Auxiliaries to the Perception of Intelligibles; Concerning Homer's Cave of the Nymphs; Taylor on the Wanderings of Ulysses. 978-1-898910-01-5

3 Collected Writings of Plotinus

Twenty-seven treatises being all the writings of Plotinus translated by Taylor. 978-1-898910-02-2

4 Writings on the Gods & the World

Sallust On the Gods & the World; Sentences of Demophilus; Ocellus on the Nature of the Universe; Taurus and Proclus on the Eternity of the World; Maternus on the Thema Mundi; The Emperor Julian's Orations to the Mother of Gods and to the Sovereign Sun; Synesius on Providence; Taylor's essays on the Mythology and the Theology of the Greeks. 978-1-898910-03-9

5 Hymns and Initiations

The Hymns of Orpheus together with all the published hymns translated or written by Taylor; Taylor's 1824 essay on Orpheus (together with the 1787 version). 978-1-898910-04-6

6 Dissertations of Maximus Tyrius

Forty-one treatises from the middle Platonist, and an essay from Taylor, The Triumph of the Wise Man over Fortune. 978-1-898910-05-3

7 Oracles and Mysteries

A Collection of Chaldean Oracles; Essays on the Eleusinian and Bacchic Mysteries; The History of the Restoration of the Platonic Theology; On the Immortality of the Soul. 978-1-898910-06-0

8 The Theology of Plato

The six books of Proclus on the Theology of Plato; to which is added a further book (by Taylor), replacing the original seventh book by Proclus, now lost. Extensive introduction and notes are also added. 978-1-898910-07-7

9 Works of Plato I

Taylor's General Introduction, Life of Plato, First Alcibiades (with much of Proclus' Commentary), Republic (with a section of Proclus' Commentary). 978-1-898910-08-4

10 Works of Plato II
Laws, Epinomis, Timæus (with notes from Proclus' Commentary), Critias. 978-1-898910-09-1

11 Works of Plato III
Parmenides (with a large part of Proclus' Commentary), Sophista, Phædrus (with notes from Hermias' Commentary), Greater Hippias, Banquet. 978-1-898910-10-7

12 Works of Plato IV
Theætetus, Politicus, Minos, Apology of Socrates, Crito, Phædo (with notes from the Commentaries of Damascius and Olympiodorus), Gorgias (with notes from the Commentary of Olympiodorus), Philebus (with notes from the Commentary of Olympiodorus), Second Alcibiades. 978-1-898910-11-4

13 Works of Plato V
Euthyphro, Meno, Protagoras, Theages, Laches, Lysis, Charmides, Lesser Hippias, Euthydemus, Hipparchus, Rivals, Menexenus, Clitopho, Io, Cratylus (together with virtually the whole of Proclus' Scholia), Epistles. An index to the extensive notes Taylor added to his five volumes of Plato. 978-1-898910-12-1

14 Apuleius' Golden Ass & Other Philosophical Writings
The Golden Ass (or Metamorphosis); On the Dæmon of Socrates; On the Philosophy of Plato. 978-1-898910-13-8

15 & 16 Proclus' Commentary on the Timæus of Plato
The Five Books of this Commentary in two volumes, with additional notes and short index. 978-1-898910-14-5 and 978-1-898910-15-2

17 Iamblichus on the Mysteries and Life of Pythagoras
Iamblichus On the Mysteries of the Egyptians, Chaldeans & Assyrians; Iamblichus' Life of Pythagoras; Fragments of the Ethical Writings of Pythagoreans; Political Fragments of Archytas, Charondas and other Pythagoreans. 978-1-898910-16-9

18 Essays and Fragments of Proclus
Providence, Fate and That Which is Within our Power; Ten Doubts concerning Providence; The Subsistence of Evil; The Life of Proclus; Fragments of Proclus' Writings. 978-1-898910-17-6

19 The Works of Aristotle I
The Physics, together with much of Simplicius' Commentary. A Glossary of Greek terms used by Aristotle. 978-1-898910-18-3

20 The Works of Aristotle II

The Organon: The Categories, On Interpretation, The Prior Analytics; The Posterior Analytics, The Topics, The Sophistical Elenchus; with extensive notes from the commentaries of Porphyry, Simplicius and Ammonius. 978-1-898910-19-0

21 The Works of Aristotle III

Great Ethics, Eudemian Ethics; Politics; Economics. 978-1-898910-20-6

22 The Works of Aristotle IV

Rhetorics; Nicomachean Ethics; Poetics. 978-1-898910-21-3

23 The Works of Aristotle V

The Metaphysics with notes from the Commentaries of Alexander Aphrodisiensis and Syrianus; Against the Dogmas of Xenophanes, Zeno and Gorgias; Mechanical Problems; On the World; On Virtues and Vices; On Audibles. 978-1-898910-22-0

24 The Works of Aristotle VI

On the Soul (with much of the Commentary of Simplicius); On Sense and Sensibles; On Memory and Reminiscence; On Sleep and Wakefulness; On Dreams; On Divination by Sleep; On the Common Motions of Animals; On the Generation of Animals; On Length and Shortness of Life; On Youth and Old Age, Life and Death; On Respiration. 978-1-898910-23-7

25 The Works of Aristotle VII

On the Heavens (with much of the Commentary of Simplicius); On Generation and Corruption; On Meteors (with much of the Commentary of Olympiodorus). 978-1-898910-24-4

26 The Works of Aristotle VIII

History of Animals, & the Treatise on Physiognomy. 978-1-898910-25-1

27 The Works of Aristotle IX

The Parts of Animals; The Progressive Motions of Animals, The Problems; On Indivisible Lines. 978-1-898910-26-8

28 The Philosophy of Aristotle

Taylor's four part dissertation on the philosophy of Aristotle which outlines his primary teachings, the harmony of Plato and Aristotle, and modern misunderstandings of Aristotle. 978-1-898910-27-5

29 Proclus' Commentary on Euclid

Proclus' Commentary on the First Book of Euclid's Elements; Taylor's four part Dissertation on the Platonic Doctrine of Ideas, on Demonstrative Syllogism, On the Nature of the Soul, and on the True End of Geometry. 978-1-898910-28-2

30 The Theoretical Arithmetic of the Pythagoreans

The Theoretic Arithmetic of the Pythagoreans, Medicina Mentis, Nullities & Diverging Series, The Elements of a New Arithmetic Notation, Elements of True Arithmetic of Infinities. 978-1-898910-29-9

31 & 32 Pausanias' Guide to Greece

Pausanias' Guide to Greece (in two volumes) with illustrations and extensive notes on mythology. 978-1-898910-30-5 & 978-1-898910-31-2

33 Against the Christians and Other Writings

The Arguments of Julian Against the Christians; Celsus, Porphyry and Julian Against the Christians; Writings of Thomas Taylor from his Collectanea, his Miscellanies in Prose and Verse, and his short works On Critics, An Answer to Dr Gillies, A Vindication of the Rights of Brutes, and his articles from the Classical Journal. Included is a Thomas Taylor bibliography. 978-1-898910-32-9

Students' Edition Paperbacks

The Sophist

Trans. Thomas Taylor. Includes extensive notes and introductory essays.

978-1-898910-93-0

The Symposium of Plato

Trans. Floyer Sydenham & Thomas Taylor. Includes Plotinus' *On Love* (En III, 5), and introductory essays.

978-1-898910-97-8

Know Thyself – The First Alcibiades & Commentary

Trans. Floyer Sydenham & Thomas Taylor. With introductory essays.

978-1-898910-96-1

Beyond the Shadows - The Metaphysics of the Platonic Tradition

Guy Wyndham-Jones and Tim Addey 978-1-898910-95-4

The Unfolding Wings - The Way of Perfection in the Platonic Tradition

Tim Addey 978-1-898910-94-7

The Meno

Trans. Sydenham & Taylor. With introductory essays 978-1-898910-92-3

Other titles available from the Prometheus Trust

Philosophy as a Rite of Rebirth – From Ancient Egypt to Neoplatonism

Algis Uždavinys 978-1-898910-35-(

The Philosophy of Proclus – the Final Phase of Ancient Thought

L J Rosán 978 1 898910-44-2

The Seven Myths of the Soul

Tim Addey 978-1-898910-37-4

Release Thyself – Three Philosophic Dialogues

Guy Wyndham-Jones 978-1-898910-56-5

Platonism and the World Crisis

John M Dillon, Brendan O'Byrne and Tim Addey 978-1-898910-55-

Towards the Noosphere – Futures Singular and Plural

John M Dillon and Stephen R L Clark 978-1-898910-60-2

Song of the Solipsistic One

Deepa Majumdar 978-1-898910-63-3

Selections from the Prometheus Trust Confernces 2006-2010

978-1-898910-66-

An Index to Plato - A Subject Index using Stephanus pagination

978-1-898910-34-

For further details please visit the Prometheus Trust website at:

www.prometheustrust.co.uk